Hannibal & the Second Punic War

HANNIBAL.

Hannibal & the Second Punic War
Rome & Carthage at War for the Dominance of the Ancient World, 218-201 B.C.

ILLUSTRATED

Hannibal
William O'Connor Morris

With a Small Biography of Hannibal
Henry William Herbert

Hannibal & the Second Punic War
Rome & Carthage at War for the Dominance of the Ancient World, 218-201 B.C.
Hannibal
by William O'Connor Morris
With a Small Biography of Hannibal
by Henry William Herbert

ILLUSTRATED

FIRST EDITION IN THIS FORM

First published in the titles
Hannibal
and
Captains of the Old World (Extract)

Leonaur is an imprint of Oakpast Ltd
Copyright in this form © 2025 Oakpast Ltd

ISBN: 978-1-916535-78-7 (hardcover)
ISBN: 978-1-916535-79-4 (softcover)

http://www.leonaur.com

Publisher's Notes

The views expressed in this book are not necessarily those of the publisher.

Contents

Preface	7
Chapter 1: Rome Before the First Punic War	13
Chapter 2: Carthage Before the First Punic War	30
Chapter 3: The First Punic War	51
Chapter 4: Hamilcar, and the Youth of Hannibal	67
Chapter 5: The Pyrenees the Alps the Trebia	85
Chapter 6: Trasimenus and Cannae	114
Chapter 7: Rome in a Death Struggle with Hannibal	149
Chapter 8: The Struggle Slackens—the Metaurus	189
Chapter 9: The Struggle Closes—Zama	213
Chapter 10: The End of Hannibal	236
Hannibal *By Henry William Herbert*	257

Preface

Hannibal, like Napoleon, and even more decidedly than Napoleon, towers over all the figures of an age of war in its grandest aspects, and of the shock of nations in conflict. Except his father, who died when Hannibal was still a youth, no Carthaginian of his time had a pretence to greatness; he is supreme over the soldiers and statesmen of Rome; he is the master spirit of the Mediterranean World. Nothing in the period of the Second Punic War can be compared to Hannibal, save the great people which at last overthrew the great man. We possess hardly anything which has emanated directly from this extraordinary personage, scarcely a phrase, not a line of correspondence; his achievements and character have been described by bitter enemies, with the doubtful exception of one historian who understood his genius, yet inclined to the side of Rome.

Yet through the mists of calumny and detraction we can see the form and the lineaments of that gigantic figure, one of the most commanding that has appeared in history. Hannibal was a consummate warrior, an illustrious statesman, a patriot, sustained through a career which proved every extreme of fortune by devotion to his country, and intense hatred of its implacable foe, and that too apparently without a thought of ambition and self-aggrandisement. The triumphs of Hannibal do not increase his stature, as he stands on the tracts of the past; his misfortunes do not diminish it; he seems superior to fate itself. The success of his arms would have been a calamity to mankind; but this does not lessen his greatness, or the admiration it deserves.

Our information respecting Hannibal is far from adequate; we know very little about the daily round of his conduct in the camp and in council, and about his domestic and private life. Nevertheless, history has been busy with him; it is possible to form a sufficiently just estimate of the epoch he fills, of his mighty deeds and his character. There is not much in the writings of Appian, Plutarch, Cornelius Nepos, Sallust, and others who have cursorily dealt with his time and his career, that deserves attention, and the feeble poem of Silius Italicus is chiefly interesting as it affords proof how Hannibal's memory impressed the Romans with awe, even after the lapse of centuries.

But two historians of the ancient world did describe the Second Punic War in detail, and did dwell fully on the exploits of Hannibal; we can obtain from their works a tolerably accurate idea of the period and of the great man who overshadows it. Polybius is rather a dull writer; he was a bad geographer; he was under Roman influence, especially under that of the Scipios, but he is tolerably impartial; he has a true military eye; he understood war, especially on its moral side; he sincerely admired Hannibal; he was not far removed from Hannibal's time. We only possess his complete narrative of the Second Punic War to the end of the Battle of Cannae; but considerable fragments of the lost books remain; these are of the greatest value; and all that he has written about the institutions of Rome and of Carthage, the composition and the characteristics of the Roman Army, and the art of war in that age should be carefully studied.

The second historian is Livy; his whole account of the Second Punic War has fortunately come down to us; it is scarcely necessary to refer to the brilliancy of his style, the beauty of his descriptions, the animation and charm of his pages. But he was indifferent to truth, and a superficial enquirer; his narrative is often untrustworthy, full of omissions, almost incredible; he continually strains after effect and gives too free a rein to rhetoric; above all he is a persistent, mendacious, and unscrupulous slanderer of Hannibal. Still Livy is a great writer; his description of the Second Punic War is of the greatest use to the student of the time, were it only that it perfectly illustrates the strength, the pride, the confidence, and the indomitable constancy of the Roman character.

The modern historians of, and commentators on, the Second Punic War and on the career of Hannibal are very numerous; they may be said to extend from the days of Raleigh to the present time. Many of these works, however, are worthless or obsolete; many are chiefly conversant with antiquarian researches, as, for instance, with the itinerary of Hannibal's march across the Alps. I shall briefly glance at recent authorities which appear to me to be of peculiar value. The great work of Mommsen, owing to its proportions, necessarily contains rather a brief account of the Second Punic War; the eminent author has, I think, fallen into error in his description of more than one battle, notably of the Trebia. But no modern historian has reproduced so perfectly the genius and tendencies of his age, and of the institutions of Rome and of Carthage; and Mommsen has placed in full and striking relief the grandeur of Hannibal's nature and achievements.

My idea of Carthage has been mainly derived from Mommsen's *History of Rome*, but Mr. Bosworth Smith's *Carthage and the Carthaginians* is an admirable work which should be diligently perused, Arnold's *Second Punic War* is a posthumous fragment; Arnold is, I believe, quite wrong in his account of the Battle of Cannae, and in his estimate of Scipio Africanus; but he is an excellent geographer; he is very intelligent in describing military operations; he thoroughly understands Hannibal's greatness; his narrative is clear, full, and rich in information. Every student of Hannibal ought to possess and to master the *Annibal* of Colonel Hénnébert. I do not concur in his account of the route taken by Hannibal in his Alpine march, and in several of his conclusions; but he is a most conscientious and learned biographer; he has ransacked all available sources for his materials; his work is very valuable and attractive.

The *Hannibal* of Colonel Dodge of the United States Army is also a very able and interesting work; it is especially good in the description of the military organisation of Rome and of Carthage, and of the Roman and the Carthaginian Armies; he has described carefully and very well the strategy and the tactics of Hannibal and of his adversaries in the field. MacDougall's *Campaigns of Hannibal* is a good epitome, well written and containing able criticism; the same may be said of the "Trasimenus" of Colonel Malleson in his *Ambushes and Surprises*. There are some pregnant remarks in the *Sea Power* of Captain Mahan, on the importance of the command of the sea in the Second Punic War, and the few lines Napoleon has devoted to Hannibal, if deficient in knowledge, reveal a master's hand. I cannot close these pages without expressing my sense of the ability and the courtesy of Mr. Evelyn Abbott, the editor of this and the other volumes of the "Heroes Series."

William O'Connor Morris.

7th July, 1896.

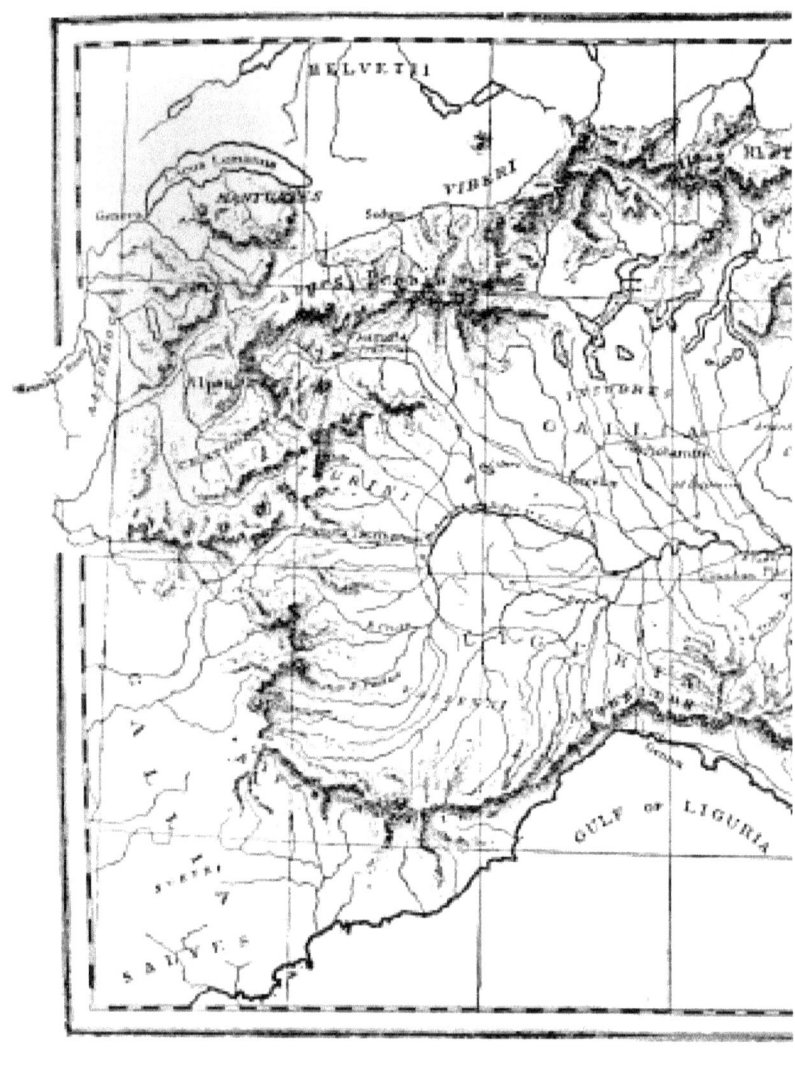

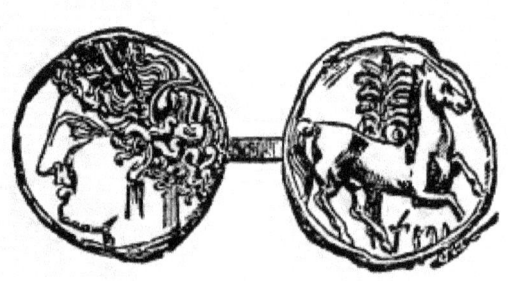

Chapter 1: Rome Before the First Punic War

History has verified the words of the Sacred Writings; the sons of Japhet dwell in the abodes of the sons of Shem. The march of Alexander to the Indus was only a raid; but England has effaced the empire of the Moguls at Delhi; she has long ruled from the Ganges to the Himalayas, amidst the wrecks of Asiatic dynasties. Russia has advanced into the lands of Zinghis and Timour; she is supreme on the Oxus and the Jaxartes; she menaces the fast-decaying Chinese world. Yet the conflicts between the descendants of Shem and Japhet have been many and prolonged for ages; their ultimate issue has often appeared uncertain. Rome never permanently established her power in the Parthian or the Bactrian deserts, though the legions on the Tigris and the Araxes kept back, for centuries, the barbarians of the East.

But, as the empire began to decline and fall, these hordes pressed on the civilisation of the West, the Huns of Attila made their way into the heart of Gaul; the Saracens overran Spain, and appeared on the Loire; they sat down, more than once, before the city of Constantine. Even the crusades hardly checked the course of invasion; the Turks made themselves masters of Asia Minor; seized the seat of imperial power on the Bosporus and, from the fifteenth to the end of the seventeenth centuries, were the terror of European Christendom. Islam is now in the last stage of decrepitude; but it is hardly more than two hundred years since the hosts of the Crescent spread around Vienna, and its navy was dominant, in the Mediterranean, before the great day of Lepanto.

The most memorable, however, of these contests, and perhaps the most momentous for the estate of man, was that which took place between Carthage and Rome, at the close of the third century before the Christian era. The great Phoenician state, supreme on the northern shores of Africa, had, by this time, been for years in decay; it had lost the ascendency at sea, which was the main source of its power; it had been driven out of Sicily, after a disastrous war; it had been almost overthrown by rebellion at home; it was undermined by corruption and bad government.

The Roman republic, on the other hand, was in the prime of youthful national vigour and strength; it had long ruled Italy, south of the Apennines; it had triumphed over its declining rival, and wrested the Mediterranean from its grasp; and it was extending its dominion to the verge of the Alps, was subduing the Celtic tribes in the valley of the Po, was turning its gaze towards Hellas and the East, and was the best ordered community then in existence. Should the two powers be engaged in a death struggle, the fall of the weaker power appeared already certain.

Commanding genius, nevertheless, came, at this juncture, to the aid of Carthage, redressed the balance of adverse fortune, struck down Rome over and over again; and all but achieved her complete destruction. Hamilcar—the chief of the great house of Barca, (corresponding to the Hebrew Barak)—the Nassaus of the Carthaginian commonwealth—had been the hero of his countrymen in the First Punic War; he had resented, with stern patriotic wrath, the calamitous results of that ominous contest. Like William of Orange, in another age, he made it the work of his life to prepare the means to confront an infinitely more powerful enemy; and, having shaken off the ignoble peace party at home—it had paralysed and almost betrayed the state, like the rich Dutch *burghers* of 1671-2—he set off from Carthage, with an armed force, to carry into effect his audacious purpose. He made the Phoenician settlements in Spain a seat of empire, collected immense resources and subdued whole provinces; above all created an army of formidable strength, to become the instrument of his scheme of vengeance.

A worthy successor continued his task; ere long his mantle fell on his eldest son, one of the most extraordinary of the figures which stand out in history. Deceiving Rome by the very grandeur of his design, Hannibal crossed the stupendous barrier of the Alps, where an army had never been seen before; in battle after battle, he overthrew the legions hitherto almost always invincible in the field; and though the tenacity of the republic enabled it to resist, he maintained the contest for many years in Italy, making the result uncertain, almost to the last. And it was Hannibal, and Hannibal alone, who achieved these great deeds, for his army was much less numerous than that of his foes, and he received little or no support from an ungrateful country; and despite difficulties and discouragements of every kind, success wellnigh crowned his gigantic efforts. The fate of the world trembled, in fact, in the balance, for many months, after the terrible rout of Cannae.

Before we follow the career of Hannibal it is necessary, in order to understand its wonders, to glance at the previous history of Rome and of Carthage. The petty community that, in the eighth century B.C., had gathered around the Palatine Hill, and was laying the foundations of the Eternal City, was possibly superior to the other Latin tribes, in certain elements of essential greatness, as the Salian Franks were to the other Germans, or the Normans to the kindred Danes and the Saxons. But it was the neighbour of the trading Etrurians; it was seated on the sea, and acquired power by commerce; its kings, mythical as their figures are, were probably really great rulers; to these causes, perhaps, we may chiefly ascribe the sources of the future grandeur of Rome.

The monarchy lasted nearly two hundred and fifty years; and before it passed away the little town near the Tiber had expanded into a great fortified city, of which imposing remains are still in existence. Rome had become wealthy, prosperous, great in peace and war, as the legends about Numa and Servius prove; she had already taken the first step in the march of conquest. She had subdued some tribes of the Sabellian stock; and she was the recognised head of the Thirty cities, which, extending to the upper course of the Anio, formed the confederacy of the Latin name.

For more than a century and a half after the fall of the monarchy, owing to protracted civil and social discord, Rome made little progress beyond her borders. During this period her fortunes appeared uncertain; she was more than once on the verge of ruin. She was assailed and often defeated by the Etrurian league; the victory of Porsena is not a fable; the tale of the Fabii attests her disasters. Her own sons, too, were found among her enemies, as the pathetic story of Coriolanus proves; and the feuds that divided her citizens were a continual source of danger. But the greatest calamity that befell her came from across the Apennines; she was nearly overwhelmed by a horde of the Gauls; the sword of Brennus all but cut short the thread of her destiny.

Still her power increased on the whole, even in these years; with the assistance of her Latin allies, she conquered two of the Sabellian clans, and advanced her dominions near the heads of the Liris. When her intestine troubles had been composed, and the elements of her constitution had become harmonious, she moved rapidly forward in the path of conquest, and ere long made herself the dominant state of

Italy. She broke up the declining Etrurian power; reduced the Latin league to subjection; made the fertile land of Campania her own; exacted terrible vengeance from the Celts on the Po, and after a fierce and prolonged struggle, conquered the Samnites, the flower of the Sabellian people.

In this conflict she had to resist a league of warlike and brave enemies; she often suffered bloody reverses; the catastrophe of the Pass of Caudium might have unnerved a race of less sterling qualities. But the perseverance, the craft, and the power of Rome in war prevailed; and, after the earlier years of the third century before the Christian era, Italy, from the Rubicon to the Gulf of Tarentum, was at her feet.

The republic had, hitherto, fought Italian tribes only, and the rude, if formidable, levies of the Gaul; it was next to encounter the armed force of Hellas, led by the most brilliant commander of his age. A quarrel between Tarentum and Rome brought Pyrrhus and a Greek army to the southern verge of the peninsula filled with Greek settlements, and the king had been promised the support of a great rising of the subject races, and of the Celts of Italy. But the insurrection was crushed in the bud; a tremendous example was made of the Gauls; a small force proved sufficient to keep down the north; and Rome was enabled to put forth her strength against the invader, who had challenged her power.

The presence of the elephant in the Greek ranks—these huge animals, with their towers of archers and slingers, formed a kind of heavy cavalry and artillery combined, to which the consuls had nothing to oppose—gave Pyrrhus the victory in two great battles; but the *phalanx* could not break the flexible legion; and it deserves notice that the king learned to imitate the tactics of the barbarians he had at first despised. A Pyrrhic victory has become a proverb; the dashing soldier endeavoured to march on Rome, but he found of what stuff his enemy was composed. The aged head of the proudest of the nobles of Rome struck the keynote of the foreign policy of the state; the senate haughtily declared that it would not treat with an invader upon the soil of Italy; and the king fell back, amazed and discomfited.

He had now embarked in the great venture in which he hoped to become the lord of a Sicilian kingdom; but here again he failed, after passing success; and, having returned to Italy to confront Rome once more, he was completely defeated in a decisive battle. The republic had again proved unconquerable in the field.

Nor was the steady advance of Rome to empire more remarkable than her wisdom and skill in consolidating and maintaining her conquests, and in securing the obedience—nay, the goodwill of her subjects. Her territory was enlarged to the utmost bounds consistent with her rule as a sovereign city; the domain of her people was widely extended. But she was not the tyrant of the Italian races; she made her power and her influence supreme by modes of government and administration that attained her ends, but were not unnecessarily harsh or severe. She treated, indeed, the Celt as an enemy, and crushed him out wherever she could; but she allowed the subject communities of her own stock, to retain their institutions, usages, and laws, and gave them a large measure of self-government.

She obliged the Italians to follow her standards; but she never exacted tribute from them; her *suzerainty* was limited, but well defined; it chiefly consisted in her prerogative to declare war, and to make treaties. As regards some populations of other parts of Italy, she kept them, so to speak, in more strict tutelage; and throughout the peninsula she took care to establish military colonies, at points of vantage, which formed centres of her power, and upheld her armies. Italy, by these means, became, by degrees, welded into a great and united nation, ruled, in different ways, by one supreme state, but not generally discontented with its lot; in the main it loyally obeyed Rome; it hardly ever ventured, at least, to rebel. And this structure of empire was bound together by great roads, fortresses, and strong garrisons, even now preparing the way for the Roman Peace to be made perfect only after centuries of war.

The development of the institutions of Rome must also be noticed in this rapid survey. The kings were the masters of the Roman state, as the Roman father was of his own household; but they were only the foremost men of a noble order; they were advised by a senate, or Great Council; they were, in some degree, controlled by a patrician assembly. They were supposed, too, to govern according to law, and it must be borne in mind that reverence for law was a special characteristic of the Roman citizen; the conceptions of Public Justice and of Crimes against the State became very soon manifest in the Roman commonwealth. The kings, therefore, were not mere despots; but, as was the case with every Roman magistrate, they were depositaries of very great power; and, able rulers as some certainly were, they no doubt occasionally abused their immense authority.

Yet the external growth of Rome, we have seen, was remarkable during the regal period, and her internal progress was not less decisive.

As the territory and the possessions of the city increased, the little community that formed its ruling caste was gradually surrounded by a population of sojourners, of dependents, of subject vassals; and numbers of these acquired wealth and influence, though as yet shut out from the full rights of citizens. The military necessities of Rome probably caused these classes to be largely introduced into the ranks of the national army; a political revolution in time followed.

The exclusive aristocracy of birth, that had been dominant, was supplemented to a certain extent, by an aristocracy of landed possessions and wealth; the supreme assembly of purely noble houses had set by its side a new assembly of a broader and more popular aspect. The strongest barriers of privilege were thus broken; the foundations of the state were made wider; and the combined aristocracy formed by these means in all probability caused the fall of the monarchy which had lately shewn arbitrary and unjust tendencies.

The new aristocracy of Rome, however, was very inferior in position and rank to the old aristocracy of patrician blood. It was excluded from the chief offices in the state, and from rights and distinctions of many kinds; it was in some respects what the Nobles of the *Terra Firma* were to the Nobles of the Golden Book of Venice. It was only the head of the plebeian multitude; and, accordingly, it soon began to regard the order placed above it with jealousy and dislike. The feud between the patricians and the plebeians of Rome was envenomed by social distress and grievances, especially as regards the domains of the state, of which the more humble classes vehemently complained; and it lasted, we have said, more than a century and a half.

During this period of trouble, the young republic was repeatedly torn by fierce dissension; the plebeians fled, in a mass, it is said, from the city; the tyranny of the *decemvirs* was formed, and perished; and Rome was divided into two bodies of citizens exasperated against each other by angry passions. The means adopted to put an end to these disorders were curious and strange; dictator after dictator was made supreme; the magistracy of the *tribunes* was even invested with the power of paralysing on the spot the march of the government.

Yet the respect for authority, and the keen political insight which were marked features of the Roman national character, brought these evil times at last to a close; the plebeians were made eligible to nearly all dignities; their social wrongs were, in some measure, redressed; and the assembly of the city was placed on a more popular basis. These great reforms, which removed what was most iniquitous and peccant in the institutions of the state, gave new life to the Roman commonwealth; thenceforward, we have remarked, it advanced from conquest to conquest.

The transformed constitution of Rome, in fact, was well ordered and worked well; it combined stability of government with large popular rights; it was favoured, in a remarkable way, by circumstance, The admission of the plebeian leaders to power in the state healed a *schism* of classes which had been most disastrous, and animated the republic with ever growing energy. The Duilii and the Icilii led armies in the field and filled the highest places in peace, as ably as the Postumii or the Furii of the old *noblesse*; the twofold aristocracy did Rome equally good service. A common sentiment of patriotism extinguished faction, and gradually fused all orders of men together; at the same time the whole system of government and administration was greatly improved.

The extravagant powers which had been entrusted to single magistrates and had proved dangerous, were divided among many, and made more safe; the individual became less potent, the law stronger; the tribunate which might have wrecked the commonwealth, became the loyal and docile ally of the senate. Rome was knitted together as it had never been before; and the results were seen in the expansion of the state, in the diffusion of content through nearly all classes, in the cessation of civil trouble and discord. There was much, indeed, in the existing state of society, which contained the germs of evils to come; the late social reforms had been superficial only; the class of small owners of land was being diminished; the public domain was being more and more engrossed by wealthy men of the ruling orders; a population of slaves, if not yet very large, had been for centuries on the increase.

But the extension of the territory of Rome, which had been the result of conquest, and which enabled thousands of citizens to acquire land, had made these mischiefs comparatively little felt; and slavery had not yet become a national peril. The republic was seated on firm foundations; and the establishment of civil equality and of enlarged franchises had the happiest effects on the whole community.

The constitution of Rome, however, although national, and popular in a real sense, had very little of a democratic character. The assembly of the citizens was nominally supreme; but the senate possessed the substance of power; and the government belonged to the upper classes. The senate, composed of the most eminent men in the state, selected with great care by a very powerful board, practically declared war, made treaties, and proposed the measures which ultimately were to become law; and the assembly at this period never crossed its purpose. It had thus the highest legislative and executive functions; it was recognised abroad and at home alike as the true embodiment of the majesty of Rome.

The great officers of the state, whether generals in the field or heads of embassies, or chief judges, might be indifferently of patrician or plebeian origin; but they were chosen, with scarcely an exception, from the ruling orders of men. The institutions of Rome were, therefore, aristocratic in essence; they were not yet affected by the will of the multitude, or by the influence of mere popular leaders. The causes of this were threefold; political influence in Rome centred in the owners of the soil; and these have usually been conservative in all countries, and ready to obey the powers in existence.

Again, an assembly of citizens engaged in successful wars, in husbandry, in the pursuits of industry, was willing enough to put its trust in another assembly, drawn from its very best men, especially as this had marvellous tact in falling in with the general sentiment; and this tendency increased as the affairs of Rome became more complicated, and had a wider scope. But the most decisive cause is to be found in the peculiarities of the Roman character. The Roman looked up with reverence to his natural leaders; had profound respect for authority, law, and usage; could resent practical wrongs and grievances; but had no ideas about the abstract rights of man; and thought that the people should be governed, not govern. And hence it was that the republic, at this stage of its being, had the strength and the constancy of an aristocratic state; and was loyally upheld, also, by the undivided will of a community prosperous on the whole, and contented.

We pass from the civil to the military institutions of Rome, of special interest in a review of the career of Hannibal. The first Roman Army was drawn from the aristocracy of birth, which formed the people of the original city; it was composed of 3,000 footmen heavily armed, of 300 horsemen, and of 1,200 light infantry; it received the celebrated name of the Legion. As the territory of the state was enlarged, and its population gradually increased, a new and alien element was brought in to augment and strengthen the force of the state; the ranks of the soldiery of noble blood were multiplied by the addition of another soldiery, for the most part, possessors of land; and the single legion grew into four, each modelled upon the pattern of the first, and containing about 4,500 men.

The Confederacy of the Latins, allies, and afterwards subjects, contributed four legions of this type, save that the horsemen were double, perhaps threefold in number; and thus the military establishment of Rome consisted of eight legions, Roman and Latin, comprising 33,600 infantry, and probably 4,000 cavalry or more. In addition to this, the regular army, composed mainly of holders of land, there were bodies of supernumeraries, as they may be called, made up of men lower in the social scale; and as the republic extended its conquests, and became ruler of Italy south of the Apennines, its military strength was prodigiously increased. The vanquished Italian peoples were forced to send contingents to its army; these may have retained characteristics of their own, but probably were organised, armed, and disciplined after the fashion of the legion in nearly all respects; they certainly held the same order in battle.

By these means the armed forces of Rome became the most numerous and formidable in the then known world; she had 70,000 infantry and 8,000 horsemen, at the great Battle of Ausculum fought against Pyrrhus; in a contest with the Gauls, before the Second Punic War, she put, it seems, more than ten legions on foot. (Polybius, ii., estimates the entire armed strength of Rome and of Italy before the Second Punic War at 777,000 men, including 70,000 horse. These figures have been adopted by Napoleon III., *Hist, de Jules César*, i., and by Colonel Dodge, *Hannibal*.)

In the last years of the third century B.C., she could place 200,000 men in her first line; and these were supported by powerful reserves, it has been said, more than 400,000 strong. Besides these arrays, swarms of Gallic auxiliaries, on many occasions, followed her standards, giving aid to a mortal enemy, with the recklessness of the Celt, in their savage quarrels with neighbouring tribes.

The legions, before the First Punic War, seem to have remained at their original strength, that is, the Roman at 4,200 foot and 300 horse, the Latin at the same number of foot, and at least 600 horse—some writers say there were 900;—and to these should be added the supernumerary force, some perhaps light footmen, archers, and slingers, others attendant on the trains and the impedimenta, others possibly a kind of special reserve. We may next briefly consider the nature and qualities of the legion, the principal unit of the Roman Army, corresponding to the "division" of our day; we assume that the Latin and the other Italian legions, known by the general name of "allied," were essentially of the same character. The old Roman legion was, for the most part, a dense mass, analogous to the Greek *phalanx*; the 3,000 heavy infantry, from sixteen to twenty deep, were arrayed for battle on a compact front, the 1,200 light foot, thrown as skirmishers forward, the 300 horsemen placed upon either wing.

This formation, however, was ill adapted to the hilly and broken country of Italy; and at a remote period—the date is unknown—the Romans, with their natural instinct for war, replaced it by another formation better suited to their land and themselves, and shewing a marked progress in the military art. The light footmen, now called *velites*, perhaps supported by supernumeraries, armed with bows and slings, retained their position and occupied the extreme front; but the heavy infantry was divided into three classes of troops, the *hastati* and the *principes*, each 1,200 strong, men in the vigour and flower of life, and the *triarii*, 600 picked veterans; and these bodies were formed into three lines, at fixed distances, passing from the front to the rear, and each probably ten deep. The order of battle of these lines was remarkable, and requires attention.

Each line was composed of a number of *maniples*, the counterparts of the modern "company"; the *maniples* were drawn up on the field, with gaps between them, at measured intervals; and the lines were so arranged that the *maniples* of each could move, through the gaps, to the support of the others, advancing or falling back as the case might be, and even, conceivably, that the three lines could be marshalled on a single extended front. This order of battle, which must have required troops of extreme steadiness, and of the highest discipline, was, given this condition, very flexible and strong; and armed and trained as the Roman infantry was, it was most formidable in attack and defence, especially against a mass like the *phalanx*, resembling the unwieldy French columns of the last days of Napoleon. The cavalry of the legion, weak in numbers, and not reckoned an important arm, remained, as before, on both wings. The organisation and the order of battle of the allied legion was, no doubt, the same as that of the Roman legion, in all essential respects.

The legionary soldiers wore defensive armour; but this hardly requires notice; it was of excellent quality and fit for its uses. The *velite* had a helmet and a light shield; but the heavy infantry man was well protected; he carried an admirably designed shield, and wore greaves and a flexible coat of mail; his helmet, nodding with red or black plumes, guarded his head, and seemed to add to his stature. The offensive arms of the footmen deserve to be mentioned; for they explain and illustrate the Roman methods in battle. These troops made little use of missiles of far range; they had not yet the *balista*, the ancient field-gun, (perhaps in use during the Second Punic War, but does not seem to have been very effective, it proved useless at the Trebia, if it was really employed); their slingers and archers were few, and of small account; they had nothing resembling the English long-bow, which levelled the haughty chivalry of France with the dust.

They trusted wholly to close hand-to-hand fighting; for this their weapons were of extraordinary power. The *velite* carried a short sword, and six or seven light darts; but these, thrown by the hand, could not have had a long flight; his sword was probably much more effective. The offensive arms of the heavy infantry were, on the other hand, peculiar, and formidable in the extreme. The *hastati* and *principes*, besides spears, had the *pilum*, a javelin of great weight and strength, and the *gladius*, a cut and thrust sword, short, sharp, and of the best workmanship; these decided the issue of many a battle. The *triarii* were armed with a long pike, a relic, perhaps, of the exploded *phalanx*; but they had the *gladius*, and two spears; the duty of these veterans in the last line, in the rear, was to avert defeat or to follow up victory; their arms were adapted to this purpose. The weapons of the comparatively neglected cavalry were less distinctive; they carried a lance, a sword, and a few javelins.

The legion, organised and armed in this way, was divided into numbers of *cohorts*, (some writers have maintained that the *cohort* was a formation later than the Second Punic War), similar to the battalions and squadrons of these days; each *cohort* was composed of a *turma* of horsemen, and of *maniples* of heavy and light infantry; but this unit was not of special importance. As has been the case in all good armies, the Romans had many officers in well-defined grades; the legion was commanded by a *tribune*—a general of division, of brigade, and a colonel in one; and it had *centurions*, *signifers*, *decurions*, the captains, lieutenants, ensigns, and sergeants of modern times. Every legion, too, had its regular staff, its hospital and commissariat services, its artificers, bands, carriages, trains, and beasts of burden; but it should be specially noticed that the legionary carried a pack heavier than that of any soldier of our age, and yet made astonishing marches, a decisive proof of his excellent training and health.

We may next see how a Roman Army was formed out of a union of legions. A Roman and allied legion usually marched together; the two were often reckoned as a single legion; and two of these double legions, really four, formed a Consular Army, as it was called, an army, including fighting men, and men of other services, from 20,000 to 21,000 strong at this period.

★★★★★★★★★★

At and after the time of the Second Punic War, the strength of the legion, Roman and Latin, was increased; a Consular Army would then be from 24,000 to 26,000 men, and Two Consular Armies double their numbers.

★★★★★★★★★★

A consul, as a rule, was at the head of this force; the two consuls, the military chiefs of the state, thus commanded from 40,000 to 42,000 men in this way; but these numbers could be enormously increased by the addition of other legions, and auxiliary troops, such, for instance, as friendly Gallic warriors. A dictator, however, at grave crises, occasionally was invested with supreme command, and represented the consuls in the field; and the military duties of a consul were often devolved on a *praetor*, or a *legatus*, especially when there were many armies on foot, and a retiring consul was sometimes re-appointed, and served as a proconsul. (Some commentators, e.g., Hénnébert, think that a *legatus* was a commander of a later period, Livy, however, refers more than once to a *legatus* in the Second Punic War. The point is not important.) The highest commands in the Roman Army were always confined to Roman citizens, but the allied legions probably had their own officers.

We may now observe how a Roman Army, say a consular one, engaged in battle. It was, we have seen, usually composed of two double legions, that is, two Roman and two allied; the Romans held the centre, the allies the wings. It often marched from its camp, across a river to meet the hostile force in its front, a grave error, the results of which it learned by tremendous lessons, when before Hannibal. A Roman Army always assumed the offensive, with the true instinct of a conquering race; its whole system of tactics was designed for attack and that at the closest possible quarters; but its attacks were usually in front simply; it seldom manoeuvred.

The *velites*, when it formed its order of battle, detached themselves from the rear, and moved to the front; the cavalry was stationed at the edge of either wing: the heavy infantry was marshalled in its comparatively thin lines, which supported each other from the front to the rear. After discharges of arrows, stones or bullets from bows or slings—these seem to have been feeble and not effective—the *velites* threw their darts to harass and shake the enemy; the *hastati* then advanced in their divided *maniples*, flung their spears and launched the terrible *pilum*, and then instantly closed with the fatal *gladius*, the onset resembling a volley of musketry, followed by a determined charge of the bayonet.

If the attack of the first line was not successful, the *principes* moved forward in their *maniples*, through the gaps that had been left open for them; or the *hastati*, if repulsed, fell back on them; the *triarii*, the last line, followed the same tactics. The enemy's masses were thus exposed to formidable attacks by three lines, which assisted each other with practised skill; the three lines had the means of deploying on a broad front, and attaining the hostile flanks; and armed and disciplined as the Roman soldiery were, this method of fighting repeatedly secured victory. The cavalry, as a rule, was held in reserve, until the infantry had made success probable; it then fell on the enemy's flank and rear.

An army, however, like this, and these modes of tactics, successful as they were, over and over again, were not without several well-marked defects; and advantage might be taken of these, especially by a great captain. The Roman Army had very little means of projecting missiles, at far distances; its slingers and archers were an insignificant force; it was thus liable to defeat at the hands of an army, superior in this respect; and this was to be proved by notable instances. A Roman Army, again, was weak in cavalry; this arm was seldom more than a seventh or eighth part of the infantry, perhaps not a tenth in the shock of battle, for it was largely employed as an exploring force; and the footmen of the legion would be necessarily exposed to formidable and perhaps fatal attacks, if assailed by cavalry better and more numerous than their own, particularly if these were ably directed.

The Romans had already felt the power of the elephant; an array of "the huge, earth-shaking beasts"—heavy cavalry and artillery we have said, combined—might lay them open once more, as in the days of Pyrrhus, to a reverse. The methods besides by which their lines of foot were formed on the field, admirable as they were against such a mass as the *phalanx*, were perilous in the face of a skilful enemy, possessing good cavalry; the gaps between the *maniples* would afford the horsemen an opportunity to strike in; and crush the ranks; and, marvellous as the Roman discipline was, it sometimes failed to endure a trial of this kind, and the legionaries were broken up, and routed.

We should add, what was, perhaps, most important of all, that the system of supreme command in the Roman Army was faulty. The consuls held their offices for a year only; this term was too short to make them masters of war, trained to arms as they had been from boyhood; and though the term was sometimes renewed, and a dictator was now and then made general-in-chief, in a few instances, for a series of years, this was not the way to create great commanders.

When the consuls, moreover, were in the field together, they commanded, as a rule, on alternate days, a thoroughly bad and dangerous practice, which was, however, followed in the Army of France, until it was exploded by the powers of Turenne. It should be remarked, too, that the institutions of Rome, both civil and military, were not adapted to bring out supreme individual genius; its statesmen and soldiers were rather able men, than of the first capacity in peace or in war. It was reserved for Hannibal to shew, by immortal examples, what were the defects of the Roman Armies and their chiefs.

The Roman legion, we have said, was mainly composed of owners of land—peasant freeholders probably in most instances—and so doubtless were the allied legions. The army, therefore, was drawn from the classes which have nearly always produced a breed of hardy men, amenable to discipline, and ready to obey; it was formed of the elements which were seen in the archers of Crecy, and the mighty Ironsides of Dunbar and Worcester. The Roman soldier was liable to serve from seventeen to forty-five, in the field; and after that age he might be employed in garrisons; he was, therefore, bound to an extremely long service, though probably he received his discharge, in ordinary times, while still a young man.

The army has been most incorrectly called a militia; it was a standing national army of the best quality, embodying what was strongest in the Roman people, and trained to the highest point of perfection. The boyish recruit was drilled with extraordinary care, especially in the use of his arms, and marching; his military education was always going on; from his teens, until he became a veteran, he was kept to a round of incessant duty. The Roman soldier was liable to the severest punishments; death was the penalty of insubordination, desertion, and cowardice in battle; but his country could appeal to his patriotic pride; and he was eligible for different rewards and honours. The army, constituted and fashioned in this way, like every creation of man, was not faultless; it went down before a great genius in war; but it was indomitable, and it subdued the civilised world.

The Romans, at this period, had not attained the proficiency of the Greeks, in the art of sieges. The fortifications of Rome, and of other Italian cities, were formidable, and apparently well designed; but they were certainly inferior to those of Carthage; the Romans, like all races that excel in war, relied more on armies in the field, than on the skill of the engineer. The methods of besieging in use, before the invention of gunpowder made them in part obsolete, were, however, understood by the Romans of this time; they drew lines round a beleaguered fortress, constructed approaches, and employed mines; they possessed the battering ram and the catapult, the wooden tower and the *agger* to command the walls they assailed.

The Roman camp was a special feature of the Roman system of war; it largely contributed to the progress of the arms of Rome. The legions, we have said, always attacked in battle; but they usually had a fortified camp in the rear to fall back on, in the event of defeat; this great work was sufficient to keep the enemy at bay, and to enable them to resume the offensive. The Romans, too, made camps, when they were on the march, especially in a hostile country; and these constructions, admirably planned, though hastily thrown up from materials on the spot, and resembling an Italian town in a state of defence, formed points of vantage for resistance or attack, and laid the foundations, so to speak, of conquest. A Roman camp probably baffled Hannibal more than once; and encampments hold a conspicuous place in the campaigns of Caesar. (Polybius and Livy, especially Polybius, are still of course the best authorities on the military institutions and the Army of Rome.)

In one most important part of the art of war, Rome was, at this time, behind other nations of the age. The Mediterranean was, for the ancient world, the great highway of commerce, and the road to empire. The possession of naval power had made the Etrurians, for many years, a formidable state; had spread Greek colonies, and the civilisation of the Greeks, from the shores of Asia Minor to the Gulf of Lyons; had made Carthage supreme at sea, from the Adriatic to the Pillars of Hercules. Rome had a fleet, and a trading marine in the regal period; but between her intestine strife, and her Italian conquests, she had neglected these elements of strength and wealth; her flag in the Mediterranean, to use modern language, was seldom seen in the century before the First Punic War.

By this time Carthage was mistress of that great basin, and though nominally she was an ally of Rome, she took care to exclude the republic from commerce between the coasts of Hellas and the Atlantic, and looked with jealousy at her petty and few war-ships. Rome, afraid of the naval power of the Phoenician empire, began to fortify parts of the coast of Italy; but with her instinctive comprehension of war, she perceived ere long that a fleet alone would secure her the means of effective defence, or prevent the annihilation of her foreign trade; thenceforward she began to construct a navy. Her efforts were, however, weak and tentative for a long time; had her rival known what the future was to bring forth, she would have left nothing undone to make them fruitless; for, as we shall see, maritime power was a decisive element in the contest with Rome, and was, perhaps, a paramount cause of the ultimate defeat of Hannibal. (I shall, of course, dwell on this subject afterwards.)

The civil and military institutions of Rome, of which we have tried to sketch the outlines, were, taking also circumstance into account, visible signs and growths of the Roman national character. That character was one of the most striking that has appeared among the families of man; we need not say what a mark it has left on history. The Roman citizen, of this period at least, possessed the qualities that assure the greatness of a state, and that send it upon the path of empire. He feared the gods, whom he devoutly worshipped, bound by the religion (*ligare*) which he sincerely felt; but he was not a coward to immolate human victims; and he had not a trace of the scepticism of the Greek. He had the profoundest regard for law and the powers that be; the very authority his magistrates possessed is a proof that it was not often perverted; he went through life a loyal and obedient subject.

He was attached to his farm, as his chief pursuit; he did not care much for the stir of the city; he took comparatively little part in its din and its turmoil. He scorned mob rule, and would have laughed at a demagogue; he knew nothing about democratic theories; he would have thought the natural equality of man nonsense. The ideas of Greek philosophy never entered his mind; but deep down in his heart was the proud conviction that Rome was the ruling state of Italy, and that nothing should be left untried to secure her aggrandisement. For this he freely shed his blood in battle; for this he endured hardships however severe; before everything else he was a true patriot. He thought foreign nations his inferiors; the destiny of Rome was to make them her footstool; but he could conciliate them, when he had become their master; he was their sagacious ruler, not their cruel tyrant.

He was stern, and even implacable in war, but he was sometimes magnanimous, seldom bloodthirsty; he was a conqueror who did not abuse conquest. At home he was master in his own household, but he was a good husband, a good father, even not pitiless to his slaves; he made a righteous use of his immense authority. For the rest, he was dogged, tenacious, conservative in thought, not ready to take new ideas in, somewhat commonplace, and seldom endowed with genius, but manly, of a genial and happy temper, and usually contented with his lot in life. He was in many respects the very opposite of the brilliant, keen-witted and light-hearted Greek, the chief inventor of the arts that adorn life, the parent of philosophy and poetry of the highest order, but not the founder of stable and enduring government.

Such very briefly was the position of Rome before she entered the lists with Carthage. Though not always victorious in the First Punic War she, nevertheless, did wonderful things; she showed an easy superiority over her declining rival, in patriotism, in energy, in essential power, in all that constitutes a vigorous and a rising state. She made remarkable progress after this contest; expanded nearly to the extreme verge of Italy; evidently began to aspire to far-reaching empire. Yet, just when she thought she was about to subdue and annihilate her detested enemy, she was suddenly arrested in the path of conquest. Hannibal very nearly compassed her ruin; and, notwithstanding Zama, and the fall of Carthage, the memory of his tremendous exploits lay heavily on the minds of her people, even through the centuries of her imperial grandeur.

Chapter 2: Carthage Before the First Punic War

The Phoenicians, a people of the Semitic stock, of which the Hebrews were doubtless the finest specimen, seem to have originally wandered in lands to the east of the Tigris. At a period, however, before the birth of history, they had settled upon the plains of Syria, and they held a strip along the coast that received their name. The Mediterranean lay open to their enterprise; their great cities of Tyre and Sidon arose; they had establishments in Hellas, still half barbaric; they became the first nation of traders on record. (The legend told by Herodotus, that Hellas owed many elements of her first culture to the Phoenicians, may be rejected; but it attests their relations with the early Hellenes.)

The Phoenician sails were seen in the Erythraean sea, along the Persian Gulf, in the Bay of Biscay; Phoenician merchants trafficked in the tin of Britain, in the ivory of Africa, in the gems of India; Tyre became the Venice of the early ancient world. A Phoenician colony, probably setting out from Tyre, in the ninth century before the Christian era, seated itself—perhaps beside another colony that had already formed an abode at Utica—in the fertile territory around the bay of Tunis; and Carthage, (to be compared with Kirjath), the "new town" of the latest settlers, became gradually a large and flourishing city.

Its position on the Mediterranean, upon the northern coast of Africa, a few leagues only from the shores of Sicily, and within easy reach of Italy, of Greece, of Spain, marked it out by nature as a great centre of trade; and the rich inland plains along the Mejerda—still abounding in the olive, and waving with corn—gave it an ample store of agricultural wealth. In a comparatively short time Carthage had spread her dominion over the adjoining region occupied by the Libyan tribes, and had sent colonies of her own along the verge of Africa, into the Algeria

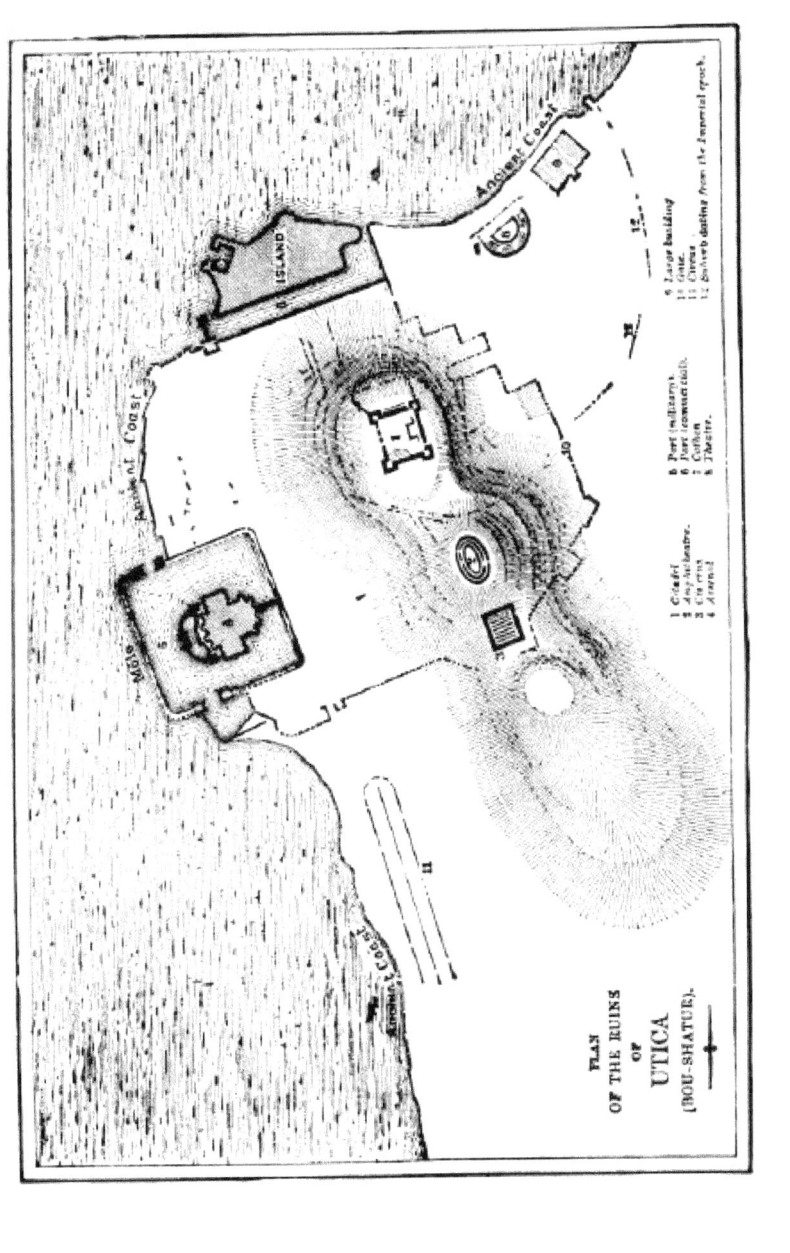

and Morocco of modern days, which mingled with other Phoenician settlements, and seemed to have reached the distant Atlantic.

The Phoenicians were a strong and adventurous race; the mariners who first braved the ocean of the West must have possessed qualities of a very high order. But their energies were devoted to trade only; they did not aspire to foreign conquest; they were not destined to become great rulers of men. They founded numerous settlements on the Mediterranean coasts; but these were factories like the Madras and Bombay of the East India Company before the advent of Clive; they paid tribute to Assyrian and Egyptian kings; even in the Mediterranean they had few war-ships. Carthage followed the example of the race from which she sprang; she acknowledged, perhaps, for three or four centuries, the *suzerainty* of the chiefs of the Libyan *nomades*; she was a vassal of the Great King of the East; she co-operated, with the men of Sidon, in the expedition of Xerxes. Sheer necessity seems to have made her a warlike state, and to have directed her in the paths of conquest.

Her commerce in the Mediterranean was crossed and thwarted by the powerful maritime Etrurian league; the settlements she had formed in Sicily, and along the verge of Tripoli, were threatened by the swarms of Greek colonists, which had begun to emigrate from the lands of Hellas. She was thus compelled to build fleets and to fit out armies; and she maintained a protracted contest with the foreign races, which had made themselves, against her will, her enemies. The dominion of the Etrurians at sea soon passed away; but Carthage had to contend, for centuries, with the Greeks, for empire in the Mediterranean, and along its borders. The chief theatre of the strife was Sicily, where the Phoenician state had large possessions in the west, and the great city of Syracuse was at the head of the Hellenes, in the east, and the south: it was waged with the fury which has usually marked conflicts between the Semitic and the Aryan races.

We cannot follow its many vicissitudes; more than once the Greek power in Sicily had almost fallen; more than once Carthage was in grave straits; but from the great battle of Himera, fought, perhaps, on the day of Salamis, to the failure of Pyrrhus, after he had set foot in Sicily, that is, for a period of upwards of two centuries, these wars raged with few large intervals of time between. The trial made Carthage a great naval and military power; she had, on the whole, proved superior in strength to the disunited and misgoverned Greek cities. She had kept the Hellene back to the east of Tripoli; she had maintained and enlarged her bounds in Sicily; and she was the mistress of the Mediterranean and its waters.

In the first years of the third century B.C., Carthage had become the seat of an imposing empire. The original colony had become greatly enlarged by emigration from the parent city of Tyre, after it had fallen to Alexander's arms; the Carthaginians were the recognised heads of the Phoenician name. They had completely subdued the Libyan peoples, whose lands they had once held as vassals; they had extended their territory near to the great African desert. They had swallowed up and reduced to subjection their own and the earlier settlements on the north African coast; their rule was absolute from the verge of Greece to regions far beyond the straits of Gibraltar. They were masters of Sardinia, and the Balearic isles; they formed the dominant power in Sicily; they possessed settlements in the Iberian Peninsula, as far as the course of the Guadalquivir.

But the chief symbol of their grandeur was Carthage herself; the city, the London of the ancient world, had a population probably of a million of souls, and was infinitely the largest of the Mediterranean cities; the renown of its edifices and fortifications had spread far and wide. The wealth and resources of the state were immense, they were upheld by formidable military and naval power. Carthage had placed armies in the field of great numbers, which had repeatedly fought, not without success, against the best troops of the Greek race; her soldiery had more than once overthrown the fine infantry of the Dorian name. And her fleets, at this time, had no rivals; they were probably superior to those of all the Greek cities combined; in the Mediterranean they were easily supreme.

The Carthaginians, however, were not fitted to be the architects of a permanent empire. They remained a Phoenician colony, of Phoenician qualities, planted in the midst of inferior African races; this did not conduce to the vigorous growth of the state. A nation of traders, their souls were given to the accumulation of riches, especially by sea; they had not the genius of well-ordered government; they were cruelly oppressive to the peoples they had made their subjects. They reduced the Libyan *nomades* around the city to the condition of abject and degraded serfs; the lands of their great merchant nobles were tilled by thousands of slaves, or by a population resembling the *fellahs* of Egypt. The magnificent plains around the Mejerda formed a slave plantation of immense extent; very different from the hills and valleys of Latium, the seat of free and hardy owners of the soil, they yielded

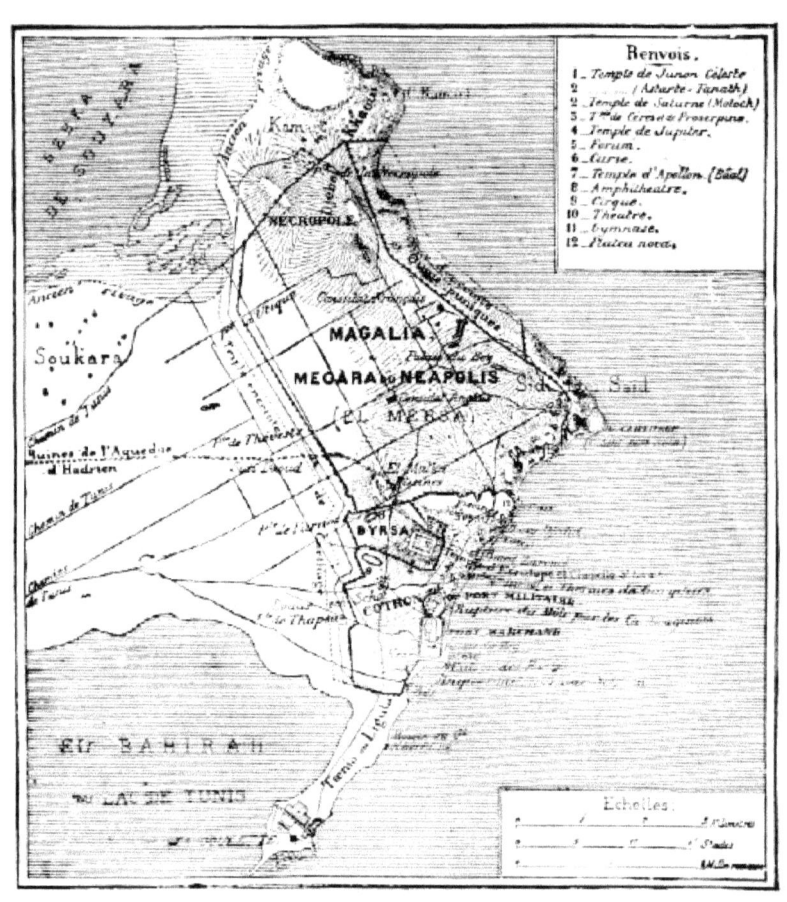

MAP OF PENINSULA OF CARTHAGE.

their increase to alien masters; they were filled with elements of discontent and wretchedness.

The rule, too, of Carthage over the settlements of her own race was that of a selfish, grasping, and short-sighted tyrant. Unlike Rome, she exacted tribute from the cities and colonies she called allies, and governed them with suspicious harshness; she did not allow them to build walls; she gave them no municipal rights; she kept them under the yoke of her own citizens. Her African empire was thus not loyal; the people of mixed Phoenician and Libyan origin, which spread from the Syrtes to the Atlantic, regarded her with terror, not with affection; she could not rely on them in the stress of national peril.

As for her subjects in Spain, and the Mediterranean islands, she dealt with them in the meanest trading spirit; she extorted from them as much as she could, and made use of them to man her fleets and her armies; but she treated them as mere half-tamed barbarians, and never tried to attract their sympathies. In Sicily alone her rule was milder; she could not afford to be in too marked contrast with the civilisation and the free isle of Hellas.

Aristotle has praised, to a certain extent, the civil institutions of the Carthaginian state; but that great thinker has looked chiefly at their mechanism and external aspect. Even theoretically they had marked defects; but they were most worthy of notice for this: they most strikingly shew how modes of government that conceivably might have worked well, in a public-spirited and patriotic nation, were made vicious and evil by the selfishness, the corruption, and the venality of rulers and subjects.

Two magistrates of Carthage had the title of kings; but though representing perhaps a monarchy of the past, their authority seems to have been almost nominal; the *suffetes* were honorary chiefs of the state, like the *doges* of Venice. The government was carried on by an elective council, formed of two bodies, one large, one small; the whole, in Roman language, was called a senate; but the small body, composed of a few members, apparently always wealthy magnates, had the general work of administration in its hands, declared war, made treaties, prepared the army and navy, and appointed the leading functionaries of the state. This body, however, was, in turn, controlled by a board, selected from aristocratic families, and resembling the Venetian Council of Ten; it exercised supreme judicial powers; and in this capacity it could try and punish even the most exalted personages, who had held office.

These institutions were thus narrow, and exclusive in the highest degree; and the executive government was checked and hampered by a dominant and irresponsible order of men, who repeatedly gave proof of a most cruel spirit, and inflicted unjust and terrible vengeance on generals, ministers, and others, who had been unfortunate. This order of things, however, possessed stability, and might not have been essentially bad, had the national life of Carthage been different from what it was, more healthy, vigorous, and able to throw off disease. But the commonwealth was divided into a class of ruling merchants, who made selfish profit the aim of their being; into a great city populace, which could be stirred with passion, but, in ordinary times, could be bought and sold; and into a multitude of miserable serfs; the results were what might have been expected.

Tyranny, maladministration, a cowardly and injudicious policy, truckling to the strong, and cruel to the weak, suspicion, jealousy, and vindictiveness in high places, were characteristics of Carthaginian Government, except at crises of grave importance; and the state was honeycombed, so to speak, by corruption. Yet the most significant feature, perhaps, of this state of things was that, in theory at least, the whole system depended upon the will of the citizens; a popular assembly at Carthage, as at Rome, had the right to exercise sovereign power; but it was practically impotent, for it was regularly bribed, and reduced to nothingness by the mercantile *noblesse*. Fierce faction and democratic passion were certain to arise out of these evil elements; but, in the case of Carthage, they failed to restore a falling state.

An empire powerful on land, and mighty at sea, but unjust to alien and subject races, and therefore weak in the hour of trial and danger; an aristocracy of wealthy and noble merchants, exhibiting the vices traders have always shewn where they became absolute in a state, and carrying out the ideas of the shop and the counter, not of the minds fitted to rule nations; a harsh government of privilege secured by riches, severe to its own members, and lording it over a vast population of bondsmen and slaves, and the rabble of a city bought by its gold—such was Carthage in the days of her highest grandeur. Her "princes," in the words of the great Hebrew prophet, (Ezekiel), "were like wolves, ravening for prey, and to get dishonest gain; the people of the land exercised robbery, vexed the poor and needy, and oppressed the stranger."

It may appear surprising that Carthage, in circumstances of this kind, should have produced a breed of really great men; but the Semitic races have had many examples of warriors and rulers of a high order; we may refer to the renowned monarchs of the tribe of Judah. The Carthaginians, too, like other peoples of their stock, were brave, stubborn, even heroic in terrible crises; and the very weakness and decline of a state has sometimes favoured individual genius. Caesar appeared in the decay of the Roman republic, Napoleon when France was in the throes of anarchy; the house of Barca was most conspicuous in the last years of Carthage.

The military institutions of Carthage are little known; but they were wholly different from those of her great rival. The Carthaginians never possessed a national army composed of the flower of their citizens, like that of the Romans and their allies; and they had no peculiar military organisation of their own. The Phoenician element in the state was not very strong; a great colony of traders, devoted to the sea, did not keep a powerful army permanently on foot. Carthage was able to muster a kind of militia, of considerable size, for the defence of the city, she occasionally sent a small body of choice troops, called the "sacred band," to serve in the field; but she had nothing resembling the legions of Rome; and if her allied and subject states were even bound to supply contingents to aid her in war, it appears probable they had a right to commute this laborious duty by a fixed money payment. The empire, in fact, was one of trade, and brave as the Carthaginians were as a people, they relied chiefly on their riches, and what these could effect, to obtain the military resources required for the state.

They had great arsenals to store up arms, and manufactured them in immense quantities; but their armies were, for the most part, formed of mercenaries collected from the provinces they ruled, and from foreign and even barbarian lands. Carthage bought her troops as she bought everything else; she gathered them in like her commerce, from many parts of the earth. The pure Phoenicians in her service were certainly few; but these, apparently, were her best troops; they were animated by the pride of a dominant race; they had the Semitic daring, and stubborn courage. The mixed population of Phoenicians, and of the Libyan tribes, spread along the seaboard of north Africa, supplied great levies of warlike men, resembling the *Zouaves* and *Turcos* of modern France; and to these should be added swarms of Numidian horsemen, light cavalry of the very best quality.

The Spanish settlements and the other parts of Spain sent thousands of Celts inured to Avar; the Balearic isles gave excellent archers and slingers; and the martial races of Gaul—born soldiers in all ages—

CARTHAGINIAN WARRIOR.

flocked, in masses of foot and horse, to the Carthaginian standards. Great mercenary armies were formed by these means; and though, even in mere numbers, the military power of Carthage was very inferior to that of Rome, she had more than once, in her Sicilian wars, put at least 100,000 men into the field.

An army thus made up of many races and tongues, differing from each other in modes of life and usage, unlike the Roman Army, could not have had a uniform organisation in the field, the same formations, the same order of battle. A Carthaginian Army must have, in fact, presented an extraordinary and strangely irregular aspect. The Phoenician citizens, civilised men, must have formed a marked contrast to the dusky hordes of Africans, the savage children of the far-spreading plain, to the kilted and half-naked clans of the Gauls, and to the Balearic and Spanish levies. Attempts, however, appear to have been made to combine these motley elements of military power into something resembling a fixed system.

Carthage, so different from Rome, had no instinct for war; the organisation of her armies in the field was largely borrowed from the Greek model. The Phoenicians and the Spaniards were probably her best infantry; they were usually marshalled in a *phalanx*, that is in a dense mass sixteen or twenty deep, and composed of about 6,000 footmen. We find, however, Africans and Gauls placed in bodies of this kind; and the *phalanx*, like the legion, probably was the principal unit of a Carthaginian Army. The *phalanx* combined heavy and light infantry, and had some 500 horsemen to cover its flanks; a number of *phalanx*es, like a number of legions, made up, when united, an army, in its main strength at least.

But a Carthaginian Army certainly possessed other large formations of a different kind, adapted to the habits in war of its numerous mixed races. The African footmen, for the most part, were light troops; these doubtless provided great arrays of skirmishers, who fought in open order, or charged home in masses. The Numidian cavalry, often in immense numbers, formed separate bodies, perhaps like the Cossack horsemen; they had their own tactics, and their own modes of fighting. The Gauls were drawn up in the field in their clans, they rushed forward to battle, perhaps in strong lines like the Highlanders of Preston Pans, and Falkirk; their formidable cavalry seems to have been a real "equestrian tempest." It should be added that Carthage possessed in the elephant a powerful element of support to her army in the field.

The defensive armour and the weapons of the Carthaginian Army were different, like its dissimilar races; but they were far from as good as those of a Roman Army. The light and heavy footmen of the *phalanx* were protected for the most part like those of the legion, but their shields were not to be compared with the Roman scutum. The African levies not in the *phalanx* wore only a tunic, or a burnous cloak; the Numidian horseman had a leopard skin thrown over his shoulders. The Spanish infantry had helmets, and perhaps coats of mail, over a uniform of white, with red borders; but the Gauls fought in their kilts, or naked to the waist, and seem to have despised all defensive armour, except a huge shield of inferior quality. The light infantry of the *phalanx* carried darts like the Roman *velite*; but the heavy infantry did not possess the *pilum* and *gladius*—the most destructive of Roman weapons; they were armed with long pikes, and perhaps spears; and they were certainly supported by infantry less heavily armed.

The arms of the African levies, and of the Numidian cavalry were darts and lances; the Numidians, like the Saracens of a later age, were admirably skilled in the use of the lance. The Spanish soldier was well armed; he carried a spear, and a cut-and-thrust sword, the nearest resemblance to the Roman *gladius*; the slings of the Balearic islanders in their hands were very effective. The Gaul was armed with a spear, and a long broad sword, the claymore of the highlander of another day; he often did great things with these weapons; but their temper was bad, and their shape clumsy; they were most formidable in the first rush of battle.

Hannibal more than once armed his troops with the weapons of legionaries slain, or made prisoners; this is a conclusive proof of their superior excellence. The array of elephants in a Carthaginian Army bore towers, filled with archers and slingers, on their backs; and, as we have said, it united the power of heavy cavalry and artillery in a single arm.

It is not easy to describe the features of a battle fought by a Carthaginian Army; they were less strongly marked than those of a Roman battle, and they seem to have been much less uniform. It may be possible, however, to understand them, generally at least, by examining a number of known instances. The deep *phalanx* formed the strength of the Carthaginian line; but its depth apparently was much varied; this seems to have been reduced by Hannibal. The *phalanx* presented a narrow front; but on either side were arrayed strong lines of the less heavily armed infantry, to take advantage of the effects of its shock, and to make the order of battle more extended; swarms of archers, slingers, and other light troops, much more numerous than those attached to the legion, were thrown forward, to act as skirmishers.

The auxiliary forces doubtless held the ground in formations of their own; beside the cavalry which belonged to the *phalanx* there were great masses of other cavalry in the field; all these were usually on the wings of the army, but sometimes were placed on points of vantage, and the array of elephants, as a rule, was on the flank, or in the rear. A Carthaginian Army was thus drawn up less regularly than a Roman Army; its tactics in battle were very different. After the skirmishers had discharged their many volleys of missiles, and made an impression on the hostile force, the *phalanx*es advanced in their dense arrays, with probably infantry on both flanks; reliance was chiefly placed on the imposing size and the weighty shock of the close column, and should it succeed in forcing the enemy back, the supporting infantry fell on, to make his overthrow complete.

This method, however, furnished a single attack only, unlike the threefold attack of the legion; it was less really formidable because the weapons of the soldier of the *phalanx* were inferior, especially in a hand-to-hand fight; and should the unwieldy mass be defeated, it ran the risk of being broken up and cut to pieces. The infantry battle of a Carthaginian Army was feeble compared to a Roman infantry battle; the troops engaged, too, were of different quality, for nothing was equal to the Roman footman; but it was otherwise as regards the cavalry. This arm, we have said, was weak in the Roman service; in the Carthaginian it was extremely strong; and the Gaulish, and especially the Numidian horsemen, repeatedly performed admirable feats in the field; annihilated the squadrons, and even the legions of Rome, and secured for Carthage most splendid triumphs. The elephant seems to have been usually employed in crushing the enemy when once shaken; the archers and slingers on the towers harassed him when in retreat. (It will, of course, be understood that these attempts to describe a Roman and a Carthaginian battle are meant only to explain its broadest and most general characteristics. No two battles can be exactly the same.)

The Army of Carthage, considered as a whole, was not a trustworthy, or even a good army. A huge mercenary assemblage of mixed races, it did not possess the patriotic feeling, the regular order, the systematic training of a well-organised, national army; it was wanting in moral power, and could not bear defeat. Crowded as it was with

RESERVOIRS OF CARTHAGE.

levies of barbarian tribes, its discipline must have been very imperfect; its subordinate officers were probably bad; it was difficult to make the troops obey orders; it was liable to break up, and scatter into fragments. The infantry, the backbone of an army in every age, were not the "*robur peditum*" of the Army of Rome; few certainly were of the best quality, and the *phalanx*, in its formation and its mode of giving battle, was very inferior to the lines of the legion, armed as these were with much better weapons, more easily handled and less cumbrous, and much more powerful for attack and defence.

Still a Carthaginian Army had excellences of its own, and these in the very points in which a Roman Army was most defective. Its power of projecting missiles was great; its archers and slingers were not only more numerous than the Roman, but much better; the Balearic slingers had no equals; the tower on the elephant was not unlike a battery. Its cavalry, however, was by far its most formidable arm; this was superior to the Roman in every respect; and, as we have said, it achieved wonders. It was admirable in reconnoitring and scouring a country, and in carrying into effect stratagems; it sometimes burst through the gaps in the legions, and broke them up, iron as was their discipline; its charges on the enemy's flanks were often fatal; and it was terrible in following up a victory.

Cavalry, in fact, was Hannibal's talisman in war; his prodigious successes were mainly due to his horse men. In another respect a Carthaginian Army had a great advantage over an army of Rome. The command of a Carthaginian general was usually for a length of time; Hannibal and his chief lieutenants commanded the army, that invaded Italy, during many years. This single circumstance, in marked contrast with the short and divided commands in a Roman Army, told strongly in favour of a Carthaginian Army; in fact, Hannibal would not have won his most decisive victories had he been opposed by a single general, even of inferior powers, but inured to war, and of long experience in the field. It is unnecessary to add that the Carthaginian Army, like every army directed by a great captain, surpassed itself when Hannibal was at its head.

The Greek was better versed in the theory of war than the Roman, and in the elaborate knowledge of the engineer. A Greek was the great "destroyer of cities"; Carthage learned fortification, and the art of sieges from Hellas. The fortifications of Carthage were the wonder of the world; the citadel was of enormous extent; the ramparts and walls were of great strength, were furnished with all appliances for

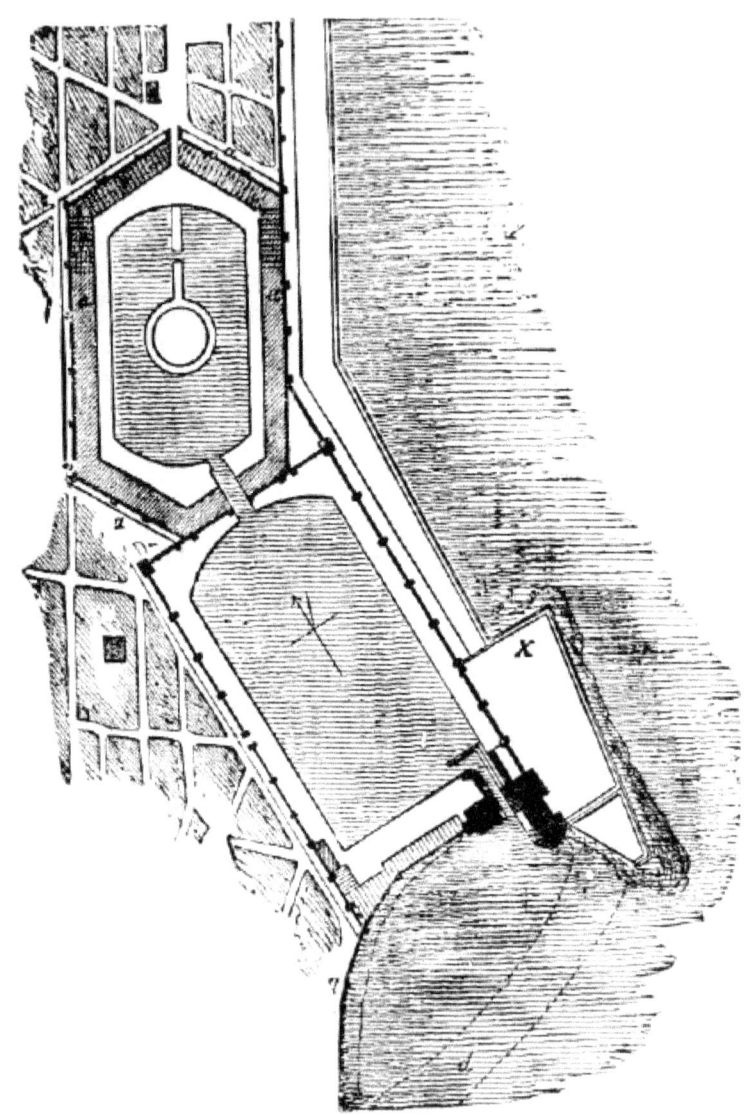

HARBOURS OF CARTHAGE
(ACCORDING TO DAUX).

defence, and, as far as we can judge, were constructed with admirable skill. But the fate of empires seldom depends upon that of a city unless they are already in decline; and the power of a military state has, at all times, consisted rather in the strength of its armies in the field, than in its fortresses, and its scientific arms. Carthage did not possess the Roman camp; a nation that had no genius for war was not one to invent and perfect the marvellous system of field defences, which so powerfully contributed to Roman conquest. A Carthaginian Army, of course, encamped; but its camp was merely a resting-place for the time.

The supremacy, however, of Carthage at sea was, at this period, we have said, absolute. Her war galleys filled the harbours and docks of the great city; her transports crowded the expanse of the bay of Tunis. She possessed numbers of craft with five banks of oars, like the great battle-ships of a modern power; she had hundreds of three-banked triremes; she sent fleets into the Adriatic and Tyrrhene seas, beyond the straits, and along the west of Africa; she had enormous resources for naval construction. At this time, we have seen, she was watching Rome with suspicion, and keeping Rome within narrow bounds; and had she maintained her maritime power, she might have become the mistress of the civilised world. In that event Hannibal would not have lost more than half an army in crossing the Alps; he would have been able, after his first great victories, to keep his communications with Spain and Carthage open, and his countrymen could not have failed to give him ample support.

But Rome was already creating a navy; it was possible, under the existing conditions of building vessels, especially in the smooth Mediterranean, to make and fit out a fleet in a very short time; and the material was abundant in the fine woods of Latium. Rome was to conquer her rival on her own element; Carthage lost an opportunity that she might have secured.

Carthage was not a nation in the true sense of the word; she was a colony that had made an empire, and that ruled allied and subject races; there was no Carthaginian national character. But we can see what the Carthaginian citizens were; and what the qualities of the population spread around the city. The Carthaginian was superstitious and cowardly in his faith; he propitiated Moloch by human sacrifice; he bowed before the licentious and perhaps cruel Ashtaroth. The Carthaginian noble had little thought of the moral forces that uphold states, of law, order, or just government; he belonged to a dominant caste of traders, and was the master of slaves by tens of thousands; he was a narrowminded, selfish, corrupt, and oppressive ruler.

His position did not encourage manly virtue, the sense of duty, the patriotic spirit; his great pursuit was to make money; and, accordingly, the government of which he was the leader, was seldom energetic in public affairs; and, as we have said, usually adopted a bad and timid policy, that cringed to the strong and wronged the feeble. The mass of the citizens resembled their betters; and the lower orders formed a great urban populace, bought and sold like sheep in the mart of politics, but arrogant, domineering, passionate, and addicted to the most odious vices. As for the subject population directly ruled by Carthage, it was, we have seen, a multitude of slaves and *fellahs*, it exhibited, of course, the degraded qualities of men in a state of ignominious bondage.

The genuine character of the Carthaginian race was nevertheless, we repeat, brave, stiff-necked, like that of the Hebrew, and capable of great deeds; and Carthage, many as were the obstacles, produced illustrious men. The peoples governed by the Carthaginians, but at a distance, seem not to have felt their influence deeply; their nature, habits, and usages were hardly changed. The language of their rulers has left no traces among them; like the exotic literature and art of Carthage, it has altogether perished.

A Greek historian has written that Rome and Carthage were not unequally matched before the First Punic War. This, however, is a superficial view; there was no real comparison between the inherent power, the vitality, the influence of the two states. The ascendency of Carthage at sea was no doubt a great thing; but in every other element of national strength, she was hopelessly inferior to her vigorous rival. Rome was a great nation, mainly of one great race; Carthage was a colony at the head of a half barbarian empire. Rome was a wise, even a merciful ruler of her allied states; they were usually not only submissive, but loyal; Carthage was the oppressor of downtrodden peoples eager for an opportunity to throw off her yoke. Rome, backed by at least half Italy, had defeated Pyrrhus; Agathocles and a handful of Greeks had placed Carthage in peril.

Rome was a community of free landowning citizens, not yet divided by sharp differences of class; Carthage was an aristocracy of merchants, and great slaveowners, ruling the mob of a demoralised city, and races sunk in degraded thraldom. The government of Rome was essentially good, was animated by a patriotic spirit, regarded the state as its first object; the government of Carthage was essentially bad, was pervaded by the narrow selfishness of a caste, was ready to sacrifice every interest for mere *lucre*. The Roman Army had certainly defects; but it was far superior to the Carthaginian as an instrument of war, especially in the qualities that ensure success. The Roman was god-fearing, law-abiding, manly, conservative; the Carthaginian was superstitious, vindictive, corrupt, venal; the great body of his subjects was misruled or savage.

It is easy to see which of the two states was destined to take a leading place in the march of humanity. Rome was to overcome Carthage in the First Punic War; if the struggle was to be fierce and long, she was then rapidly to make her way to empire. Yet she was to meet Hannibal like a destructive, irresistible power; the edifice of her greatness nearly toppled down; and though the mighty Carthaginian fell, and his country disappeared from the eyes of men, his exploits have preserved the name of Carthage, and will live forever in the page of history.

PUBLIUS CORNELIUS SCIPIO AFRICANUS.

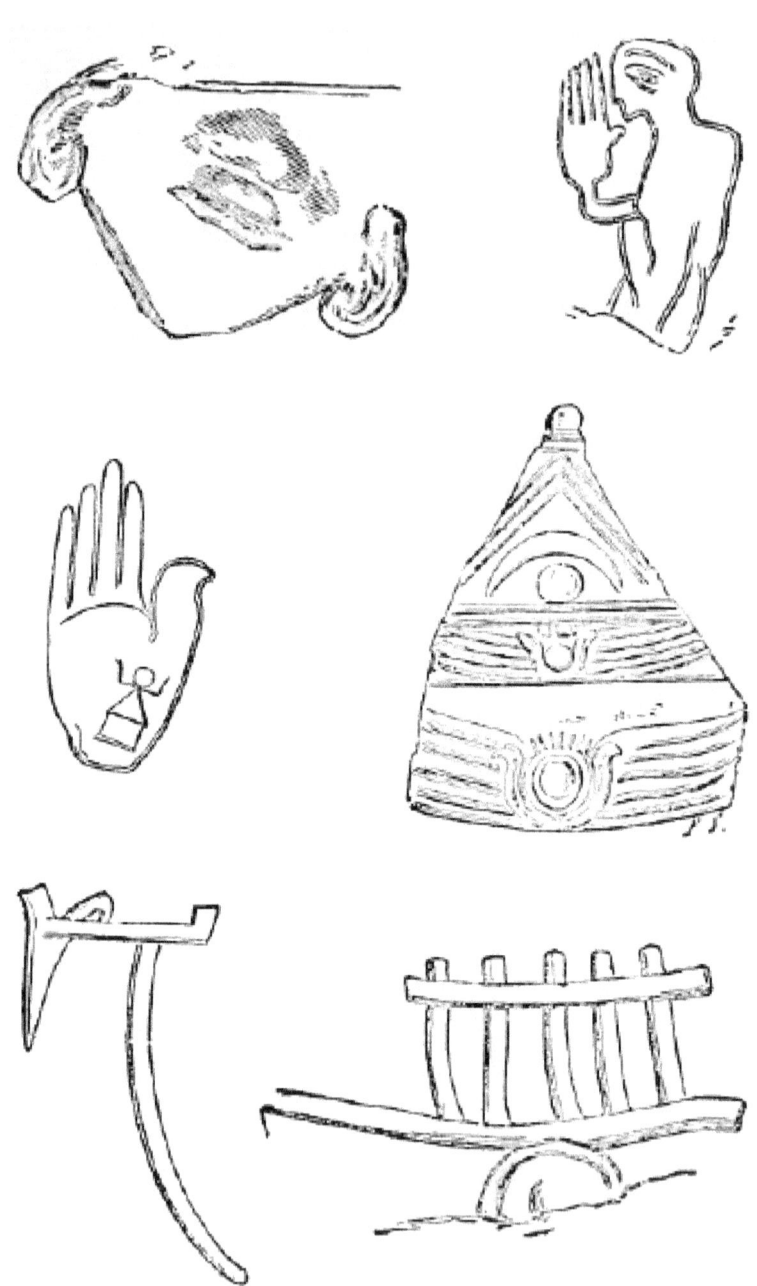

REMAINS OF CARTHAGINIAN ART.

Chapter 3: The First Punic War

Pyrrhus, when leaving Sicily, exclaimed, it is said, "There is a fair battlefield for Carthage and Rome." It was becoming evident, indeed, that the two powers, one supreme on the land, the other at sea, would ere long be engaged in strife, and that Sicily would probably be a scene of the conflict. Rome had been hemmed in more and more by Carthage; she was being shut out from Mediterranean commerce; her trading mariners, if the story be true, were often murdered by crews of Phoenician vessels. She had begun, too, we have seen, to build a war fleet, for the coasts of Italy were exposed to Carthaginian insult; after her recent triumphs in the south of Italy, she had become the ally and the head of most of the colonies of "Great Greece"; and her attention had already been turned to Sicily, a part really of the land of Italy, and where the Hellenic race was being subdued by her rival.

Carthage, on the other hand, was resolved to maintain the ascendency at sea she had long secured; she was mistress of many of the Mediterranean islands; in the east of Sicily she threatened Syracuse, and the declining power of the other Greek cities; and she desired to make the great island her own, in order effectually to curb the naval power of Rome, and to hold a position which would completely command the Adriatic, the Ionian, and the Tyrrhene seas. Although an ally of Rome in name, she had lately sent a fleet to Tarentum, in the hope probably of occupying that fine port and station; and this had given the senate extreme umbrage. The two states, in a word, were drawing towards each other, to meet in stormy shock, like thunder clouds in a lowering sky.

The great contest, however, known as the Punic Wars, like other great contests of which history tells, was brought to a head by a trifling incident. A filibustering band of armed marauders, who had left the Campanian plains in quest of adventure, had seized the Greek city of Messana, and had for some time been extending their forces along the Greek region bordering the eastern coast of Sicily. Hiero, a brilliant soldier, who, in the many changes that had befallen the great state of Syracuse, had been placed at the head of its affairs, thought it foul scorn that a horde of freebooters, even in the decay of the Greek name in Sicily, should hold the key of the Sicilian straits; and having overthrown the Campanians in a decisive battle, he proceeded to attack and besiege Messana.

The Mamertines, or "Men of Mars," as the besieged called themselves, after hesitating whether they should apply to Carthage, resolved to seek the assistance of Rome; they despatched an embassy to the senate (265 B.C.), just ten years after Pyrrhus had been driven out from Italy. It seemed scarcely probable that Rome would give aid to a lawless body, little better than pirates, especially as she had lately made an example of a party of raiders of the same kind, who had sacked Rhegium, and done horrible deeds; and the envoys at first received but little countenance.

But it was gradually perceived that great issues were involved; Messana was a bridge head, so to speak, that would give its possessor easy access to and from Sicily, and the peninsula; Carthage would occupy it, if it was not held by Rome; would not this be a standing menace to Italy? Besides, the Hellenes of Sicily were friendly to Rome; nature had made the island an Italian land; and to assist the Mamertines really meant to set limits to Carthaginian power, to sustain the cause of the Greeks in Sicily, and to extend the sphere of Roman influence, perhaps of conquest.

The sovereign assembly of the citizens, to whom the senate referred the question, confident in the power and the future of Rome, embarked in an enterprise boldly conceived but of which it could not foresee the results. The defenders of Messana were promised relief; Hiero was peremptorily ordered to abandon the siege; a Roman Army was despatched to Rhegium and a Roman fleet to command the straits. To secure the possession of Messana, and to place a check on Carthage, were, doubtless, the objects of this energetic policy.

Carthage saw through the designs of her enemy; but she had not the determination of Rome; she tried to negotiate, but the attempt failed. She succeeded, however, in patching up a peace between Hiero and the Mamertines; a Carthaginian fleet was sent to guard the straits; a Carthaginian garrison was placed in Messana. But Rome was not to be thus baffled; the officer in command of the van of the Roman Army contrived to elude the relieving squadron; and having landed

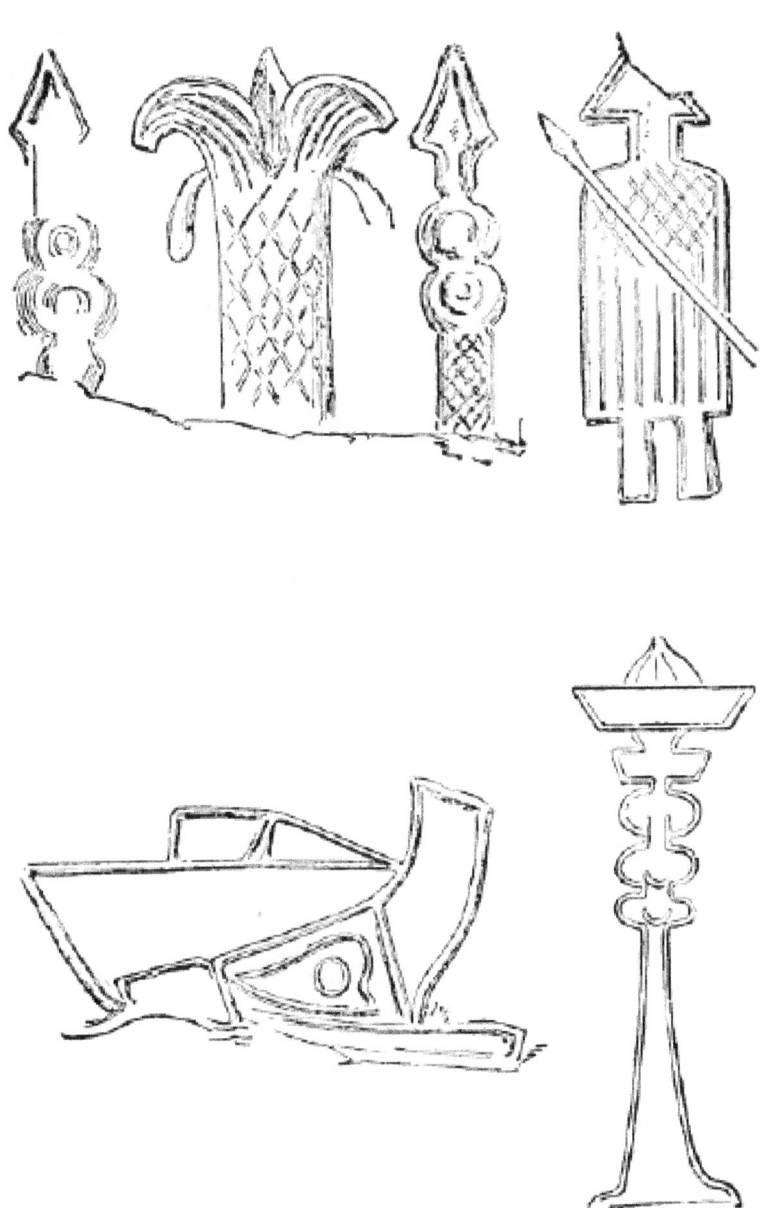

REMAINS OF CARTHAGINIAN ART.

with a few troops, so wrought on the fears of the Carthaginians on the spot that Messana was evacuated, and fell into his hands. A consular army now crossed the straits; the Carthaginian admiral was doomed to the cross, the fate of many an unfortunate Carthaginian chief; and Carthage reluctantly declared war, (264 B.C.); the beginning of the mighty struggle with Rome, more than half a century in duration and of grand vicissitudes, which involved the destinies of the ancient world.

Sicily was the theatre of the first scenes of the contest; and for three years Rome was easily triumphant in the field. A Carthaginian Army and fleet laid siege to Messana; but the passage from Rhegium had been secured; and the Romans compelled the siege to be raised, after inflicting a heavy defeat on the enemy. There were soon two consular armies in Sicily; the progress of the arms of Rome was thenceforward rapid; nearly all the Greek cities joined her standard; Hiero, her late adversary, became her loyal ally, and supported her with all the power of Syracuse. A great victory was won on the eastern coast; and though Carthage maintained her hold on her fortresses in the west of Sicily and on some of the maritime towns in the north, the island seemed about to pass under the dominion of Rome, and a not doubtful contest to approach its end.

The Roman Army was actually reduced one-half; and when the great Greek city of Agrigentum fell, the power of Carthage in Sicily appeared lost. In a battle fought under the walls of the fortress, the contrast between a Carthaginian and a Roman Army had been made strikingly manifest, perhaps for the first time. The Numidian cavalry had lured their enemy into a trap; but the Phoenician infantry were scattered like chaff by the legions.

Successful, however, as Rome was on land, Carthage maintained her ascendency on her own element. "We will not let you wash your hands in the sea," a Carthaginian envoy had boasted at Rome; the prediction hitherto had been fulfilled. The commerce of the Romans and their allies had been strangled by Phoenician cruisers; raids had been made on the coasts of Italy; not a Roman warship had dared to leave its harbour. Rome, with the intuition of a great conquering race, resolved to put an end to this state of subjection, and to create a marine able to cope at sea with Carthage.

She had been constructing a fleet, we have seen, for some time; but her efforts had been comparatively small; she had no ship larger than the *trireme* of three banks, she did not possess the great *quinquereme* of her foe. But hers was the indomitable energy of a great people, and excellent material was at hand; with the assistance of her allies on the coast—she laid the principal charge on these—she launched a hundred *quinqueremes* in less than two years, and was strong enough to confront her rival at sea. This was one of the most astonishing efforts ever made by a state in the annals of mankind. It was no doubt much less difficult to improvise a fleet in that age, than in modern times; the war-ship propelled by oars, and without artillery, was very different from the war-ship moved by sails or steam; the one could be made ready to manoeuvre and fight in very much shorter time than the other; and there are but few storms in Mediterranean waters.

The result, nevertheless, was one of imposing grandeur; and it is very remarkable that the Romans gave proof of consciousness where they would be inferior at sea, and made admirable preparations to redress the balance. The crews of the Carthaginian fleets were expert seamen; they were trained to handle their ships in battle with effect; their success usually depended on their practised skill in striking the enemy's vessels with the beaks of their own, and ramming them until they were disabled or sunk. But the Carthaginian galley had few fighting men on board; and its formidable onset might be paralysed, by numbers, brave hearts, and mechanical aid.

The Romans placed many soldiers on the decks of their ships, relying, as always, on close quarters; an ingenious contrivance was made by which the attack of the formidable hostile beak might be thwarted, and the enemy might be assailed in force hand to hand. A machine, something resembling a crane, was set in the bows of each Roman war-ship; huge grappling irons, easily let down by pulleys, hung from the extreme top, to entangle a hostile war-ship's rigging, and to prevent or retard its onset; and strong flying bridges, fitted to bear armed men, were so attached to it that they could be swung and thrown on the decks of the Carthaginian vessels. By these means the ramming attack might be rendered useless, and the enemy's ships might be carried by boarding.

★★★★★★★★★★

The French seamen of the great Revolutionary war, and indeed Napoleon himself, repeatedly dwelt on the naval contest between Rome and Carthage. Like the Romans, the French admirals crowded the decks of their ships with soldiers and relied much on grappling and boarding. Villeneuve and Lucas tried to board the Victory at Trafalgar, but there was no real analogy between the two cases.

★★★★★★★★★

The occasion ere long came when the new maritime power was to try its strength with the ancient ruler of the seas. The skill of the Carthaginian seamen at first prevailed; a Roman squadron was cut off and captured, in an attempt to seize the little island of Lipara. But the Roman methods of fighting proved successful in a sharp engagement off the coasts of Italy; and this was the prelude to a general and decisive battle. The Roman and Carthaginian fleets encountered each other off the promontory of Mylos, (now Milazzo, the battle was fought 260 B.C.), to the north of Sicily; each had more than a hundred war-ships of the largest size; the results seem to have astounded the Mediterranean world.

The Carthaginians advanced with reckless confidence, trusting to their superior power of manoeuvre; but their ships were ill ordered, and not in their places; they thought they had only to close on their prey. Their efforts, however, to ram and run down the enemy, were baffled in many instances, by the Roman *corvi*, (the name of the crane and its grappling irons); the Roman flying bridges did their work well, and threw boarders in hundreds on the hostile decks; and when the struggle, in the historian's words, (Polybius, his account is careful, even spirited), had become "like an infantry fight in the field," fear fell on the Carthaginian leaders, they became demoralised and sought refuge in flight. The admiral escaped in an open boat; but thirty *quinqueremes* were made prizes; the victory of the Romans was complete.

The Romans had little experience of naval warfare, indeed of war upon a grand scale; their operations at sea were at first tentative, notwithstanding their late extraordinary success. For some years they confined themselves to making descents on Italian islands, and to strengthening their position in Sicily, where the Carthaginian fortresses still bravely held out. At last, after another engagement at sea, the issue of which seems to have been uncertain, they made an effort more worthy of a great race of conquerors. They had doubtless learned from their Greek allies how weak Carthage really was on land; the example of Agathocles was not forgotten; an immense expedition was fitted out to strike at the heart of the enemy, in the seat of his rule in Africa.

The armament was composed of 330 vessels, including transports and ships of war; two Consular Armies were placed on board; the soldiers, seamen, and rowers, it is said, were not less than 140,000 men. Carthage, however, conscious of her vulnerable points, prepared an armament of even greater size; this stood out to sea to confront the enemy moving down along the southern coast of Sicily. The encounter took place off Cape Ecnomus; it was one of the greatest seen in Mediterranean waters. (Now Cape Licata. The battle was fought 256 B.C.) Hard fighting was again opposed to manoeuvring skill; hard fighting gained a triumph once more. The Roman vanguard, led by the two consuls, forced, like a wedge, the centre of the Carthaginian line which gave way by express orders; the Carthaginians closed in on either side, a fierce and well contested engagement followed, in which the Carthaginians were at last worsted.

Meanwhile, two Roman squadrons, lying in the rear, were boldly assailed by two hostile squadrons; the Roman ships on the right were driven, in part, on shore; those on the left suffered heavy losses. The consuls, however, hastening back after their successful fight, came, with their victorious ships, to the aid of their hard-pressed rear; this decided the final result of the battle. Some thirty ships were sunk on either side; but sixty-four Carthaginian ships were captured; and the Carthaginian fleet was scattered in flight.

Africa was now laid open to the attacks of Rome; the consuls Regulus and Volso—tradition and poetry (the legend of Regulus, told by Horace, *Odes*, iii. is a fiction), have thrown a halo over the first name—effected a landing in the Bay of Clupea, (now Kibelia), near Cape Bon, the eastern head of the Gulf of Tunis. They had with them 40,000 troops at least, flushed with recent triumph; and having thrown up a great camp, they proceeded to scour and ravage the adjoining country, part of the subject domain of Carthage. No hostile army shewed its face in the field; the essential weakness of Carthage was now made manifest.

A servile insurrection broke out; 20,000 slaves sought Roman protection; the Libyan *fellahs* found leaders, and rose in arms; some oppressed towns cook part in the revolt; others, being unfortified, had no choice but surrender. The men in office at Carthage, powerless and terrified, sued for peace, but the consuls refused their offers; and had Rome vigorously prosecuted the war, she could have laid her enemy at her feet. She stood in the position, in fact, in which she stood more than fifty years her strength, she would have escaped the tremendous strokes of Hannibal.

But, great as the Roman nation was, it seldom produced individual genius; the government made an unpardonable mistake; in the over-confidence of assured success, it recalled one of the consuls and the mass of its forces; and Regulus was left in Africa with only about 16,000 men. This gave Carthage the breathing time she needed; like other nations of the Semitic stock, she showed energy in the extreme of misfortune. The troops she had in Sicily were recalled; her gold gathered a mercenary army together, and large bodies of active Numidian horsemen; she placed Xanthippus, a skilful Spartan officer, at the head of the forces thus quickly assembled. The days of Lacedaemonian supremacy in arms had passed; but the traditions of Brasidas and Gylippus had not been forgotten. After a few months Xanthippus was in command of an army more than 20,000 strong, comprising 100 elephants and 4,000 horsemen, a force dangerous in the extreme to ill-protected infantry.

Regulus had long ago broken up from his camp, had moved into the open plains around Tunis, and had even approached the walls of Carthage. He had some 15,000 footmen in hand, but not more than 500 horsemen; yet he offered his enemy battle on the very kind of ground where his inferiority in a rapidly moved force would be most felt. He seems to have been aware of this; and, in order to break the shock of the elephant, and the tempestuous charge of the Numidian horsemen, he placed his infantry in an order of battle by which he hoped to attain his object. He arrayed the *maniples*, in his three lines, in succession, so that the *maniples* of each line could not move through, in the ordinary way, the gaps made for them, and support the *maniples* in the others, (Polybius lays stress on this); his front thus presented a line of columns, with a handful of horsemen on either wing; and not only was the threefold attack of the legion rendered almost impossible, but the soldiery were put out by the new formation, bad in itself, and of which they had no experience.

Xanthippus, on the other hand, made excellent use of the advantage given him by the ground and his special arms. He arrayed his elephants before his front, in order to baffle the rush of the legion in the smooth plain; behind them he placed his massive *phalanx*es, with light infantry on the wings, thrown rather forward, and he drew up on the extreme edges of his line his admirable cavalry, beyond comparison more numerous and better than the Roman horsemen. The result was what was to be expected when skill is pitted against incapacity in war, and also possesses preponderating strength. The matchless Roman infantry of the left wing, outflanking the narrow line of the elephants, burst through, indeed, the mercenaries in their front, and pursued them, utterly routed, to their camp.

But the legionaries of the centre and right, no doubt hampered by a strange and unwonted order of battle, were stopped by the elephants and thrown into disorder; and though they fought on in spite of heavy loss, they were unable to shake the serried *phalanx*, and fell in great numbers. Meanwhile, the Numidians had driven the few Roman horsemen from the field; they closed in swarms on the enemy's rear; Xanthippus bade his whole line advance; and a scene of murderous carnage followed. The Roman foot, huddled in a mass, held out to the last gasp; but they were surrounded and attacked in front, flank, and rear; only 2,000 escaped to tell the terrible tale. (The battle was fought 255 B.C.)

No such disaster had befallen the arms of Rome since her legions had passed under the yoke at Caudium. The nation, however, was equal to itself, whatever had been the faults of the government; a fleet of 350 ships and transports was sent to sea; it completely defeated a Carthaginian fleet off Cape Bon. But the Roman commanders threw their victory away; they did no more than re-embark the survivors of the army which had been lately destroyed; with a want of resolution difficult to understand, they abandoned the enterprise, and set sail for Italy. The armament almost perished from the effects of a tempest which struck it on the western coast of Sicily, the inexperienced landsmen in command having rejected the advice of the pilots to make the course through the straits; and more than 250 vessels were lost.

Meanwhile, the cruel Carthaginian government had exacted hideous vengeance from its revolted subjects; three thousand leaders of the rebels were set writhing on the cross; enormous sums were levied from the districts around the city; atrocities were committed big with evil results in the future. Carthage, however, elated at unexpected success, sent a fleet and army into Sicily again; 140 elephants were placed on board to make up for the inferiority of the infantry in the field. Rome, rising above disaster once more, met her enemy on the old battlefield; the great fortress of Panormus, (now Palermo), fell; nearly the whole of the northern coast of Sicily passed, in a short time, into Roman hands.

But the arrogant ignorance of the commanders of the Roman fleet involved them in another catastrophe at sea; they insisted on making from Panormus straight to the Tiber against the entreaty of practised seamen on board; and 150 war-ships were sunk by a storm. After this fresh misfortune the senate held its hand for a time; but the Roman arms in Sicily were crowned by a most welcome triumph. Since the great defeat of Regulus, even the Roman soldier feared to encounter the elephant in the open field; he lost heart when these ponderous animals appeared in line. (Polybius is not a brilliant historian, but he understood the moral forces that have such influence in war. He dwells on the demoralisation the elephant produced.) But in an attempt made to retake Panormus, the elephants were nearly all slain, or captured; the Carthaginian infantry thenceforward could not face their foes.

The power of Carthage in Sicily seemed again destroyed; she retained only the two great fortresses of Lilybaeum and Drepana on the western coast; she had no army that could contend with Rome. She made proposals of peace, for the second time; but the senate, in its exultation, rejected these, and made a great effort to finish a war, which had dragged on its length for fifteen years. A fleet and army were fitted out to master the strongholds still in the hands of the enemy; Lilybaeum was singled out for the first attack. The city, directly opposite to Cape Bon, was the chief place of arms Carthage possessed in Sicily; it had been fortified, after the Greek fashion, with all the resources of engineering art; it was defended by a numerous garrison; and it lay open to the sea, of which Carthage had had absolute command until the present war. (Lilybaeum was close to Marsala.)

The siege was the first, upon a really great scale, which the Romans had hitherto undertaken, at least when attacks by land and sea were required; it was conducted with stubborn constancy, if perhaps with little skill. The Roman Army drew lines round the place, and succeeded in closing the harbour, at least in part, by the superiority of their more powerful fleet. For a time, their triumph appeared at hand; their catapults, rams, and other engines beat down ramparts and towers in several places; a large practicable breach was made; the garrison, its supplies cut off, was reduced to grave straits. The *commandant*, however, retrenched the breach, and repelled a series of fierce assaults; though beset by a conspiracy within the walls, set on foot by his mercenary troops, he kept the besieging forces at bay; and at last a Carthaginian squadron ran the blockade, and threw food and reinforcements into the place. Ere long the garrison made a well-planned sally, and destroyed the works of the siege by fire; this compelled the Romans to abandon the attack, and to confine themselves to a mere investment.

While this difficult siege was being prolonged, the consul in command of the Roman fleet—landsmen were still at its head spite of late disasters—made a bold effort to destroy a large Phoenician fleet lying within the harbour and bay of Drepana. (Now Trapani. The battle was fought 249 B.C. The harbour resembles a sickle—hence the Greek name Drepana.)

* * * * * * * * * *

Landsmen, it is well known, held the highest commands in the English naval service until late in the seventeenth century. Blake was a distinguished soldier before he became a great admiral

* * * * * * * * * *

He set off at night, and reached the spot by sunrise; his ships formed a semicircle within the port extending thence to the open sea; he made preparations for immediate attack. But his adversary, Adherbal, was a trained seaman; he had no notion of being caught at anchor; he drew out rapidly from his moorings on the opposite side of the port, making seawards, in order to accept battle where his ships could readily move and manoeuvre.

* * * * * * * * * *

The student of naval history will recollect how Brueys failed to weigh when Nelson bore down on the French fleet at the Nile. The words Polybius, puts in the mouth of Adherbal would have been good counsel to Brueys. The cases, however, are different; the Carthaginians had oars, the French sails; the wind was blowing against the French; and a large part of the French crews was on shore. Still several French officers urged Brueys to weigh, and he seems to have entertained the idea. See Mahan, *Sea Power*.

* * * * * * * * * *

When the fleets engaged, the line of the Roman ships, for the greatest part of its length, was close to the land, and, towards the sea, was outflanked by the enemy; the Carthaginians had thus every advantage of position, and scope for their superior skill; mere hand-to-hand fighting was given hardly a chance, and could hardly avert almost certain defeat. The Roman ships were jammed up against the shore and driven aground in numbers, by their nimble enemies; the Carthaginian ships purposely gave way to any that endeavoured to break their line, and closed on them with fatal effect; the wing that had been outflanked was surrounded and crushed. It was a triumph of power of manoeuvre and seamanship over want of skill; but it was the only great naval victory of Carthage in the First Punic War. The Romans lost nearly one hundred war-ships; their fleet, in fact, was almost destroyed.

The wreck of the Roman fleet, after this disaster, returned to Lilybaeum to renew the blockade, but it was blockaded at sea by a Carthaginian fleet. The army outside the fortress remained in its lines; but the place had practically been set free; the investment became little more than nominal. Meantime Rome had suffered another great reverse, due again to superior Carthaginian seamanship. A consul had been placed at the head of a large fleet, attended by a number of transports, with orders to send supplies to the army at Lilybaeum; he most unwisely divided the armament, and despatched a part of his transports along the southern coast of Sicily, while he remained at Syracuse, with the mass of his forces.

The Carthaginian admiral, Carthalo, drew off the squadron, watching the enemy's fleet at Lilybaeum, and advancing with all possible speed, pounced on the isolated array of transports; and though the crews effected a landing on shore, and defended themselves, by missile engines, their vessels, observed by the enemy standing out to sea, were ere long caught by a storm, and perished. Carthalo made next for the consul and his fleet; he met the Romans who had weathered Cape Pachynus, (now Cape Passaro), and were pressing forward to join hands with their comrades; and—it would appear by skilful manoeuvres—he compelled them to take refuge in bad anchorage, not far from the city of Camarina, The experienced seaman, foreseeing a tempest at hand, doubled Pachynus, and got into smooth water; but the Roman fleet was exposed to the fury of the wind and the waves; and, like its detachment, it was utterly destroyed. (The disaster occurred 249 B.C.)

These reiterated disasters shook the senate's purpose, and, for a time, made even Rome hesitate. The war had lasted half a generation of man; its victories had been balanced by defeats; its ultimate success seemed now improbable. The Roman arms had been checked in Sicily, where at first, they had carried all before them; if a Roman Army had landed in Africa, and shaken the power of Carthage to its base, it had perished in a frightful catastrophe; Carthage which had lost the command of the sea was apparently about to regain it again. The losses, too, of Rome had been immense; the roll of the citizens had been largely diminished; and, owing to mismanagement and rare Mediterranean storms, the Roman war-fleet had suffered far more than that of her enemy. (The Romans at the end of the war had lost 700 *quinqueremes*, the Carthaginians only 500; Polybius i. The Roman loss was at present in larger proportion.)

The stress of the contest, at least at sea, had also chiefly fallen on the allied states; these had been compelled to build and man most of the Roman ships; their soldiers had fallen in tens of thousands; sounds of murmuring and discontent were heard. Rome ceased to prosecute the war with energy; for a long time, she did little more than retain what she had won in Sicily, keep up the investment of Lilybaeum where her troops were really thrown away, and endeavour to injure Carthaginian commerce by petty expeditions that effected little. Now if ever was the time when her enemy had an opportunity to strike a tremendous blow, which might have anticipated even the blows of Hannibal. The enormous resources of Carthage were still intact; she had still her vast trade, and vast stores of gold; her prospects at sea had again become bright; she might easily have arrayed a great armed force and fitted out a fleet of formidable strength, which might have effected a landing in Italy, and placed Rome, in her present condition, in the gravest danger.

But Carthage never understood war; her half-hearted government of trading nobles procrastinated, temporised, lost the occasion; they even allowed their maritime power to decay, completely neglected their land forces, and actually starved the still doubtful contest in Sicily.

Yet Carthage possessed, at this time, a man, who might have changed the course of her fortunes, had she known how to second his noble efforts. In the eighteenth year (247 B.C.), of the now lingering war, Hamilcar, the leader of the house of Barca, the most illustrious of the Phoenician name, obtained the command of all the forces, on land and at sea, which Carthage had still in Sicily. He was eminent in a small party of nobles opposed to the vacillating conduct of the state; he had already formed profound designs; and though only in the flower of youth, he was a great soldier, nay, a great statesman. The government at home refused him the aid of its good Phoenician and Libyan infantry, and left him a comparatively small fleet; he had only an assemblage of mercenary troops, and, apparently, two or three armed squadrons. But a great captain can make and inspire soldiers; mercenaries follow a leader who can shew them victory.

The very men who, under other chiefs, had deserted their standards, and mutinied for pay, were fashioned by Hamilcar into staunch warriors capable of daring, and even heroic efforts. He devoted some time to preparing his levies; he then made persistent attacks on the Romans thrown round Lilybaeum, harassing the besiegers with effect and skill; he pursued the same course before Drepana, which had been, also, invested by a Roman force; and he employed his war-ships in making descents on the coast, in some instances not without success. By these means he created an army and a fleet, which became formidable instruments of war; his troops were at last not afraid of the legionaries in the field, a result never attained before. Hamilcar now seized the town of Eryx, near Drepana, and made the siege hopeless; but his greatest effort was seen in another direction.

Monte Pellegrino rises seawards above Palermo; it commands far and near the adjoining lands; its top is admirably fitted for a great entrenched camp; it is not easily approached by an enemy; and the neighbourhood can supply all the wants of an army. (Polybius.) Hamilcar occupied this strong position in force; threw up fortifications carefully planned; and made Mount Ercte, as it was then called, a Torres Vedras from whence to defy the power of Rome, and to defend Sicily. At this point of vantage, he menaced every one of the Roman stations at hand, Panormus, Lilybaeum, and Drepana; he was well-nigh invulnerable to his foes; and his fleet was within easy reach of Italy. It was a stroke of genius worthy of his still more renowned son.

The war languished for a considerable time, but the position of Hamilcar continued to improve as regards his operations, at least on land. His army had begun to hem the Romans in, and to lessen their hold in all parts of Sicily; he seems to have contemplated a descent on Italy. This, however, required a large addition to his fleet; and the weak and short-sighted Carthaginian Government not only refused to supply this; but reduced by degrees his available naval force, and left him almost isolated in his camp. He was, however, a most formidable menace to Rome; should he obtain the reinforcements at sea he required, he might yet carry the war into the heart of Latium. Rome once more made one of those marvellous efforts, in which no nation has ever been her equal. The senate, dreading the terrible drain on the state, still hesitated to adopt a bold policy; but the citizens, backed, it appears, by many of the men in power, (Polybius), fitted out another great fleet at their own cost, and despatched it to Sicily to strike with effect.

Two hundred *quinqueremes*, constructed, so to speak, by magic, appeared suddenly off the north-west of the island, drove off the small Carthaginian squadrons, seized the harbours of Drepana and Lilybaeum, and joined hands with the army on land which was thus enabled to press forward the double siege. Hamilcar was unable to risk an attack; Carthage was completely taken by surprise. After a delay of some months, she sent out a fleet, which seems to have been of very bad quality, and to have consisted, in the main, of transports; it was intercepted, in an attempt to relieve Drepana, off the little island of Favignano; it was almost annihilated in a battle in which it never had a chance. (The battle was fought 241 B.C.) Roman energy and patriotism had at last triumphed over the supineness of the ruling class of Carthage; the great work of Hamilcar was undone; nothing, could now save Sicily from the grasp of the conqueror.

Hamilcar, however, did his country most important service at this grave conjuncture. There is no more distinctive mark of a true statesman than to be able to negotiate in adverse fortune, to measure accurately the enemy's strength, to know what resources are still at hand, to perceive what to insist on, and what to yield. Hamilcar was little more than thirty; but he gave conspicuous proof of political insight. Rome years before had demanded terms which would have made her enemy a vassal state; Carthage was to cede Sardinia and Sicily, to surrender her fleet, and to furnish war-ships to her conqueror's marine. She, doubtless, tried to impose these conditions again, but Hamilcar had received the fullest powers to treat; he acquitted himself admirably of a most difficult task. He gave up Sicily, for it had been hopelessly lost; but he stipulated for the integrity of the rest of the Carthaginian empire, and for the independence of Carthage as a state; he rejected every proposal of a humiliating kind; he steadfastly maintained an undaunted attitude. (Polybius dwells especially on the political tact and wisdom of Hamilcar.)

After long negotiations, and much opposition at Rome—the senate consulted the assembly again—peace was practically made on these bases, save that Carthage had to pay a large indemnity for the war. Here also the father as it were foreshadowed the son, if at a less terrible and momentous crisis.

★★★★★★★★★★

Mommsen, *History of Rome*, ii, grows eloquent in describing Hamilcar's diplomacy. "Thus at length they came to terms. The unconquered general of a vanquished nation descended from the mountains which he had defended so long, and delivered to the new masters of the island the fortresses which the Phoenicians had held in their uninterrupted possession for at least four hundred years, and from whose walls all assaults of the Hellenes had recoiled unsuccessful."

★★★★★★★★★★

The First Punic War was a prelude to the Second; but with much less grandeur and tragic effect, indeed, the protracted contests of powerful states have, in most instances, a marked resemblance. Rome did not produce a single great man; her government made very grave mistakes; the senate, engaged for the first time in a trying foreign war, conducted to a considerable extent at sea, was repeatedly wanting in its characteristic energy. Had the descent on Africa been steadily carried out, Carthage might have met the fate she met years afterwards; Rome would not have known Trasimenus and Cannae. The war, too, was sometimes ill planned, and badly directed; and it was unwise to entrust whole fleets to inexperienced landsmen, and to court a series of immense disasters.

But these considerations vanish before the magnificent spectacle of the heroic determination of the Roman people, which secured victory spite of the faults of its government. The community that could fit out war-fleets, in rapid succession, undeterred by reverses that might have destroyed hope, and that, ignorant as it was of naval affairs, could defeat a mighty enemy on its own element, was destined to triumph in the strife with Carthage; it was to withstand even the giant power of Hannibal. Carthage, on the other hand, already shewed that she was no match for her young and invincible rival. Her government was effete, her aristocracy worthless; she threw away every opportunity Fortune gave; her policy was at once vacillating, cowardly, and odiously cruel.

Her inherent weakness on land was soon made manifest when an enemy had set foot on her coasts; with her natural and overwhelming superiority at sea, she was defeated even at sea by Rome. Nevertheless, a man of genius appeared in her midst, and had she made an earnest effort to support Hamilcar the First Punic War would have had a different end. The phenomenon was to recur, but with more marked significance; Rome, though stricken to the earth, was to overcome Hannibal, by her indomitable constancy and strength of will; Carthage was to abandon her mighty defender and to perish, the victim of her own folly and weakness

Chapter 4: Hamilcar, and the Youth of Hannibal

The First Punic War had deprived Carthage of her great domain in Sicily, had placed Rome almost at her gates in Africa, above all, had destroyed her supremacy at sea, and annihilated her monopoly of Mediterranean trade. She had been reduced, in fact, to an inferior power; it was easy to foresee that her victorious rival would seek an opportunity to renew the contest. The struggle with Rome had hardly ceased when terrible troubles beset Carthage, and all but overturned the already tottering state. Hamilcar, admirably as he had conducted the war, had been almost left to his own resources; a large arrear of pay was due to his mercenaries when peace was made.

Foreseeing danger, he had sent these troops off in detachments, to enable the government to treat with them in detail, but the men in power at Carthage probably waited until the whole army had landed in Africa; and then, with the true shopkeeping spirit, began to haggle about the debt they owed. The mercenaries broke out in furious revolt; they found leaders in a Campanian free-lance, and in an African soldier of real parts; and ere long they formed an army 70,000 strong, which mastered the region around Carthage, and even approached the walls of the city. The pernicious result of the misrule of the past, and especially of the crimes perpetrated after the defeat of Regulus, became, as was to be expected, manifest.

The oppressed Libyans rose in masses and joined the mutineers; the women tore off their ornaments to make money to give them support; subject cities threw off a detested yoke; Numidian tribes sent their horsemen, in thousands, to take part in an insurrection promising liberty, at least plunder. Even Utica and Hippo, Phoenician colonies—the first the mother perhaps of Carthage herself—were drawn into the universal movement, attracted by sympathy, or compelled by terror. The rebellion, in the historian's words, had become even more threatening than the power of Rome. (Polybius.)

The Carthaginian Government was taken by surprise, and for a time made scarcely a sign of resistance. It collected, however, by degrees, an armed force, largely composed of the city militia; it set at its head one of the leading merchant nobles, who had risen to a bad eminence in suppressing the previous revolt. But "Hanno the Great," as he was called by his partisans, if a tyrant, was in no sense a soldier; he was beaten by the mercenaries, in two battles; the progress of the insurrection became so decisive, that even the fall of Carthage appeared at hand. In this extremity the *Junta* at the head of affairs turned at last to the one man who could save the state; they recalled Hamilcar and sought his counsels; but with the jealousy and suspicion of short-sighted faction, they insisted that Hanno should share his command, and have a prominent part in conducting the war.

A leader of men, however, makes his presence felt, especially in a national crisis; Hamilcar succeeded in putting an army together, in a great measure through his commanding influence; he defeated the enemy near Utica; and then, by a movement of peculiar skill, contrived to drive him, in rout, far away from Carthage. These exploits raised him to his true position; even the government had to thrust Hanno aside; Hamilcar was placed, by the voice of the army, which at this juncture had seized the substance of power, in undivided and supreme command. The war raged, with many vicissitudes, for more than three years; it was marked by barbarities frequent in contests of the kind. Envoys were murdered; men in beleaguered camps devoured their captives before laying down their arms; hundreds of prisoners perished in torture on the cross. But the military skill and tact of Hamilcar prevailed; he defeated the rebels over and over again; gradually detached from them the Numidian leaders; induced the Libyan population to return to its homes; in short, by uniting severity and clemency with true insight, brought at last the hideous struggle to an end.

Carthage emerged with difficulty, and exhausted, from this desperate contest. And yet the peril she had only just escaped was but part of the perils which menaced the state. The garrisons she still kept on foot in Sardinia, felt the contagion of the mercenary revolt, and offered the island to observant Rome, when they found themselves unable to subdue it without their aid. Rome hitherto had maintained a doubtful peace with her rival; but she accepted the gift that had been proposed; she seized the Phoenician settlements on the Sardinian coasts; and when Carthage ventured on a reluctant protest, she not only cynically declared war, but extorted a large sum of money as the price of a humiliating peace.

This degradation had little effect on the mercantile noblesse which had regained power, and thought only of commerce and pelf; it licked the dust, and sued for concessions at the feet of Rome; it actually conspired against Hamilcar, because it thought this would please the Roman senate, which instinctively felt who was its real enemy. But it was otherwise with the people of Carthage; corrupt and venal as it usually was, it still knew that Hamilcar had saved the state, that he alone could avert impending dangers, that the aristocracy in power was corrupt, nay, false to its country.

The unpatriotic peace party, supreme in the senate, in the dominant board, in a word, in the government, was set aside by the small war-party of nobles, and by what seems to have been a strong popular movement. Hamilcar was placed at the head of all the forces of the commonwealth on land or at sea, and in Roman phrase was made a dictator, responsible to no higher authority. The illustrious chief addressed himself to the task of making his country ready to confront an enemy, whose deadly designs were but too evident. Hamilcar hated Rome with true Semitic hate; he had long wished to strike at her power with effect; but he was cautious, and knew how to conceal his purpose. Rome, at Lilybaeum, held close watch on Carthage; she might pounce down on her foe from that point of vantage, and complete the work she had left undone; she might overwhelm the Phoenician empire, should warlike preparations be made on the northern coasts of Africa.

But Carthage had settlements in Spain and the far West; she might elude the eyes of Rome in these distant regions, regain much of the power she had lost, above all form a great army and fleet; when the opportunity arose, she might then strike. The country of Hamilcar was to be restored by his efforts made beyond the Pillars of Hercules.

Hamilcar set off on his arduous mission, a few months after the insurrection had ceased. (236 B.C.) He took with him Hannibal, his first-born son, having made the boy, then in his tenth year, vow vengeance on Rome before the Phoenician gods; Hasdrubal and Mago, two of his younger sons, of the "Lion's Brood" of the Barege, were in their father's train. The expedition shewed how weak Carthage had become at sea; the army, in previous years, would have been borne along the African seaboard by a great fleet; it was now obliged to make its way by land, accompanied only by a petty squadron. Hamil-

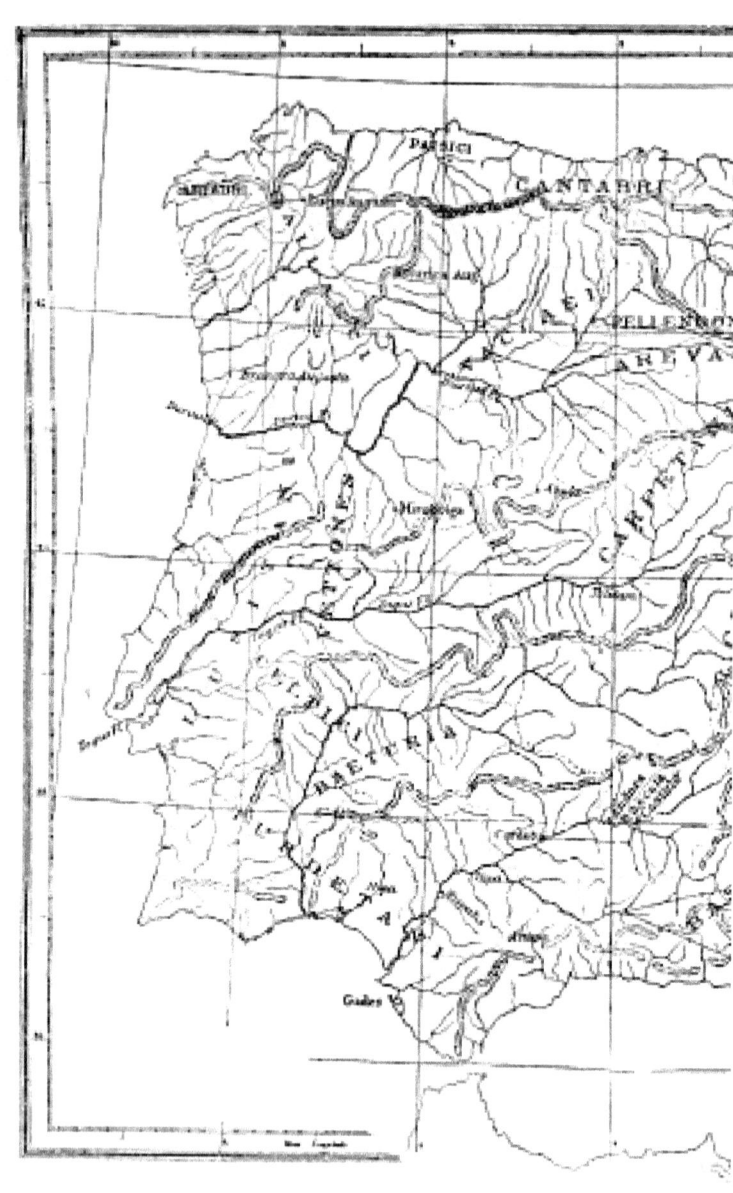

car, however, reached Spain in safety; during the nine years of life that remained to him, he succeeded in carrying out the first part of his design, and in preparing the way for its complete fulfilment.

He found the Carthaginian settlements mere seats of trade; he made them outposts of a fast-growing empire; and by a policy of blended conciliation and force, he turned Iberian chiefs into docile vassals, reduced whole provinces to loyal submission, and extended his dominion to the line of the Ebro. At the same time, he took care to form, what was his great object, a fleet and an army; war-ships were constructed from the Spanish forests; thousands of the Iberians ranged themselves around him, with the eagerness of the warlike Celt; even tribes of the distant Gauls were drawn to his camp. By these means an army of formidable power, trained to service in the field by long experience, and equipped and disciplined by a great leader of men, was, in a few years, assembled and arrayed; Phoenician cities and Libyan tribes sent numerous levies of high quality; and multitudes of the Numidian horsemen left their plains to follow a chief they loved.

Hamilcar, too, knowing what the government at home was, supplied its wants or its greed out of the resources he had formed; he contrived even to secure its safety, for he put down another attempt at rebellion. The records of all that he accomplished are lost; but a deadly enemy of Carthage—the elder Cato—is known to have exclaimed after a journey through Spain, that "no king was the peer of Hamilcar Barca." The illustrious soldier and statesman died a warrior's death, but he died in the full fruition of hope; and he bequeathed his task to a son-in-law, Hasdrubal, who worthily trod in his heroic footsteps.

Rome, meanwhile, had been steadily growing in power and advancing upon the road to empire. She left her ally, Hiero, to rule at Syracuse, and treated the Sicilian Greeks as friends; but he and they were alike her vassals; she was really supreme throughout the island. Corsica was soon added to her last prize, Sardinia; and though she did not subjugate the interior of either land, she held the coasts of both, and the adjoining sea. Rome had thus taken the place of Carthage in the Mediterranean; she was all but absolute throughout its waters; from her base in Sicily, she could not only land an army in Africa in a few hours, and threaten her rival with complete ruin, she could stretch her arms equally towards Hellas, Syria, and Spain. Her aggrandisement did not as yet cause any marked change in her foreign policy; she felt that she had to master Italy up to the Alps, and probably to annihilate Carthage, before she could venture on large further conquests; her statesmen, indeed, were still, perhaps, not eager to enlarge her dominions.

A change, however, was made in her domestic policy; speaking generally the peoples of the lands she had annexed, were treated not as allies, but as conquered subjects; they were left their own laws, but had to pay tribute; they sent no contingents to the armed force of Rome, like the Italians under the old rule of Austria; they were governed by officials from Rome; the system of provincial administration, which was to give birth to such odious abuses, was thus established. Rome, at the same time, was casting a watchful eye on Greece, where the best Hellenic influences were dying out, and Hellas was divided and weakened by her perennial discords. The glory of Athens, of Lacedaemon, of Thebes, was a thing of the past; the empire of Alexander had fallen to ruin; if it had diffused elements of Greek civilisation and life as far as the Araxes and the Upper Nile, it was rapidly decaying, in its great seat, Macedon. The chief representatives at this period of the Hellas of Miltiades, of Leonidas, of Epaminondas, of Pericles, of Æschylus, Sophocles, Plato, and many other great names, were the league of the Achman towns, and the military adventurers of obscure Ætolia.

Rome, however, was brought into contact with the affairs of Greece, in the first instance at least, through her interests at sea. She had made Brundusium, (now Brindisi), a great naval station, before the close of the First Punic War; her object was to rule the Adriatic waters. The Illyrians, however, a half-barbarous race, settled on the eastern shores of the gulf, from near Trieste to the straits of Otranto, had made the Adriatic the domain of piracy; their Liburnian galleys, famous even in the Augustan age, preyed on the commerce of the adjoining lands; they repeatedly made raids on the Greek settlements extending along the coasts of Epirus, and even on the Greek islands in the Ionian Sea; their sails spread terror as far as the Peloponnesian seaboard.

Some years after Rome had made peace with Carthage, they had seized Corcyra and held it by force; they had sacked Dyrrachium, (now Durazzo), almost within sight of Italy; they carried on their depredations to such an extent that even Roman traders feared to put to sea, and Roman colonists were kept in a state of danger. The Italians and the Achaean league had endeavoured in vain to protect the Greeks; their fleets were defeated off the island of Paxos; the Adriatic, in a word, had passed into the hands of freebooters. Rome took the matter up with characteristic energy; sent a great fleet and army to the Illyrian coasts, set the Greek islands and settlements free from their dreaded enemies; purged the Adriatic from piracy, for a time; threw it

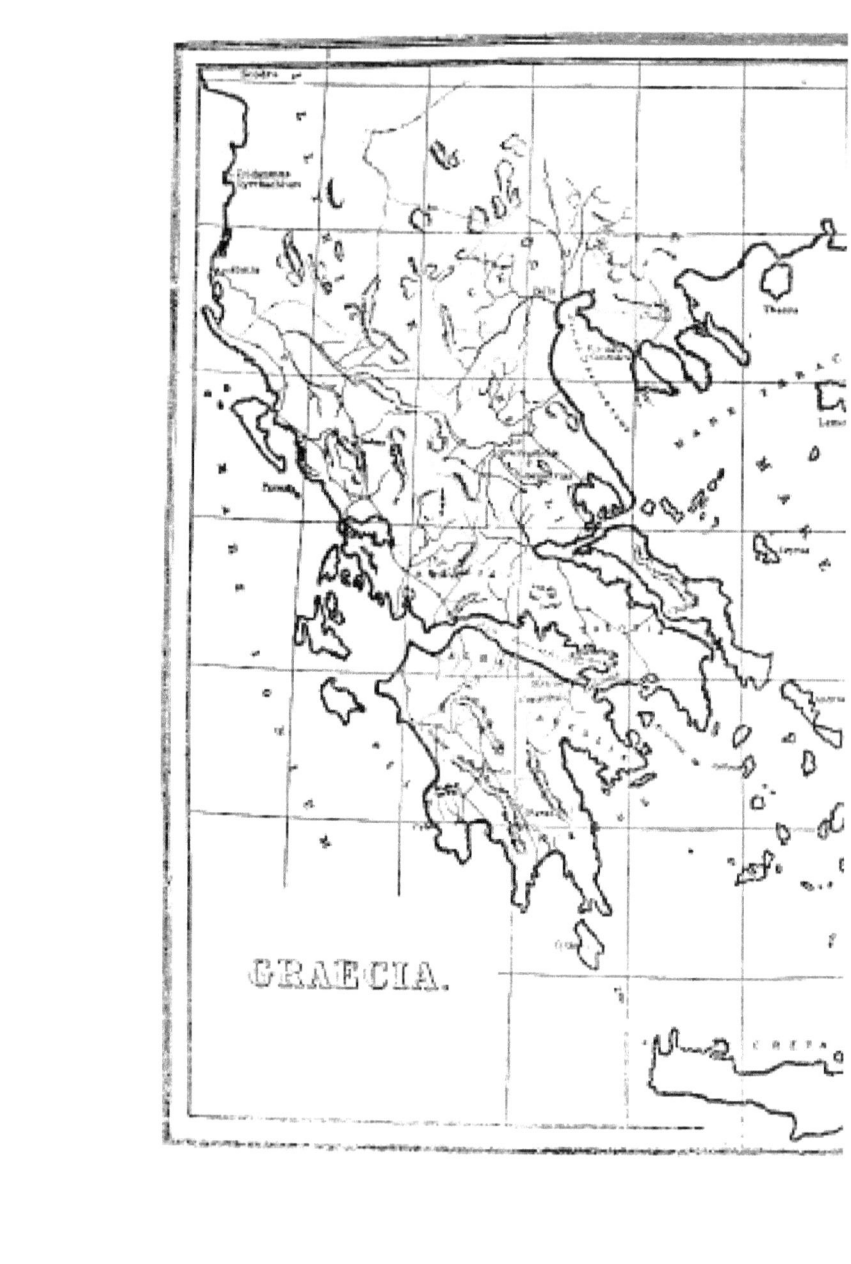

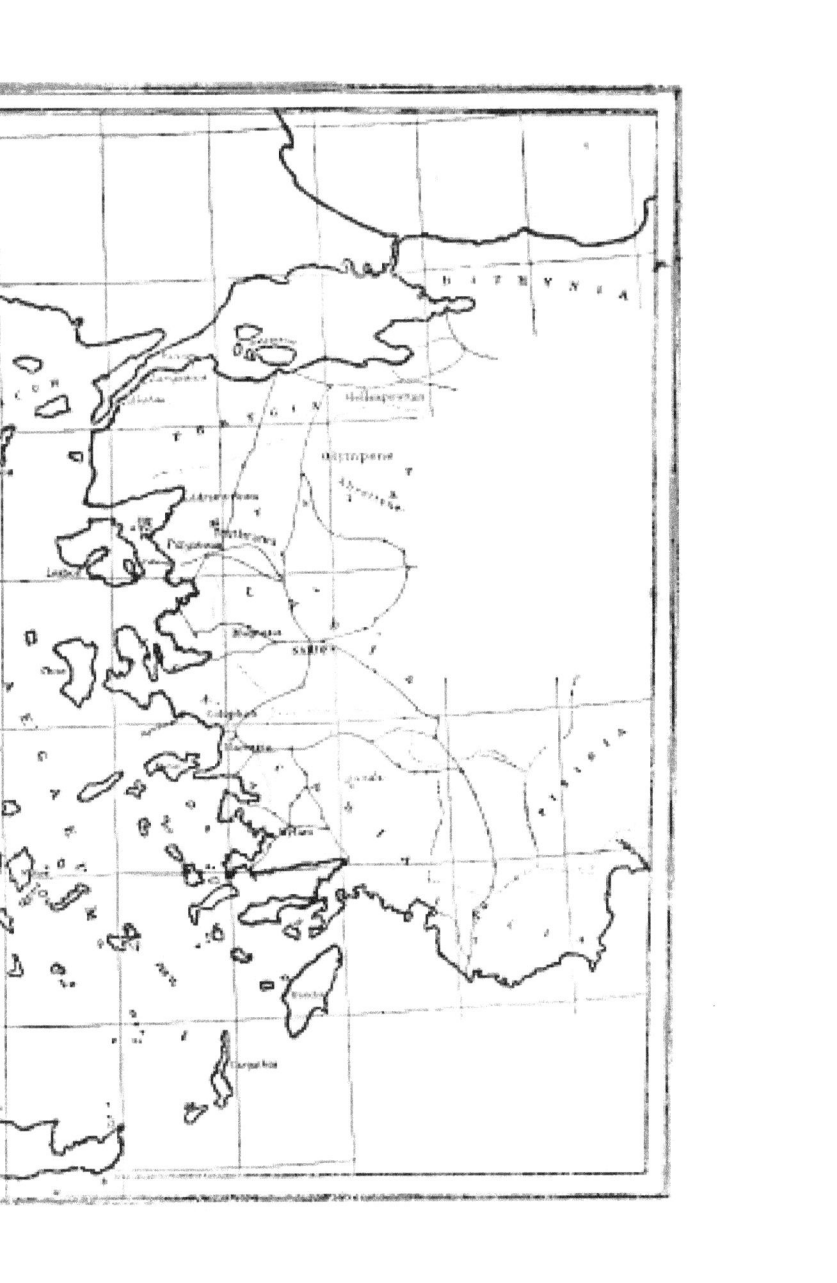

completely open to Italian traffic, and made it, as she had determined, a Roman lake.

She adopted, besides, a more aggressive policy; she dictated peace to the Illyrians under the walls of Scodra, (now Scutari, on the verge of Dalmatia), the capital of her terrified foes; she compelled them to cede large districts on the coast, and to become tributary vassals to Rome; and she established her power firmly in Dalmatia, and the regions to the south. (B.C. 229, 6), She was welcomed as a deliverer by many of the states of Greece, and—a most signal mark of Hellenic honour—she was made free of the Eleusinian mysteries, and allowed to send aspirants to the Isthmian games. But she had planted herself at the gates of Macedon, and shut Macedon out from the sea; and this necessarily provoked the jealousy of a power ambitious and proud even in decay.

Ere long northern Italy became the theatre of an internecine struggle of race. After the defeat of the Gauls before the war with Pyrrhus, Rome had seized part of the lands of the Senones, a tribe dwelling near the heads of the Tiber; the name of Senigallia still attests the presence of the colony she planted in their midst. She had then gradually extended her power to the Rubicon and had made settlements at Ariminum, (now Rimini), and other places; it was becoming evident that she entertained a design to conquer the Gauls in the valley of the Po, and to stretch her victorious arms to the line of the Alps. Italy, north of the Apennines, was at this time occupied by a medley of wild and barbarian races; the Veneti held the tract between the Adriatic and the Adige; the Ligures the territory around Genoa; but the Gauls were the predominant people; they were masters of all the plain of the Po, and of its numerous feeders.

Like all Celts, the Gauls were repeatedly at feud; the Cenomani near Brescie and Verona were enemies of the Insubres spread around Milan; the Boii settled around Bologna quarrelled with their neighbours on the spurs of the Apennines; even the menacing aspect of aggressive Rome did not unite them for years to resist a common danger. The Italian Gauls, however, with the Celtic memory of the past (Polybius dwells on this), treasured a proud recollection of the great deeds of their fathers, and of the march of Brennus on Rome; and just about this time their kindred beyond the Alps were moving through the passes, and adding to their strength.

A short time after the First Punic War, a combined assemblage of the Transalpine Gauls and of the Boii made a raid into Umbria, and even encamped before Ariminum; but Celtic dissensions saved the colony; the invaders savagely fell on each other; and Rome, not ready as yet, gave them a favourable peace. Some years afterwards, (B.C. 225), however, an attempt to found another Roman settlement in Gallic land combined most of the Gauls in the valley of the Po, to make a stand against the advancing spoiler; the Cenomani indeed held aloof; but the Insubres, the Boii, and other lesser tribes made a determined effort to assail Rome; and these were seconded by the warlike races of the lands watered by the Rhone. Leaving detachments to hold the Cenomani in check, the Gallic chiefs burst into the Etrurian plains, at the head of a formidable host 70,000 strong, of which 20.000 were fine cavalry, supported by the well-known war chariot.

The military strength of Rome at this time was gigantic; she could put, we have seen (in chapter 1), 200,000 men into her first line, sustained by reserves perhaps double in numbers; and before the war ended, she made a formidable display of her power. But, on this occasion, she was taken by surprise; time was required to collect her forces; though all her Italian allies and subjects flocked eagerly to arms, when they received her summons, she was at first inferior in the field to her barbarian enemies. She had only two ordinary Consular Armies on foot, that is about 43,000 men, and a kind of militia arrayed on the spur of the moment; one of the Consular Armies was in Sardinia; the other in Umbria, near Ariminum. The greatest terror prevailed in the city, when the Celtic watch-fires lit up the hills of Clusium; with a barbarity uncommon in Roman annals, and significant of extreme panic, a Gaulish man and woman were offered up to the gods.

The Gallic leaders, however, fell back towards Fiesole, perhaps fearing the consuls now on their flank; but they drew the Roman militia upon ground they had chosen for a fight, and routed it with considerable loss, Rome, possibly, was for a time in danger; but the invasion was only a huge raid, not a systematically planned attack; the Gauls, victorious as they were, turned their steps homewards, intent chiefly on securing the fruits of their plunder, (compare the similar conduct of the Highlanders even as late as 1745), and advancing along the southern coast. By this time the consul Atilius Regulus had landed at Pisa with his Sardinian legions; the other consul Lucius Æmilius Papus came into communication with him, after a skilful march; the two Roman Armies brought the invaders to bay, moving against the enemy in front, and from the rear at Telamon, near the stream of the Umbro.

The Gauls bravely accepted battle; but their lines were compelled to form back to back, in order to face the Romans from both sides; their horsemen and chariots had but scant space to manoeuvre. In this unfavourable position, the cross volleys of the darts thrown by the light Roman footmen, (Polybius, ii., particularly notices this, his account of the battle, fought 224 B.C. is clear, even vivid), had, as seldom happened, terrible effect; and when the legions closed on their foes in a converging attack, the *pilum* and the *gladius* were easily superior to the claymore. The Gauls fought with heroic courage, but they were gradually heaped together into a dissolving mass, and penned in like sheep to the slaughter. 40,000 clansmen perished in the field; 60,000 captives graced a Roman triumph; several of the chiefs slew themselves in despair.

After this great and decisive victory, Rome poured in force through the Apennine passes; the time to crush the Celtic barbarians had come; the *gens togata* and the *gens braccata* could not coalesce; Italy joyfully seconded her leading state. (The Italians had already the common name of *togati*, the Gauls of *braccati*.) The Boii and their dependents were quickly subdued; nothing in fact could withstand the Roman arms; the plains south of the Po were mastered in a few months. But the Insubres made a noble resistance; they took the standards of gold from the shrines of their gods, and swore to perish in defence of their homes; their armed levies, nearly 50,000 strong, caught the consul Caius Flaminius, who had pressed forward beyond the Oglio, in difficult straits.

The Roman commander was inferior in force; the Cenomani were in his camp; but he distrusted auxiliaries who had begun to waver; he separated them from the rest of his men; and he placed his legions, with their backs to the stream, telling them plainly that they must do or die. (Military history repeats itself. Hafiz Pacha adopted a similar course before the Battle of Nisib, and Moltke approved; *Lettres sur l'Orient.*) Roman constancy and weapons at last prevailed; but the Insubres fought heroically on; and it was not until after a series of defeats, that Milan fell into the hands of the conquerors. Rome proceeded to settle the valley of the Po; the Gauls were hunted down, and expelled from their villages; Roman colonies were planted at points of vantage, Modena, Casteggio, and Piacenza on the Po; the outposts of the legions were pushed as far as the Alps.

A stream of Italian emigration set in, and flowed over the subjugated lands; Italian civilisation passed the Apennines; and a great Roman road—the Via Flaminia—which united the Tyrrhene and the Adriatic seas, was carried on from Ariminum towards the Ticino, and opened the region between to the Roman Armies. The Gauls, trodden under foot, had no resource left but to brood over their wrongs with Celtic hatred; already Carthaginian emissaries from Spain had made them hope that the hour of revenge was near. (The struggle with the Gauls continued from 225 to 219 B.C.)

Meantime Hasdrubal had been carrying out in Spain, systematically, and with notable success, the policy and the designs of Hamilcar. He was, perhaps, rather a statesman than a soldier; he did not engage much in Iberian warfare; but he steadily kept up and increased the Phoenician army and fleet in Spain. In Cartagena, founded by his hands, he made an excellent harbour for his war-ships; and under officers trained by his great kinsman, he brought his troops to a high point of perfection. His army became devoted to chiefs, always at its head, and of long experience; it was mainly composed of the best elements which Carthage was able to send into the field; it had little of the mercenary spirit in it; it was numerous, admirably disciplined, capable of great deeds.

Yet Hasdrubal's efforts were more remarkable in diplomacy and the triumphs of peace. He overcame the Iberian princes, made treaties with them, and became their master, consolidated, in a word, the rule of Carthage; and, at the same time, drew vast resources from the silver mines of Murcia, and caused flourishing agriculture to spread. The trade between Carthage and Spain enormously increased; heaps of gold flowed into the Carthaginian treasury; and the Carthaginian Government, taking things easily, allowed Hasdrubal a free hand in Spain, indifferent apparently, as long as he sent them revenue. Rome acted in a very different way; she became suspicious of the enemy's empire in the West, and especially of Hasdrubal's army and fleet; and she endeavoured to check the progress of Carthage in Spain.

At this time, she was engaged, we have seen, in putting the Illyrian pirates down, and in her protracted struggle with the Gauls; but she found allies where she could not herself appear in arms. The patron, as usual, of the Hellenic name, she made treaties with two half-Greek colonies, Saguntum and Emporia, (now Murviedro and Ampurias, Sagonte is not on the actual site of Saguntum, though near it), on the eastern coast of Spain; she warned Hasdrubal that he was not to cross the Ebro. She did not, indeed, dream of peril from across the Pyrenees, but she wished to set a limit to Carthaginian influence in Spain.

Hasdrubal was assassinated in the prime of manhood; but he had a successor greater than himself, one of the gigantic figures that only increase in the lapse of time. Hannibal had served under his illustrious father and under Hasdrubal, from his teens; he had held the chief command of the cavalry in Spain; and, like most great soldiers in their early years, he had made his mark for conspicuous deeds of valour. He was as yet, however, known only as a brilliant officer, and as excelling in the duties and the pastimes of the camp; but he was a Barca, and the eldest son of Hamilcar; the army unanimously elected him general in chief. The choice was ratified by the government at home; and though only in his twenty-ninth year, Hannibal succeeded to all his father's commands, and was entrusted with the supreme direction of the forces of Carthage on land and at sea.

We do not possess a letter or a despatch of this extraordinary man, or of the lieutenants who made him their idol; we have no Carthaginian records to tell us what he was; we know of him only from the reports of enemies, who, while they could not deny his powers, feared and hated him, through a succession of centuries. Yet enough remains to enable history to assert that he was a mighty genius in the camp, and in council; that, considering the state of the art at the time, he has certainly not been surpassed as a warrior; that he was gifted with marvellous diplomatic skill, and with rare political insight; above all that he was a single-minded patriot, apparently without one selfish thought, and devoted, through an heroic life, to the cause of his country, spite of base ingratitude, and half-hearted cowardice at home.

Hannibal, too, was one of the greatest leaders of men, who have ever been seen on the stage of events; he ruled an army of many races and tongues, whether in victory or defeat, with absolute sway; he maintained a protracted and ultimately a hopeless contest for years, by the sheer force of his genius; he mastered the government and the people of Carthage, even in the hour of disaster and misfortune, and shewed that he could be superior to fate; he bowed kings of the East to his will, when an exile, and a soldier without a sword; he inspired Rome with terror even in his old age. And his domestic life, as far as we can judge, was as pure and honourable as his public career; nor is there a doubt that the "Punic faith" which Roman historians have made a charge against him, means simply that he had wonderful craft in war, and that he was a consummate master of the art of stratagem.

✯✯✯✯✯✯✯✯✯✯

I have lately come across a so-called writer on war who has actually charged Marlborough and Napoleon with unfair *finesse*, and who extols Wellington and Moltke for the want of this quality, as if power of surprise and of stratagem were not a distinctive mark of a great captain. (Original editor.)

****

A great writer (Mommsen) has truly said:

> Nevertheless, though anger and envy and meanness have written his history, they have not been able to mar the spotless and noble image it presents.

Hannibal was not long in affording striking proof of his capacity as the chief of an army. He had reached the Douro, in a raid upon Iberian tribes; on his return he was well-nigh surrounded by a host of barbarians, near Toledo, as he was preparing to get over the Tagus. His enemies thought they had him in their grasp; but instead of attempting to cross the river, which would almost certainly have led to disaster, he sent light horsemen to discover a ford; and when the means of passage had been found, he deceived the Iberians by a skilful feint, successfully crossed while they were sunk in sleep, and annihilated them from the opposite bank, by the admirable use he made of his favourite arm, cavalry, and by his elephants, and their towers of slingers and archers.

He soon had addressed himself to the great work of his life, the accomplishment of the designs against Rome, which he had sworn to carry out, and were a parent's legacy. Hannibal inherited his father's hatred of the mortal foe of Carthage; he had been long aware of Hamilcar's policy and views; and possibly his extraordinarily precocious judgment in affairs of state may in some degree be ascribed to this teaching. But his project of assailing Rome was probably all his own, though the original inspiration came from his father. Had Carthage retained the command of the sea, Hannibal doubtless would have effected a descent on Italy by the Mediterranean from Spain; he knew the difficulties of the attempt, if made by land; he was perfectly aware that, in an operation of this kind, he would expose his army to peril and loss, and would lose the immense advantage of what are technically called interior lines on the field of manoeuvre. (Hannibal, in his operations, shewed over and over again that he understood the value of interior lines. It is indeed self-evident.)

But the mastery of the sea had passed to Rome; all that could be expected from Carthage, on the element she had once ruled, was a mere diversion; and Rome had acquired admirable opportunities to attack her enemy, from the Mediterranean, and from her watchtower, so to speak, in Sicily. The enterprise, therefore, must be conducted by land whatever the obstacles, dangers, and risks; and it must also be conducted from Spain, for a direct attack from Africa was certain to fail, nay, practically had become impossible. (See Mahan, *Sea Power*.)

In the suddenness and unexpected nature of his attack—so often the object of great captains—Hannibal saw the prospect of safety and success. He had confidence in himself, and in his devoted troops; he would march across the Pyrenees and the Alps, a march never made by an organised army before, and would strike at the power of Rome in the valley of the Po, while she was preparing her resources for the field, and contemplating a descent upon Africa. He matured with the greatest care, but with extreme secrecy, this extraordinary plan of invasion; he negotiated with friendly Iberian chiefs, and with leaders of the tribes of Gaul, to give him a passage across their borders; he sent envoys to the stricken Gauls of Italy assuring them of action and desiring aid; he had spies even in Rome, to observe her conduct.

The sweep of his ample intelligence went even further; he knew that Macedon had resented the policy of Rome in establishing herself on the Illyrian seaboard; he endeavoured to fan the smouldering flame; he tried to rally the Macedonian dynasty to his side. Hannibal thought it possible that many races from the banks of the Guadalquivir to those of the Karasu, (the ancient Strymon), might be gathered together, under his supreme command, in northern Italy to assail Rome; and the occasion was favourable to his earnest hopes, for Rome was just beginning to disband her forces, after her long and furious struggle with the Gauls.

He could not expect much from the states of Italy, after the example they had just given of loyalty to Rome; yet even here he might ultimately find allies. The conquest of Italy was of comparatively recent date, the Samnites had not forgotten the Caudine triumph; in parts of the peninsula there were nobles, hostile to Rome, a priesthood which hated the gods of the Capitol, a population that disliked the aristocratic Roman yoke. Success might yet bring him Italian support; diplomacy and statesmanship might accomplish much. For the rest he, only expected Carthage to send occasional reinforcements by sea, perhaps to attempt descents on the coasts of Italy. In Hannibal's magnificent project of war, splendour of conception, forethought, and preparation were alike combined; in the language of a mighty kindred spirit:

"No more vast, more far-reaching plan has been carried out by man; but it was methodically conducted." Napoleon, *Corr.*

Hannibal's military and diplomatic arrangements were completed about a year after he had received his command. He now sought an opportunity to strike; he was ready, delay might reveal his purpose. But the men in office at Carthage, though doubtless unaware of the gigantic scheme he kept to himself, had become suspicious of the young general; they were alarmed at his independent and bold attitude; they tried, almost on any terms, to remain at peace with Rome. Hannibal watched an occasion to force their hands, and, at the same time, to pick a quarrel with Rome; he threatened to make an attack on Saguntum; he treated with rudeness Roman envoys, who had been sent to complain of his conduct. The government at Carthage was stricken with fear when an embassy from Rome denounced their general in Spain; but Hannibal meanwhile had seized a pretext to declare war against the men of Saguntum; he laid siege to the city, though an ally of Rome.

The place, perched on a rocky upland, resisted his efforts for many months, with the stubbornness characteristic of Spanish defence; but Rome, from whatever reason, withheld her aid; Saguntum was stormed and razed to the ground; a great mass of booty was sent off to Carthage. Rome demanded that Hannibal and his officers should be given up to her to atone for this affront; the Carthaginian senate hesitated for a time. But whether it felt that war could not be avoided, or feared the indignation of the army in Spain, or was inspired by a more patriotic motive, it gave an evasive answer to the Roman summons; and Hannibal's object was attained. The Second Punic War—one of the greatest in history—began in the two hundred and eighteenth year before the Christian era.

By this time Hannibal had made ready for the field, and was about to set off on his great enterprise. He had received pledges of friendship from some of the tribes in the tracts between the Ebro and the Rhone; he had been promised support by the Insubres and other Gauls in Italy; his envoys had been well received at Macedon. His army numbered some 140,000 men, of whom 16,000 were fine cavalry; he had about 60 elephants and 50 warships; but he was obliged to detach a large part of his forces to the defence of Carthage and other Phoenician cities; and in order to maintain his communications with Spain, which, like a real general, he kept steadily in view. He set off from Cartagena in May, at the head of 90,000 foot, 12,000 horsemen, and 37 elephants; he knew that he would have to leave part of these on the line of his march; he must have known that he could not scale the Alps without great risk and loss.

But he knew also that Rome was making delays, and was utterly ignorant of his design. He had made it certain that she was chiefly intent on fitting out expeditions to land in Africa, and had few troops in the valley of the Po, the decisive point in his theatre of war; he had calculated that his strokes would take her by surprise, would paralyse her efforts, and expose her to defeat. Even if he had lost half his army before he was in the north of Italy, he was assured of the enthusiastic support of the Gauls; and he trusted in his genius in war, and his heroic purpose. He took his departure in high hope; so, while Austria was planning an invasion of Provence, Napoleon burst on the rear of Melas, and won Italy by a march and a battle; so, while Mack was dreaming of attacking Alsace, the same great commander, moving from the Channel, hemmed in his unhappy enemy at Ulm, and discomfited the allies, largely superior as they were in force.

Chapter 5: The Pyrenees the Alps the Trebia

The army with which Hannibal began his march was, we have seen, 102,000 strong, 90,000 infantry and 12,000 horsemen, with the important addition of 37 elephants; it was the best army Carthage ever possessed. Formed by Hamilcar and Hasdrubal during many years, it was mostly composed of Spanish, Phoenician, and African troops; it contained only a handful of Gauls; it had long been commanded with great skill and care. It had been organised, too, for its grand enterprise by Hannibal, with remarkable forethought; it possessed nearly all the services of a modern army, a commissariat, hospital, and transport administration, an intelligence department, as the phrase now is, an excellent body of sappers, miners, and pioneers, long trains of impedimenta and beasts of burden, and—for the difficulties of crossing the Alps had been foreseen—it was probably furnished with an explosive of great power, resembling, it has been thought, the dynamite of this day. (This was the famous Greek invention, mistranslated by Livy and other writers as vinegar, almost certainly an explosive. See Hénnébert, *Vie d'Annibal.*)

It was, in a word, supplied with all that the material invention of the age could produce to form a good instrument of war; but it appears to have had no bridge equipage, though Hannibal knew that he would have to cross the Rhone and the Po, not to speak of numerous lesser streams; this most valuable appliance of an army of our times, in all probability was not then in use. (From several ancient historians, *e.g.,* Livy, Polybius, we may infer that the Romans at this period threw bridges over a river. But these seem to have been made of boats found on the spot; pontoons probably did not accompany the army.)

The superiority, however, of Hannibal's army consisted mainly in the greatest elements of military strength—its moral power, the genius of its chief, and the resource of its officers. It had been accustomed to victory for years, it had perfect confidence in itself and its leaders; it instinctively felt that a master of war was at its head. And Hannibal had lieutenants worthy of himself, though eclipsed, like lesser stars by the sun,—his brother Hasdrubal, left in command in Spain, another brother, Mago, a very brilliant soldier, a second Hasdrubal, an admirable cavalry chief, Hanno, Maherbal, Carthalo, and other distinguished names.

Hannibal, as his whole life shews, was a grave and earnest man; before setting out he had solemnly invoked the assistance of his gods for his mighty project. Visions and portents too, it is said, beckoned him onward on his path; but the Hector of Carthage, we may well believe, thought that the best omen for him was "to fight for his country." He bade farewell to the Spanish princess he had made his bride, and to their infant child, as he took his departure; he had his Andromache, like the hero of Troy, but he was not to see them again until his hair was grey; this is almost the only glimpse of his domestic life which we catch in his tragic career of wonders. His army, welcomed by allied chiefs, and passing through a friendly or a subject country, made its way with comparative ease to the Ebro; a Carthaginian squadron was on its flank at sea, to furnish it with supplies, and to repel attack, for a Roman descent on Spain was known to be probable; it apparently crossed the river early in July, and up to this time, it had little suffered.

But when Hannibal entered the Catalonian wilds, then, as even now, an intricate region, he encountered a fierce and prolonged resistance, and he had to fight his way with heavy loss to the Pyrenees. The Catalans, as always, proved themselves to be an independent and martial race; they had had no experience of Carthaginian rule, and the efforts they made were seconded or at least encouraged by the Greek colonists of Ampurias and Rosas, dependents of Rome, like most of the Greeks of the West, and perhaps even obeying her commands. Hannibal, however, divided his army into three columns, that marched between the Segre and the coast; he defeated and ere long subdued his assailants, and he seems to have crossed the Pyrenees without difficulty, where they slope down to the Mediterranean Sea.

But he had lost thousands of men in the late contest; and he thought it necessary to leave Hanno, a trusted officer, with a very considerable detachment behind, to keep the Catalans down, and to preserve his communications with Spain. His army was assembled at Elne, on the Tet, about the third week of September, but it had been reduced to a force that appeared quite unequal to cope with the military strength of Rome. (This is the Illiberis of Livy and the Helena of other writers, the place is still known as Ille or Elne). It numbered only 50,000 foot and 9,000 horsemen, apart from the elephants, still 37; what was this compared to the resources of a power that could easily place 200,000 men in the field? But Hannibal's word was still forward; he trusted in his genius and he was not deceived.

The Roman senate had meanwhile been making preparations for the conduct of the war, but no great soldier assisted its councils; its arrangements were ill-conceived, above all, feeble. Gigantic as was the power of Rome, the state set on foot only two Consular Armies, with an auxiliary force of little strength, and, as we have said, its first thought was to descend on Africa, and to make, as it hoped, Carthage an easy conquest. It divided, however, ere long its forces; ultimately it despatched one consul, Tiberius Sempronius Longus, with some 26,000 men and 160 war-ships, to Lilyaseum, to invade Africa; the second consul, Publius Cornelius Scipio, being intended to land on the coast of Spain—the fall of Saguntum was to be avenged—with about 24,000 men and 60 large war-ships.

This last move shews ignorance of what was going on in Spain, and of the real strength of Hannibal's army. Had Scipio made the projected descent, he would probably have been annihilated by his far superior enemy. Besides these very inadequate forces, the senate sent 18,000 or 20,000 men under a military *praetor*, Lucius Manlius Volso, to observe the position of affairs in northern Italy, which, in different ways, had become menacing, for the Gauls were astir, and the new Roman colonies were in need of help from the great mother city.

✯✯✯✯✯✯✯✯✯✯

The strength of this force has been very differently estimated. It should if possible be nearly ascertained, as the judgment to be formed on the strategy of Scipio depends much on what it was. I have in the main followed Livy; Polybius gives no exact figures.

Praetor is an officer appointed by the government to chief command in the absence of a consul, with the functions of a *legatus*. It is not quite certain, if the grade of *legatus* was at this time established.

✯✯✯✯✯✯✯✯✯✯

Sempronius was soon on his way to Sicily; but Scipio was delayed for weeks by an incident, apparently untoward, but, for him at least, fortunate. The Boii and other tribes of the Italian Gauls, excited by messengers sent by Hannibal and furious at the progress of Roman settlement, rose suddenly, overthrew Manlius, and seized two high civil officials of Rome; the senate was compelled to punish the affront, and Scipio was directed to send one of his legions to strike down the rebellious Celts in the valley of the Po. This detained the consul for a considerable time, for new levies had to be formed to join his army; and September was probably somewhat advanced before he reached Marseilles with his fleet, still bent on effecting a landing in Spain.

The Greeks of the city, staunch allies of Rome, informed him that Hannibal was already at hand; but he hesitated, and took no decided step; he wasted precious days in councils of war—that sure sign of a chief who does not know what to do—; he did not even send a man to the western bank of the Rhone to observe the progress of the enemy on his march. He probably had a fixed idea that Hannibal could never get across the river, as he certainly had a fixed idea afterwards that Hannibal could never get across the Alps. (The views and the conduct of Scipio at this critical juncture are well described by Polybius.)

Hannibal, during this time, had been pressing forward, by forced marches, from the Pyrenean frontier. He had been delayed unexpectedly by the Catalans; he knew that autumn would be advanced before he could reach the Alps; he evidently called on his army to make a great effort. His military chest was well supplied; he bought off the resistance of some chiefs of the Gauls, but found them, for the most part, friendly. He marched rapidly along the south of Languedoc, probably by the road even then connecting Narbonne and Nimes. He was on the western bank of the Rhone towards the close of September, at a point between Avignon and Orange, supposed generally to be Roquemaure; he found a huge assembly of Gaulish warriors, perhaps under the influence of the citizens of Marseilles, crowding the opposite bank to dispute the passage.

The river itself, too, a broad waste of waters still rolling down the melted snows of the Alps, was an obstacle of a formidable kind; but hindrances like these could not stop Hannibal. He made immediate preparations to cross the Rhone, seized or purchased a number of the large boats and barges, even then engaged in navigating the stream, and employed his sappers and miners, and probably many of his troops, in constructing rafts and canoes to assist in the passage. The work progressed with extraordinary speed; it was completed, we are informed, in forty-eight hours; and if this account be even nearly true, the mechanism of Hannibal's army must have been extremely good.

The great Carthaginian, however, had no notion of forcing the crossing by an attack in front, in the face of thousands of brave armed men—he had, we must recollect, no bridge equipage (pontoons, however, of even a modern army would not have sufficed to effect the passage of the Rhone at Roquemaure); he resolved to turn, surprise, and baffle his enemy. He sent Hanno, one of his best lieutenants, with a body of cavalry, up the river, to a point believed to be Pont St. Esprit; and Hanno was directed to cross the Rhone, to descend the eastern bank, and to fall on the rear of the Gauls, while the main army was to effect the passage. A preconcerted signal was to announce to Hannibal the appearance of Hanno on the scene of action.

The Carthaginian Army remained in its camp, or was only making ready for the decisive effort, while the Celtic horde, giving a free rein to noisy bravado, insulted it from across the river, by dissonant clamour, and rude and wild gestures. But on the second day after Hanno had set out, a column of smoke rose from the opposite bank of the Rhone, within sight of Hannibal and his troops; this was the signal that had been arranged; and before long Hanno's horsemen had burst on the amazed barbarians, who had never dreamed of an attack of the kind, and hewed their way into the breaking up multitude. Meanwhile Hannibal's army was steadily crossing the Rhone by the means its great leader had admirably prepared. The heavier vessels, breaking the force of the current, and towing the greater part of the cavalry horses, were ferried over, higher up the stream; the lighter boats and canoes, under the lee of the others, crossed lower down; in this way the whole army got over the Rhone, by degrees, it would seem, with scarcely any loss.

The cheers of the Spanish and African soldiers drowned the frantic yells of the Gaulish warriors; who, taken by surprise, and assailed in front, flank, and rear, made only a feeble and brief resistance; and as Hanno's attack was pressed more and more home, and the Carthaginian Army began to form in menacing strength on the bank it had won, the undisciplined and terrified Celts gave way, and had soon scattered in ignominious flight. With the exception of the elephants, the foot and horse seem to have effected the passage in about twenty-four hours, an exploit that must be pronounced wonderful. But a great chief can really do wonders; and Hannibal, we are expressly told, was one of the first to cross, and kept on encouraging his men. The elephants were carried over a short time afterwards; the huge animals having been enticed to a great landing stage, to which rafts were attached that bore them across.

****

The admirable skill and resource of Hannibal in crossing the Rhone, in the face of the enemy, may be contrasted with the pitiable weakness of Bazaine in crossing the Moselle, on the 13th and the first part of

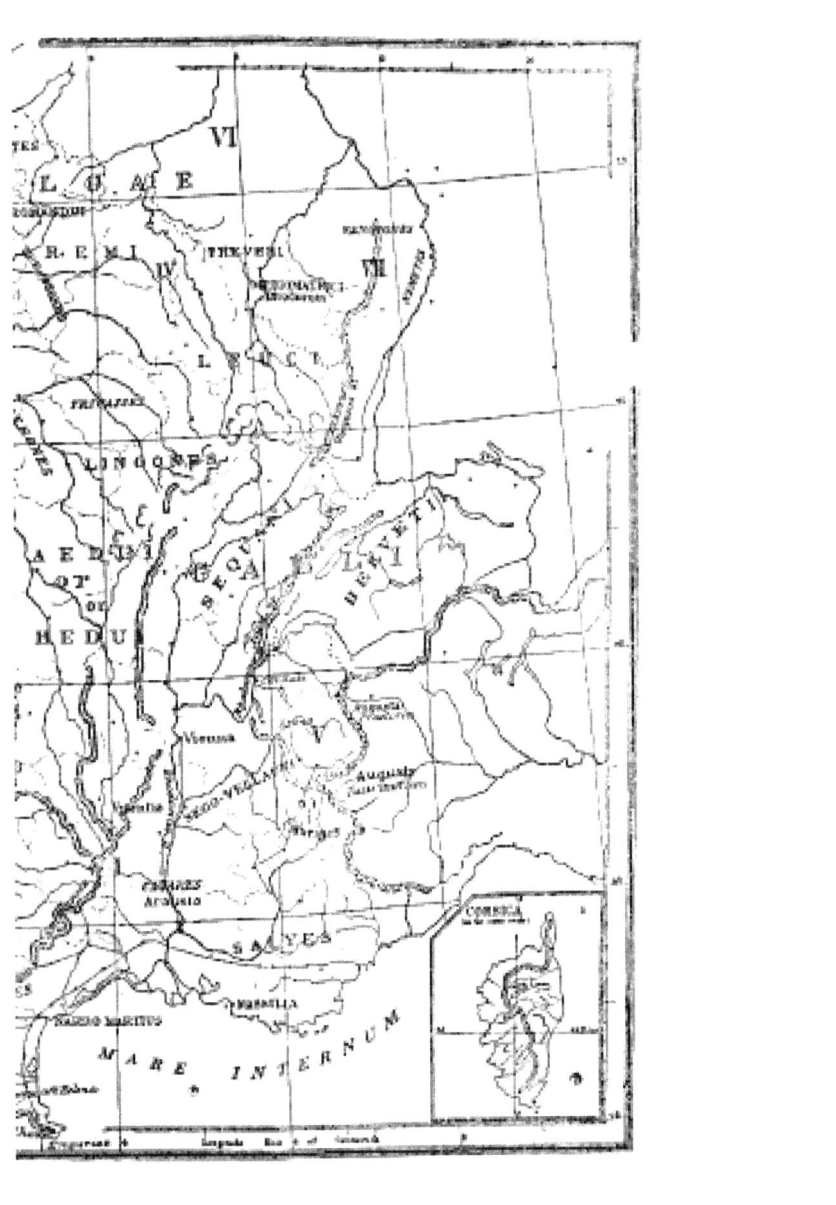

the 14th August, 1870, though the enemy was not at hand, and he had bridges, pontoons, and the material of a great arsenal at Metz.

****

The Carthaginian Army had hardly passed the Rhone when several chiefs of the Gauls of Italy—chiefs of the Insubres were among these—appeared in Hannibal's camp, having crossed the Alps, and bade him good cheer in his great enterprise. They furnished him with a number of guides for the march; pronounced the mountain range an obstacle that could be overcome; gave a brilliant description of the riches of the valley of the Po, and promised him the support of many tribes of that region. Hannibal's soldiers, it would seem, had been alarmed by the reports of the perils that lay in their way, especially of the terrors of the Alps; but their chief addressed them in impassioned language; hesitation and fears at once vanished. Meanwhile their great commander had made a remarkable move, an instance of his astonishing skill in stratagem, which probably effected the objects he had in view.

Scipio had sent a party of 300 horsemen to reconnoitre the eastern bank of the Rhone; they had drawn near the Phoenician camp before the elephants had got across; and they were on their way back to make their report, when Hannibal told off 500 Numidians to fall on their rear, and to compel them to fight. A sharp and bloody encounter followed; Hannibal's troopers, better cavalry than their opponents, and not far from twofold in numbers, retreated, and were pursued with heavy loss, to the verge of the Carthaginian lines, from which, however, no counter-attack was made. The Roman officer in command informed his chief that the hostile army was still divided on the Rhone; Scipio thought a grand opportunity had come; he instantly marched his whole army up the river, in the hope of catching his adversary at fault, and striking him with decisive effect.

The consul found Hannibal's camp abandoned, and heard that he had moved up the Rhone; he returned to Marseilles breathing empty curses against the "cowardice" of an enemy, who would not abide his attack. He lost eight or ten days by these useless movements; this enabled Hannibal to get clear away, and increased the difficulty of sending the Roman Army back, by land or by sea, in time to encounter the Carthaginians as they emerged through the passes of the Alps. The detachment of the Numidian horsemen, and their defeat, almost certainly feigned, contributed largely to this most important result; the stroke, admirably conceived and brilliant, was one of the numberless examples of Hannibal's craft in war.

★★★★★★★★★★

I agree with Colonel Dodge, *Hannibal*, that the operation of Hannibal was a dexterous *ruse de guerre*, A careful study of Polybius and Livy confirms this view. Indeed, the facts speak for themselves. Five hundred Numidian horsemen would never have retreated before 300 Roman, without orders.

★★★★★★★★★★

Scipio was now at Marseilles with a consular army; to follow Hannibal to the Alps was impossible; what was to be the Roman's next move in the theatre of war? The consul appears to have had no doubts; he sent the mass of his forces by sea to Spain, under the command of his brother Cnaeus Scipio; he set sail for Pisa, with a few hundred men, and, in a short time, was across the Apennines, to control the operations of the Roman Army in northern Italy, under the *praetor* Manlius. The direction of Scipio's army to Spain, in the long run had momentous results; it almost decided the issue of the war; and it has been extolled as a movement inspired by real genius. There is nothing in Scipio's career to warrant a supposition of the kind; it is probable that he adopted the course he took, simply because these were his original orders.

And though the movement may be justified, as affairs stood, being a blow at Hannibal's communications with Spain, it was of little effect, for any present purpose, for it was made at a very remote distance; and it is doubtful, at least, if the Roman general should not have taken a step altogether different. He could not come up with Hannibal by any march on land; but it was of the first importance to meet his enemy, as he descended from the Alps to the Po, and to strike him down with a sufficient force; and as Scipio possessed the command of the sea, this operation was probably within his reach. Had the consul embarked his army at Marseilles, landed it at Genoa, and brought the forces of Manlius into line with his own—the roads in this district were even then good—he could have opposed at least 45,000) men to Hannibal at the Italian verge of the Alps, and Hannibal could hardly have escaped a fatal disaster in the existing condition of the Carthaginian Army.

Scipio, however, never thought of this movement, and the reason is not difficult to seek. He was convinced that Hannibal could not cross the Alps, (Polybius dwells on this), or that if he did it would be with the wreck of an army, which he could easily destroy with the force of Manlius, from 25,000 to 30,000 strong, even making allowance for all losses. The consul's view was not without reason, and he did not yet know the giant he had to deal with; but it is certainly questionable whether his strategy was well conceived.

****

Whether Scipio was right in sending his army to Spain, or whether he should have taken it with him, by Genoa, to northern Italy, has been discussed by many able writers. The opinion of Napoleon, though not fully considered, is of course of the greatest value, and requires attention. The emperor points out truly that Scipio had no chance of catching Hannibal, by any march made wholly by land; but he has not noticed that Scipio might have gone by sea to Genoa, and marched from that place to the Alps, and that, in that case, he probably would have met his enemy as the Carthaginians descended into Italy, and ought to have been able to crush them, Napoleon, on the whole, rather approves of the direction of the Consul's army to Spain, *Corr.*

****

Having got rid of Scipio, Hannibal ascended the Rhone, by the eastern bank, as quickly as possible. On the fourth day after his army had left its camp, he reached the confluence of the Rhone and the Isère—there is no difference of opinion on this subject—and entered the region described as "The Island," that is the fertile tract in the northwestern part of Dauphiné, compared by Polybius to the Delta of the Nile, which may be said to extend from Grenoble to Lyons. The course he took from this point, in his march across the Alps, has been discussed, with much learning, in a number of works; we shall follow the route, which appears, on the whole, to be the most consistent with the really known evidence.

After entering the "Island," Hannibal was in the land of the Allobroges, a powerful tribe of the Gauls; he conciliated a leading chief, at feud with his brother; and he obtained from his grateful client an ample supply of food, clothing, and other necessaries for his men. He appears to have skirted the Rhone, nearly as far as Vienne; avoiding there the great bend of the river, he struck across the country until he nearly reached it again; and here he found himself on the spurs of the mountain barrier, like a rampart in front of the main chain of the Alps, which stretches from Belley, by Montmélian, to Grenoble.

The friendly chief by this time had bade him farewell; and as his army drew near a pass in the range, probably the Chevelu, just north of the Mont du Chât, it was challenged by the Allobroges of another clan, who, jealous of their wild freedom, like all mountaineers, checked the advanced guard, and crowding the neighbouring heights, assumed a menacing aspect, and seemed eager to attack. Hannibal deceived the barbarians by a skilful feint; he moved his army towards the mouth of the pass, but kept it in its camp for some hours, as if hesitating what step he was to take; and then, having ascertained that the Gauls returned to their villages at night, and kept no watch, he pushed forward a body of picked men in the darkness, seized the defile, and the highlands above, and gradually drew the mass of his troops onwards, under the cover, so to speak, of huge fires, which would make the enemy believe that the camp was still fully occupied.

The autumn morning found the Carthaginian Army in possession of the pass, and making its way, by a descent of extreme difficulty, towards the open plains leading from Chambéry, to the valley of the Isère. The Gauls had been baffled, and paused for a time; but their chiefs, who had probably sent their commands far and near, ordered their clansmen to fall in force on the enemy. Hannibal's columns were toiling along a mere track, formed in the side of the range above, and often meeting precipices that, steep as walls, went down hundreds of feet, into torrents below; the barbarians, swarming by mountain paths in their way, attacked them at these dangerous points; and as the numbers of the assailants increased, the army was beset in front, flank, and rear, and a terrible scene of disaster followed.

Horses, beasts of burden, carriages, and trains were hurled in confusion into the yawning depths beneath; hundreds of the soldiers were slain, or made captives by the Gauls; thousands perished as they were forced over the cliffs; the air rang for leagues with the savage yells of the Celts; the whole enterprise, in a word, was gravely endangered. But Hannibal's picked men had kept the crest of the heights; they moved rapidly along, at their leader's command, overlooking from above the Gaulish onset; they doubtless were accompanied by the renowned Balearic slingers, and they poured such a storm of missiles on the enemies below that an immense number of these was killed and the barbarians were compelled to abandon the prey that seemed in their grasp.

The Carthaginian Army, extricated, but with enormous loss, made its way, molested no longer, into the plain that extends to the great lake of Bourget; it seems to have made a halt for a time; and it avenged itself on its defeated enemy. Hannibal destroyed the principal town of the Gauls; laid in an ample store of provisions; and made booty of large herds of cattle. He was rejoined, probably near Chambéry, by a considerable number of wounded men and stragglers.

The army was soon in the valley of the Isère, still broad and fertile

HANNIBAL CROSSING THE ALPS.
(AFTER TURNER.)

for many miles, before the river approaches the main range of the Alps. Hannibal was received with gifts and honeyed words by the Gauls of this region; but though he accepted the guides they offered, he was fortunately suspicious, and took precautions. After a march of two or three days he reached the valley of the Reclus, a feeder of the Isère; he beheld the gigantic barrier of the Alps rising in snow, thousands of feet above, and the gap which marks the pass through the Little St. Bernard. His distrust of the Celts had only increased; he formed his army, as it was about to begin the ascent, in the manner that he thought would best ensure its safety. He placed his elephants in front of the long column, for the barbarians beheld these beasts with superstitious awe; next to these followed the cavalry and the impedimenta; his infantry, which he kept in his own hand, closed the rear, well together, and in full force.

The army had got into a narrow defile overhung by huge cliffs on either side—one of these was then known as the "White Rock," and still retains the traditional name—when it was suddenly assailed by multitudes of the treacherous Celts hidden in ambush on the top of the heights; and this attack was ere long followed by a formidable attack on its rear. The preceding disaster was repeated, but this was much worse; the Gauls hurled down rocks and even boulders from their points of vantage, and completely broke up the middle parts of the column; the destruction of men and horses was immense; the impedimenta were to a great extent lost; and the masses of the Gauls fell with desperate courage and determination on the Carthaginian footmen.

The army of Hannibal was cut in two; but the great captain overcame the storm; his infantry gradually forced the assailants back, though the ground was strewn with their dead and dying men; and ultimately he succeeded in bringing his forces together,—for the attack slackened in all directions,—having again saved his troops by his resource and energy. The army had ere long attained the summit of the Little St. Bernard Pass; it was nine days after it stood under the Mont du Chât; the date was the 26th of October, 218 B.C..

Hannibal gave his worn-out soldiers rest, on the top of the range, for two days. The region around was a desert of mountain and snow; even the bravest began to lose heart, and to murmur; but Hannibal pointed towards the east; "we have climbed," he exclaimed, "the ramparts of Italy, nay, of Rome, what lies still for us to accomplish is not difficult." The slopes, however, of the Alps, on the Italian side, are more precipitous than on that of France; and as the Carthaginians made the descent, a considerable number of men and horses were lost, though no hostile tribes attempted an attack.

At last, a point was reached where avalanches had swept away the track, and had made the mountain side a sheer wall like a cliff; the march of the column was arrested; it was pronounced impossible to make a step in advance. This was, so to speak, Hannibal's Fort of Bard, (referring to Napoleon's Alpine march in 1800); but the natural was far worse than the artificial obstacle; the November snow covered the glaciers beneath; and, in an effort to press forward, many victims perished. An attempt was made to find a path higher up the range; but this failed and had to be abandoned; a kind of gallery was then cut in the side of the cliff, blasted by the explosive to which we have referred.

The cavalry, infantry, and *impedimenta* were soon enabled to pass, but four days were required to open a way for the elephants, yet, though famished, the animals were saved. The army, having overcome this strait, moved rapidly down the valley of the Dora Baltea; and by the first days of November had reached Ivrea, and entered the lands of the friendly Insubres. It was welcomed by its allies with delight; but it presented a woeful and almost hopeless aspect. In a record supposed to have been made by himself, Hannibal has declared that of the 59,000 men he had led from the Pyrenees, there remained only 20,000 infantry, and 6,000 horsemen; and these were but the shadow of a military force, the men spectres, the horses scarcely able to stand. What must have been the result, if, as was quite possible, Scipio had met this exhausted army at the passes from the Alps, at the head of even 40,000 of the soldiers of Rome? (See note at end of chapter.)

The Insubres, thirsting for vengeance on Rome, supplied the needs of Hannibal's army with eager alacrity and good-will; but weeks were required before the worn-out troops were in a condition to move, and to face the enemy. By degrees they regained their strength and acquired once more the appearance of a well-organised force; it deserves special notice that not one of the elephants was lost in the long and arduous march, for they had been an object of peculiar attention and care. Hannibal was now in Piedmont and at the foot of the Alps, but almost without a trustworthy base; he entered the country of the Taurini, with whom the Insubres were at continual feud, in order, in part probably, to please his allies, in part to render his communications in some measure secure.

The chief town of the tribe, the modern Turin, fell to a siege conducted with great vigour, and followed by an assault, after the explosion of an enormous mine; an example was made of the hostile Gauls, who were, not improbably, in the pay of Rome. It was now time for Hannibal to march into Italy, and to proceed on his heroic enterprise, but the prospect before him was not reassuring. A Roman Army, he knew, was not far distant; and if the Insubres were his devoted friends, and other Gaulish tribes seemed eager for his approach, there had been no general rising as yet in his favour, and the Cenomani and a few lesser clans, along the south of the Po, had joined the standards of Rome. As usual, in a word, the Celts were divided; but the die had been cast, and the Carthaginian Army advanced, perhaps in the first week of December, towards the Sesia, along the northern bank of the Po.

Before this time Scipio had reached Placentia, (now Piacenza), even then a strong fortress, and a large Roman colony; he had marched, we have seen, across the Apennines, had rallied the army of the *praetor* Manlius, had obtained some reinforcements in Italy, and had been joined by a body of Gauls; he was probably at the head of more than 30,000 men. At Placentia he held the key of the north of Italy and commanded the famous Stradella Pass; had remained in that position he would have placed Hannibal in no doubtful straits. (Piacenza, and the Stradella Pass, are importance defences of northern Italy.) But though his army was largely composed of recruits, he resolved to push forward, and fall on Hannibal, when apprised that his adversary was on the march; he was full of recollections of the skirmish on the Rhone. In an unlucky hour for himself he left his point of vantage, crossed the Po and the Ticinus, (now the Ticino), as quickly as possible, and moved into the great plains eastward; it seems that he pressed his cavalry on, leaving the greatest part of his army far in the rear.

We may picture to ourselves the grim delight of Hannibal when he learned that his enemy had quitted his fine position, and was moving into the Lomellina, where the Phoenician cavalry would certainly possess a distinct advantage. He crossed the Sesia to meet the consul, with, it has been said, about 6,000 horsemen, in part heavy Spanish and Phoenician, in part light Numidian; he came in view of Scipio, a little to the east of Vercelli. The consul's force was only composed of some light infantry and perhaps 2,000 or 3,000 horsemen; at all events it was greatly outnumbered; he had recklessly advanced with a portion of his army only, into the ground where his defeat was certain.

The combat that followed, if hardly a battle, had important results, and was short and decisive. (Polybius and Livy.) The Roman *velites*, boyish recruits, gave way at once, when charged by the heavy Carthaginian cavalry; the Roman horse made a better stand; but their inexperience in their arm was clearly shewn (Polybius and Livy); numbers dismounted, attempted to fight on foot, and were trampled down by the Phoenician and Spanish squadrons. Meanwhile the admirable Numidians had closed in on the hostile wings, their favourite manoeuvre so often seen; all then became confusion and rout; the Roman detachment was butchered where it fought; few only escaped to bear the dismal news.

The consul, who stood with his men to the last, was severely wounded in the first shock of arms; he was extricated from the fugitives by his young son, the celebrated Africanus of the day of Zama, destined, in after years, to overthrow Hannibal. The Roman Army, after this reverse, retreated hastily behind the Ticinus and the Po, and took refuge, it would appear, just outside Placentia, forming a great camp near the walls of the fortress.

Hannibal made prisoners of a large rearguard, in his pursuit of the defeated army. Some critics have asked why he did not follow his enemy across the Ticinus and the Po; but the reason is sufficiently plain; he had suffered loss, and his position was still insecure. His next operations, for the few subsequent days, are remarkable for judgment and military skill. He was reinforced by some Gaulish warriors, though no general insurrection as yet took place; and he enlisted them in the ranks of his army. He then resolved to proceed on his march; but he did not advance lower down the Po; this would have led him into the lands of the Cenomani, well-known subjects and allies of Rome; the passage of the great river too would have become very difficult, as its waters extend in their course eastwards.

But the Stradella Pass, he knew, was a main defence of Italy, and must be mastered to enable him to advance safely; he was eager to join his enemy at Placentia; he had messages from the Gauls to the south of the Po assuring him of large and loyal support; and he had been informed, probably through his spies in Rome, that Sempronius, with the army which had been designed for Africa, was in full march to the north of Italy in order to effect his junction with his colleague Scipio. Hannibal's resolution was soon formed; it reveals a great captain in every sense of the word. He ascended the Po, by the northern bank, crossed the river apparently by boats and barges, as he had previously crossed the Rhone, at a point supposed to be near Cambio; the Celts, as they promised, rose at his summons, and swelled the ranks of his now rapidly increasing army.

Pushing instantly forward by forced marches, Hannibal seized and held the Stradella Pass, an avenue into the midst of northern Italy; he passed Clastidium, (now Casteggio), a Roman stronghold, either mastering it, or, as has been said, making terms with a cowardly or false commandant—this was one of the instances of his Punic faith—and he was ere long in sight of Placentia, and of the hostile army motionless in its camp. Judging admirably that his enemy was cowed and beaten, he marched boldly across Scipio's front; established his army on the banks of the Nura, a short distance to the east of Placentia; and thus, placed himself between the two consuls, holding Scipio in check, a few miles away, and preventing Sempronius from approaching his colleague, at least by the proper line of junction, the great main road from Ariminum.

He had the full advantage of an interior line; and was in the central position between divided foes, which Turenne and Napoleon so often gained, and in which both of these great commanders, especially the last, accomplished marvellous exploits of war. During these operations on the Ticinus and the Po, Sempronius and his legions had been advancing with extraordinary speed to the north of Italy, and had reached Ariminum about the third week of December. That officer, we have seen, had been sent with a consular army, and a great fleet, to make a descent on Africa; but he had been unable to fulfil his mission. Under the inspiration beyond dispute of Hannibal, the Carthaginian government had fitted out two small squadrons to make a diversion ill the Mediterranean, and to threaten Italy; and though one of these suffered loss in a severe storm, and the other was defeated off Lilybaeum, in a combat in which sheer hard fighting prevailed again over manoeuvring skill, this fleet effectually accomplished Hannibal's purpose. (Livy has described this battle in his usual picturesque manner. He points out very clearly the characteristic difference between the Roman and the Carthaginian naval tactics.)

It kept hovering near the southern shores of Italy; this detained the consul through the whole summer; and if he endeavoured to strengthen his hold on Sicily, by capturing one or two small islands, he did not even approach Africa, and his fleet and his army were almost paralysed. Early in November he received the news that Hannibal was descending from the Alps; the senate, alarmed at what they regarded as an unforeseen portent, directed him to march to the aid of his colleague, Scipio; stout soldier as he was, he did not hesitate. He embarked with his army at Lilybaeum; proceeded by sea, in person, to Rome; and landed his troops on the coast of Bruttium, with orders to make for Ariminum by forced marches.

The soldiery, bound by a solemn oath to their chief, advanced from the extreme south into the north of Italy, at a rate which must be pronounced astonishing; it is said, at an average of sixteen miles a day, for a period of probably four weeks at least. (Dodge, *Hannibal*.) The excellence of the Roman roads accounts in some measure for this celerity; but if we bear in mind the weighty burden the Roman legionary carried on a march, the exploit deserves the very highest praise.

★★★★★★★★★★

Very few modern armies have ever marched sixteen miles a day for any great length of time. The boasted marches of the German Armies, in the war of 1870, were seldom longer than thirteen miles a day for considerable distances; they have been unduly extolled by the uninformed worshippers of success. They were far surpassed by many marches of Napoleon, and even of Wellington. The march of the Grand Army from the Channel to the Danube approached that of the army of Sempronius in rapidity.

★★★★★★★★★★

Meanwhile Hannibal had been making attempts, in accordance with the true principles of war, to turn his position of vantage to account, and to fall on Scipio before his colleague could join him. He had offered the consul battle, when he had passed Placentia; but the strength of the Roman camp, close to a great fortress, enabled his adversary to decline his challenge. A short time afterwards a revolt of the Gauls in Scipio's army induced that officer to endeavour to leave the ground he held—he evidently feared contact with the Gauls in Hannibal's camp—he set out from before Placentia, and made for the Trebia, by a night march skilfully planned. Hannibal pushed forward his well-trained Numidians to follow the enemy and bring him to bay, and pursued with the great mass of his forces, (positively asserted by Polybius, the passage which proves that Hannibal contemplated falling on Scipio, when still separated from Sempronius, has escaped the notice of, as far as I know, all commentators), but the Numidians lost time in burning the Roman camp; the consul escaped across the Trebia; took a strong position not far from Rivalta, and entrenched himself in a camp on the western bank, awaiting the appearance of his now expected colleague.

Hannibal confronted him, near Settima, on the eastern bank, and did not cross the river to attack. Why did he not carry out the design he had originally in view? We may ascribe his apparent inaction in part to the formidable nature of the Roman camp, an obstacle that may be compared to a fortress; but Hannibal, superior as he was in cavalry, ought to have been able to ravage the adjoining country, and to starve his adversary out of his lines; and probably there was a more sufficient reason. Though Hannibal had been joined by numbers of the Gauls, there was still no universal rising in his aid; a great many tribes still held aloof (Polybius, and Livy dwell emphatically on this important fact); some were as yet friendly to Rome, or waiting on fortune.

His army, too, was by no means fully restored; in these circumstances he may have thought it the wisest course to further the training of his Gaulish levies, to accustom them to Carthaginian discipline, to give his troops a still needed rest, and not to attack Scipio in his well-protected lair. It is possible, besides, that he did not believe that Sempronius could reach his colleague, by a practicable road other than the great road from Ariminum; his knowledge of Italy must have been very imperfect. He did not, however, waste his time; he scoured the whole country around for supplies; and he pounced on Clastidium where the Romans had great stores, in the hope perhaps of compelling Scipio to retreat. His "Punic faith" was again seen in his trafficking with the officer in command.

★★★★★★★★★★

I have described these operations of Hannibal somewhat differently from other writers. But my conclusions are, I think, borne out by Polybius and Livy if attentively studied. It is perfectly plain from Polybius that Hannibal at first intended to fall on Scipio in force; why he paused, after Scipio had crossed the Trebia, may also be gathered from the historian's narrative.

★★★★★★★★★★

While Hannibal was thus on the watch for Scipio, Sempronius had been moving from Ariminum, to effect his junction with his defeated colleague. He certainly did not march by the great ordinary road, the Via Æmilia of a later day, for the Carthaginian chief was in his path; he may have marched along the northern spurs of the Apennines; but probably he advanced along the south of the range and reached the Trebia, from Genoa, in part by the road known, in modern times, as that by the famous Boccheta. (Though the Via Æmilia had not yet been made there certainly was a main road from Ariminum to Placentia at this time.) He had reached the camp of Scipio, in the last days of December, or possibly even a little afterwards, having again pressed forward with great celerity; he had eluded, if not out-manoeuvred

1. Scipio's camp?   2. Scene of the Battle?   3. Mago in ambush?
   Livy, Part II.

Hannibal; the two consuls were now at the head of a united army at least 45,000 strong, but composed in part of Gauls and recruits, and with scarcely more than 4,000 horsemen.

****

It is very remarkable that Napoleon does not blame Hannibal for not having attacked Scipio before Sempronius joined him, and for not having prevented the junction of the two consuls. He compares the position of Hannibal to his own in the campaign of 1796, when he stood between Beaulieu and Colli, and when he separated his adversaries, and defeated them in detail. But, he says, "*J'étais dans une situation plus favorable qu'Annibal; les deux Consuls avaient un intérèt commun; couvrir Rome; les deux généraux que j'attaquais avaient chacun un intérèet particulier que les dominait; Beaulieu, celui de couvrir le Milanais; Colli, celui de couvrir le Piedmont,*" quoted by Colonel Dodge, *Hannibal*. I have not been able to verify the passage in Napoleon's writings.

****

Scipio was still completely disabled by his wound; but the mischief of divided consuls and a divided command were felt at once in the Roman camp. Scipio urged that it was the true course to hold Hannibal firmly in check, not to offer battle with uncertain results, to await large reinforcements from Rome; the Carthaginian Army could not fail to be in want of supplies in a short time; the Gauls would not bear importunate allies; in masterly inaction was the real hope of safety. His colleague, however, was of an opposite mind; the consular elections were not distant; he burned for an opportunity to attack his enemy before he laid down his high office, (especially noticed by Polybius and by Livy); a victory would make him perhaps a dictator. Nor were plausible military reasons wanting; the Roman was superior in numbers to the Phoenician Army; and what could resist the shock of the legions on a fair field, in their own land of Italy?

Hannibal had numerous spies in the enemy's camp, and was probably informed by treacherous Gauls of the divided counsels prevailing in the Roman Army. It is one of the gifts of a great captain to understand the character of an adversary in his front; Hannibal evidently took an accurate measure of Scipio and of his ambitious colleague. By this time he had his army in hand; it was inferior in numbers to the two Consular Armies, about 38,000 to 45,000 men; but it possessed the elephant, an important special arm, 10,000 cavalry, largely Gaulish, against 4,000; a considerable force of Balearic slingers very superior to similar Roman troops; above all it was a trained and veteran army, in a very large proportion at least, directed by a master of war, and opposed to an army, in part of recruits, and under generals of conflicting views.

It was the interest of Hannibal, therefore, to fight a decisive battle, before Scipio had recovered from his wound, and had made his authority more distinctly felt; he resolved to lure Sempronius on to attack, retrieving the error, if error it was, of having allowed him to join his colleague. He sent out a detachment, chiefly of Numidian horsemen, to ravage the lands of Gauls still allies of Rome; Sempronius crossed the Trebia, with a considerable force, and drove the squadrons, probably under orders, back; this fired the consul's exulting hopes; he made up his mind to follow up what he deemed a victory. (Polybius dwells on the arrogance and over-confidence of the consul. Livy says the same thing in more measured language.) Hannibal felt that his enemy was falling into the snare; he made instantly preparations for a great and general battle.

He arranged the positions his army was to hold, superintending everything with the most minute care; and as it was the depth of winter, and the weather was very severe, he gave orders that his troops should oil their bodies, should be plentifully supplied with good food and fires, and especially that their horses should be looked after. At the same time, being perfectly aware of the great qualities of the Roman infantry, he most skilfully laid a deadly ambush for them, foreseeing, as he did, that they would cross the Trebia to attack. He placed his brother Mago, with 2,000 picked men, in part horsemen, in part foot, in the hollow of a ravine hidden by brushwood and aquatic plants, with directions to fall in full force on the enemy's rear when the battle had been thoroughly engaged in front. (Polybius notices the remarkable skill shewn by Hannibal in preparing this ambush. The Romans had been accustomed to such tactics on the part of the Gauls; but the Gauls hid themselves in woods; Hannibal, knowing this, stationed Mago in a fold of ground.)

It was the early morning of a bitter winter's day, supposed to have been the 26th of December. (Hénnébert fixes this as the date, and is followed by several writers. I think it ought to be a few days later; Sempronius could hardly have reached the Trebia from Ariminum by Genoa, so soon. The point is not of much importance.) The snow was falling, the sky lowering; the Trebia, an Apennine torrent, was in full flood, rolling its swollen waters over its broad channel. Nature concurred to second the design of Hannibal. He sent a body of his trusty Numidians across the river to the western bank; they gallantly swam the angry stream; they were soon swarming around the Roman lines, insulting the soldiery, challenging them to fight. Sempronius could not contain his wrath; he told off footmen and horsemen to sweep his enemies away; these, obeying their orders, recrossed the stream. The consul, furious at seeing the children of the desert escape, did not even ask his colleague's advice; he hastily assembled his own officers; he gave directions that the whole army should pass the Trebia, and attack Hannibal on the eastern bank.

★★★★★★★★★★

> With all the best authorities, I have placed the scene of the battle on the eastern or right bank of the Trebia. The narratives of Polybius and Livy seem to me decisive on this point, nor can we explain otherwise the escape of the 10,000 Roman infantry to Placentia, which is east of the Trebia. Mommsen, vol. ii., is here, I think, in error,

★★★★★★★★★★

The Romans and their auxiliaries discovered a ford believed to be that of Mirafiore, (Hénnébert); but the water was up to the armpits of the men; they had not even had their morning meal; they reached the scene of action exhausted and famished. Hours were spent in effecting the ill-omened passage; Hannibal beheld with delight his enemy given into his hands; a general of a lesser order would have fallen on the Romans when entangled in the stream; he allowed them to cross to a man to make his victory, (well noticed by Macdougall, *The Campaigns of Hannibal*) complete. The day was far spent when the armies, about to close, had placed themselves in their order of battle; the Romans with their backs to the swollen Trebia, worn out, and not at all fit to fight; the Carthaginians, rested, in good condition, and confronting the river that threatened to engulf their foes.

Sempronius arrayed his legions in the usual three lines, the Gaulish auxiliaries being on the left; his weak force of horsemen was on both his wings. Hannibal drew up his infantry in a deep *phalanx*; his powerful cavalry was on both his flanks; his array of elephants perhaps filled a space between his horse and his foot; perhaps occupied to the right and the left, the extreme edge of his line. (The view of Colonel Dodge, *Hannibal*. Livy, on the contrary, certainly ranges the elephants on the extremities of Hannibal's wings.)

The Romans, as always, took the offensive; their archers, slingers, and light-armed infantry advanced, in open order, against Hannibal's array. Their numbers, however, were small, and their efforts weak; the *velites* had wasted their darts in pursuing the Numidian horsemen; they were driven in, and routed by the Phoenician skirmishers, apparently nearly threefold in strength, the renowned Baleares plying their slings with most destructive effect. This, however, was but the prelude to the fight; the lines of the legions had soon reached the *phalanx*; Sempronius rode at the head of his men, encouraging them by voice and confident gesture, never doubting that victory was in his grasp.

But the stern cheers of the Romans were hollow and faint, as, starving and benumbed with cold, they endeavoured to close; the *pilum* was hurled by nerveless hands; the *gladius* was unable to do its work; the serried ranks of the Carthaginian column resisted efforts that were half paralysed. The *principes* rushed in vain through the intervals between the divided *maniples*, to aid the *hastati*; the *triarii* pressed on boldly in vain; the extending line of the assailants tried fruitlessly to outflank and surround the unshaken enemy. While this conflict was in full progress, the great masses of Hannibal's horsemen had completely routed the weak Roman cavalry, and forced it, with heavy loss, away from the field; and they had soon fallen on the exposed flanks of the legions, crushing down the men with their irresistible weight.

The Gaulish auxiliaries gave way, and were dispersed; but the noble Roman infantry still bravely fought on, though the elephants had come to the aid of the Phoenician horsemen, trampling hundreds of luckless victims under foot, and though the Balearic slingers had crept round, and were smiting the Romans in the rear with a deadly storm of missiles. (Hénnébert asserts that the *balista* was employed at the Trebia, there is no trace of this in the narratives of Polybius and Livy, and he gives no authority.) The legions, now assailed in front by the advancing *phalanx*, and hemmed in by foes gathering in on all sides, nevertheless still maintained the lost battle; when a sudden apparition was seen in their rear.

Mago, perceiving that the crisis of the day had come, issued from his lair, and fell on the doomed army; the attack of this fresh reserve was decisive; the Carthaginian spear and the Gaulish claymore wrought fearful havoc in the ranks of the beaten troops; defeat became an appalling rout. Yet even in that hour of despair and ruin, the matchless Roman infantry was worthy of itself; 10,000 men cut their way through a host of enemies, and found refuge within the walls of Placentia. The disaster, however, was not the less complete; Hannibal did not pursue the defeated army, for night had fallen, and the Trebia was not to be lightly entered; but 30,000 men of the consular armies were made prisoners, wounded, or slain. (The student of war cannot fail to perceive a marked but only general resemblance between the conduct of Hannibal and Sempronius at the Trebia, and of Napoleon and the allies at Austerlitz.)

The battle of the Trebia, if not the most tremendous, was one of the most brilliant of Hannibal's victories. He often recurred to it in his old age, as a masterpiece of his skill in the field; it is sufficient to stamp him as a great captain. It is difficult to say whether we ought most to admire his craft in arranging the ambush of Mago, his dexterity in luring Sempronius on to his fate, his careful preparation of his troops beforehand, his perfect disposition of his army on the ground, or his art in making a decisive triumph secure; and there can be little but blame for his enemy's conduct. Yet who can withhold the due meed of praise from the magnificent Roman infantry on that day; we see, in what it achieved, the heroic qualities which made it, at last, the master of the ancient world.

The wreck of the Roman Army seems to have made its way—apart from the large division shut up in Placentia—to Cremona and other Italian colonies; but it was annihilated as an organised military force; Hannibal was lord of Italy north of the Apennines. The immediate result of this prodigious success was that the Italian Gauls rose, in one great body, at last, and joined his standards; 64,000 warriors, it is said, flocked into his camp. Yet Hannibal's prospects were not all bright; his great project had only succeeded in part. He was, doubtless, aware that he had not really weakened the enormous military power of Rome; nor could he expect as yet that he could make an impression on her allies in the middle and south of Italy. But he had been disappointed in his hope of collecting in the valley of the Po a great host of many races and tongues, to attack the object of his deadly hate, and of marching against the republic at its head.

The court of Macedon made no sign, the Illyrians, along the Adriatic coast, were held in awe by a Roman fleet; the power of Carthage in Spain was being already threatened by the army in the hands of Cnaeus Scipio; Spanish troops had not come to Hannibal's aid; the immense circuit by the Alps was a most grave obstacle, especially as Rome was really supreme at sea. And though Hannibal had obtained the assistance of the Italian Gauls, how long could he rely on natures of this kind, excitable, reckless, and, as he often found out, treacherous? His army, besides, as the winter advanced, began to suffer much from disease and privations; his elephants, which had escaped the Alpine march, nearly all perished. With perfect judgment, he paused for some months before making an attempt to invade the southern parts of Italy; he employed this interval of time chiefly in forming his new levies.

The first act in the drama of the Second Punic War, ends with the great defeat of Rome on the Trebia. Seldom in the history of the world, has the decisive influence of individual genius in war been as grandly and conspicuously made manifest. While Rome was dreaming of a descent on Africa, and listlessly making ready for an easy conquest, Hannibal baffles her by the originality and greatness of his plan; seizes the initiative on the theatre of war; marches from the Ebro to the Pyrenees and the Rhone, before her feeble preparations are complete. His sudden attack disconcerts all her projects; reduces her, overwhelming as is her power, to resort to an ill-considered and passive defence; and when after his march across the Alps, the great Carthaginian descends to the banks of the Po, he annihilates the only army she can yet oppose to him.

The magnificent conceptions of Hannibal, too, were worked out by an execution not less admirable. In all his operations we see supreme excellence, skill, resource, daring, an heroic spirit, the faculty of command in the very highest degree, caution, sound judgment, extraordinary craft, and last, but not least, watchful and incessant care in providing for the requirements of his troops. Every movement from the fine passage of the Rhone to the astonishing crossing of the Alps, to the brilliant engagement on the Ticinus, to the mastery of the Stradella Pass, to the manoeuvres which separated the two consuls, and finally to the decisive blow on the Trebia, is marked with consummate power in war; it is scarcely possible to detect a single fault; and there is evidence enough to shew that, if Hannibal did not fall on Scipio and Sempronius while still apart, he was prevented from the design he had formed, by reasons which, if obscure, may be held sufficient.

As for his adversaries they were generals of the ordinary Roman type, stout soldiers, even capable men, but ignorant of the higher parts of war; mere playthings in the hands of a chief like Hannibal; and the Trebia was probably due to their divided counsels, in part the result of defects in the military institutions of Rome. Yet the Roman infantry was equal to itself; it is impossible to give it higher praise; its conduct was a presage of a more auspicious time.

Note.—

The exact line taken by Hannibal, in his celebrated march across the Alps, has been a matter of endless but ingenious controversy. The subject is one rather of antiquarian research than of historical importance, for the Alpine passes through which the Carthaginian Army may have penetrated, present similar difficulties, and were alike in the possession of Gaulish tribes. A few remarks, however, may be made, even in a brief epitome. There are only two ancient narratives; that of Polybius, not very far from contemporaneous, is, I think, much the most trustworthy. The route indicated in these pages seems to me the only one that can be reconciled with the account of Polybius.

No doubt Polybius does not refer to the lake of Bourget; and no doubt the Carthaginian soldiery could not have seen the plains of Italy from the pass of the Little St. Bernard, as Polybius hints they did; but these objections are trifling, and are far outweighed by really important considerations:

(1) Polybius says that Hannibal moved that is, I conceive, up the Rhone, through the Insula; and though he does not say that Hannibal struck across the Insula from Vienne, he asserts that "Hannibal began to ascend the Alps near the Rhone"; and this points to the Mont du Chât and the Chevelu Pass.

(2) Polybius gives it to be understood that, after emerging from the first pass, the Carthaginians entered a plain and easy country; this corresponds with the tract around Chambery and the adjoining part of the valley of the Isère.

(3) A cliff called the Roche Blanche is near the foot of the Little St, Bernard; this answers to what Polybius refers to as close to the main range of the Alps ascended by Hannibal.

(4) The distances, very specifically set forth by Polybius, agree much better with those of the route I have followed, than with those of any other route.

(5) Polybius makes Hannibal descend into the lands of the Insubres; a fragment of Strabo, indeed, contradicts this; but the text of Polybius is quite plain; and it is probable that Hannibal would, in the first instance, repair to the territory of his allies, who, it must be borne in mind, had given him guides.

On the whole, the view I have taken is apparently nearly that of the best historian of that age; it is that of Arnold, Mommsen, Niebuhr, and other distinguished men; and it is maintained by Colonel Dodge (*Hannibal*) with admirable reasoning and fulness of knowledge.

Eminent writers, however, have contended that Hannibal marched through the Insula, along the Isère; then passed into the valley of the Arc; and finally crossed the Alps, by the pass of Mont Cenis, into the country of the Taurini, who were deadly enemies of the Insubres. This, too, is the opinion of Napoleon, formed indeed on very inadequate evidence (*Corr.*), but of course valuable.

Polybius may possibly have referred to the Isère, when he wrote; but in almost every other particular his narrative can hardly be reconciled with the route just above mentioned; and he denies that Hannibal issued from the Alps into the lands of the Taurini as, indeed, may almost be assumed. It should be added that though the pass of Mont Cenis is lower, and was perhaps even then more practicable than that of the Little St, Bernard, the march of the Carthaginian Army through the valley of the Arc, would have been difficult in the extreme; and the localities do not at all resemble those described by Polybius.

The second ancient narrative is that of Livy, a better writer than Polybius, who tells us that he had carefully investigated the subject, but separated from the events in question by nearly two hundred years. Livy's account is circumstantial and precise, but, I think, very improbable. He says that, after entering the Insula, Hannibal marched towards the Alps, but not by the direct route; he turned to his left through the lands of the Tricontii, the Vocontii, and the Tricorii; he reached with little difficulty the course of the Durance; and having ascended the valley of that river, and overcome the obstacles and the attacks described by Polybius, he debouched from the Alps into the country of the Taurini, evidently by the pass of Mont Génévre. This description would indicate that Hannibal counter-marched from the Insula, into the valley of the Drôme, the territory of the Gaulish tribes he names, for this is implied in the statement that he moved to his left; and besides that, this route is open to all the objections mentioned already, this single supposition can hardly be entertained.

A series, however, of very able writers—Hénnébert is the most conspicuous—have adopted Livy's itinerary in part; they represent Hannibal as ascending the valley of the Durance, crossing Mont Génévre, and passing into the lands of the Taurini; but they make him reach the Durance, not by the valley of the Drôme, but by that of the Drac, through Grenoble, Chorges, and other places. The arguments of Hénnébert, approved by Colonel Malleson, are of undoubted weight; but, for the reasons before stated, they cannot, I think, fit in with the account of Polybius, and ought not to prevail. It should be added that Mr. Douglas Freshfield, a very competent authority, adopts the view that Hannibal marched up the Durance; but he contends that he crossed the Alps by the pass of Argentière; certainly, a passage from

Varro is in his favour.

Still the weight of evidence is, I believe, against Mr. Freshfield; and he makes Hannibal—what is not probable—diverge from the Durance, into the very difficult valley of the Ubaye. The reader may consult, on the whole question, an elaborate and very learned note in Arnold's *History of the Second Punic War*, the third volume of the *History of Rome*, in which most of the authorities are collected and compared. The description by Polybius will be found in book iii., that of Livy in book xxi. The subject, however, I repeat, seems to me rather for the antiquarian than the historian.

HANNIBAL.

Chapter 6: Trasimenus and Cannae

Hannibal had a difficult and a perilous task in preparing his levies of Gauls for the field. The Celts had flocked to his camp, we have seen, in thousands; but they found regular discipline a hateful burden; they were indignant that they were not given a free hand to devastate and plunder the valley of the Po. Their chiefs, too, were fickle, treacherous, and at feud with each other; they angrily resented that they had to find supplies for the liberating army which ate up their country. Plots, it is said, were formed against the life of Hannibal; the great Carthaginian was compelled to put on disguises, and to be always attended by a Phoenician escort; the Gauls, in a word, were true to their barbarian nature.

He gradually, however, bowed these Celts to his will; before the spring had come, he had made real soldiers of not less than 30,000 or 40,000 men of a martial race notable in all ages, for its aptitude for war, and especially excelling, at this time, in its horsemen. At the same time, he restored his old and trusted army, the ranks of which had been greatly thinned ever since it had descended from the Alps; he was at the head of probably 50,000 or 60,000 men before entering on his projected campaign. Meanwhile he swept supplies in from the districts in his power; captured one or two places of Roman settlement; and made an attempt to starve Placentia out by attacking its magazines, in forts on the Po.

The 10,000 men who had cut their way through at the Trebia, had, we have said, taken refuge in the place; they had been joined by the wounded consul Scipio; and Hannibal was beaten off, wounded himself, in turn. He may have been foiled, too, in more than one similar effort; and ultimately Scipio and his noble troops, reaching those which had made their way to Cremona, effected their escape, perhaps by the northern bank of the Po; they seem then to have been conveyed to Rome, there is reason to believe, up to Ancona, by the

Adriatic waters. (Mommsen, ii. The importance of Rome's command of the sea recurs over and over again in the Second Punic War.)

Hannibal was now established in the valley of the Po, though he had still mainly to depend on the unstable Gauls; just before setting out on his march southwards, he advanced into the lands of the Ligures, perhaps in the hope of obtaining intelligence or aid from Carthage. We may reject as idle the tales that some time previously he had made an attempt to move across the Apennines, and that he had fought a bloody fight with his old foe, Sempronius, the wrecks of whose legions had been reinforced from Rome. (Livy tells these stories in his usual picturesque way, but they are most improbable, and are not noticed by Polybius.)

It was now the spring of 217 B.C.; while Hannibal was preparing to descend on central Italy, fortune was beginning to turn against him on another theatre of war, apparently remote, but of supreme importance. Spain, we have seen, was the real seat of his military power, the base of his operations in his great enterprise, for Carthage could not attempt to attack Rome from Africa; her government, too, was weak and untrustworthy. For these reasons Hannibal had left his brother Hasdrubal in chief command in Spain; he had detached Hanno, before he had made for the Rhone, with a considerable force to maintain his hold on the Catalans; and he evidently calculated that, owing to these precautions, his communications with Spain would be kept open, and that, long as the circuit was from the Pyrenees across the Alps, reinforcements and supplies would regularly reach his army. He had been already disappointed in this hope; the assistance he looked for was not forthcoming; it was never to arrive freely, and to a sufficient extent.

Cnaeus Scipio, who, it will be borne in mind, had been sent by his brother Publius to Spain, at the head of the greater part of the consul's army, had effected a landing, and defeated Hanno; he not only subdued the Catalonian sea-board, but brought many Catalan tribes into subjection to Rome. He was surprised by Hasdrubal, sometime afterwards, and was beaten with considerable loss; but he clung to Tarragona and the coast; he received support from Marseilles, and the Spanish Greek colonies; and before long he had his revenge on Hasdrubal, and drove him back upon Cartagena. The region between the Pyrenees and the Ebro fell thus nearly all into Roman hands; the Roman senate, which possessed the command of the sea, and clearly perceived the advantage it had gained, took care to maintain a large military and naval force in Spain; an insuperable barrier was opposed to the march of troops and other requirements of war to Hannibal. (Polybius points this out very clearly. The Roman senate and the Carthaginians were equally alive to the effect on Hannibal's position in Italy, of what was occurring in Spain. But Rome was a great nation, Carthage an ill-governed state.)

His communications were, so to speak, strangled; he was left "in the air," to use an expressive phrase, in Italy. An attempt made some months afterwards by a Carthaginian squadron to land at Pisa, and to send him support was frustrated by a superior Roman fleet; his position was thus even now insecure. This perilous state of things was to become worse in time; it had a marked effect on the fortunes of the Second Punic War. (See again Mahan, *Sea Power*, First Series. Rome's command of the sea hampered Hannibal more than England's command of the sea hampered Napoleon.)

Meanwhile Rome had been steadily engaged in making preparations to renew the contest. The rout at the Trebia caused a thrill of alarm; this was not lessened by the boasts of, Sempronius—he had reached the capital with a small body of horse—that his defeat had been due to a hard winter's day; and superstitious terror prevailed for a moment. But the nation regained its stern composure, and nerved itself to continue the terrible struggle, which it had deemed at first would be brief and decisive. Two legions were sent to the army in Spain, where the prospect of the war was becoming bright; one was despatched to Sicily, one to Sardinia, a third to hold the great port of Tarentum, for the power of Carthage at sea was to be kept under, and Carthaginian descents on Italy were not to be endured.

But Hannibal and his army formed the real danger, and Rome arrayed forces against the great enemy, which might well have appeared sufficient. The remains of the legions of the Trebia were reinforced; they were left at Lucca in the hands of Sempronius; the allies were called upon to make a great effort; and four new Roman and four new allied legions were raised and placed in the hands of the lately elected consuls, Caius Flaminius and Cnaeus Servilius Geminus, with directions to hold the Apennine passes leading into the plain land of Etruria, to confront Hannibal on this line, and, if success attended their arms, to carry the war into the valley of the Po. From 60,000 to 70,000 men, taking the forces of Sempronius into account, were thus to be assembled on the old frontier of Italy, to oppose an enemy not superior in numbers; and these arrays, backed by the immense resources of Rome, might not unreasonably have been supposed adequate.

****

It is difficult to estimate the numbers of the army of Hannibal, and of the armies of the two consuls. Hannibal's army can hardly have been more than 50,000 or 60,000 strong, allowing for his Gaulish reinforcements, and his losses since he left the Alps. No two historians agree as to the numbers of the consular armies. Polybius gives no figures, but states that Rome made great efforts, and great demands on her allies. I should infer from Livy's narrative that the legions of the Trebia were reinforced, and that four new double legions, four Roman, four allied, were raised. This is apparently the view of Arnold, and it seems to me correct, I cannot agree with Mommsen, whose estimate is plainly too low. On the whole, if we take the recruited legions of the Trebia at 25,000 or 20,000 men, and the four new Roman and four new allied legions at from 40,000 to 45,000 men all told, this will give the estimate I have made from 60,000 to 70,000.

****

The appointment, however, of the two consuls was not fortunate from various causes. The reverses of the last year had, in some measure, shattered the confidence of the citizens in the senate; though nothing that could be called a rupture took place, there was some murmuring, even dissension. The senate practically made Servilius consul; he was a good officer of the aristocratic party; but the people insisted on choosing Flaminius themselves; and Flaminius was a kind of popular leader, and had made himself especially obnoxious to the *noblesse*. He was besides, a reckless, arrogant, and incapable man; he was the general who had been caught on the Oglio by the Insubres, two or three years previously; he was completely unfit for a difficult command. (Attempts have been made to vindicate Flaminius, and to represent him as an able soldier. His subsequent conduct, from every point of view, is a sufficient confutation.) The chiefs, therefore, who were to oppose Hannibal, were political foes of different natures; one at least was without military skill or judgment.

Flaminius hastened from Rome to assume his command; he was afraid that the senate, through its influence over the augurs and priests, very powerful bodies, might annul his appointment, and cross his purpose. He rallied the troops in the hands of Sempronius; and, combining them with his own forces, took a position at Arretium, (now Arezzo), in the Etrurian plains, at the head of the fertile vale of the Clanis (now the Chiana.) He had perhaps 35,000 or 40,000 men; his colleague, who left the capital later, advanced to Ariminum, on the northern verge of Umbria, probably from 25,000 to 30,000 strong. The consuls thus occupied the Apennine passes from the north, against any invader in front; they could communicate with each other by good roads; they doubtless thought themselves perfectly secure.

But their adversary was a great captain, justly called the father of scientific strategy, Hannibal set off from the plains of the Ligures, in all probability in the later days of March, in order to invade central Italy; he had ascertained the positions of the Roman Armies; his purpose was to turn the line of the consul's defences, by a bold and unexpected movement on their extreme left flank.

★★★★★★★★★★

Following Livy and the great majority of writers, I have made Hannibal start from the territory of the Ligures, and march along the coast. I cannot agree with the commentators who make him cross the Apennines advancing from between Parma and Piacenza. The march was clearly a great flanking manoeuvre.

★★★★★★★★★★

Before beginning his march, he gave signal proof of his policy in the intended invasion. He kept his Roman prisoners loaded with chains (Livy repeatedly asserts that Hannibal slew his Roman captives; but Livy is a libeller, I have followed Polybius); but set the prisoners made from the allies free (in the same way Napoleon liberated the Saxons after Jena); he had come as a liberator, he announced, for Italy. His army moved along the line of the coast, by what was to be the Via Aurelia, until it had drawn near Spezia; the Spaniards and Africans were in front; the cavalry closed the rear of the columns; the Gauls were purposely placed in the centre, a sign perhaps, that they were not quite trustworthy.

The march was not difficult in its first stages; but the winter and spring had been severe and wet; and when Hannibal reached the Auser, (now the Serchio), and the lowlands of the Arnus, (now the Arno), he was suddenly assailed by an unforeseen obstacle. The country around was a waste of flood; the roads were inundated and effaced by the waters; the army was brought for a short time to a stand. Its great chief, however, would not brook delay; the Spaniards and Africans toiled through the swamps and morasses; but the Gauls suffered greatly, and, in part, disbanded; and Hannibal was deprived of his last remaining elephant. Ophthalmia, too, appeared among the troops; their leader had one of his eyes blinded; he had to be carried for several days in a litter.

After an arduous struggle, the invading army emerged at last from the flooded plains, and reached the fair and pleasant highland of Fae-

HANNIBAL, AFTER A MARBLE BUST DISCOVERED AT CAPUA.

sulae, (now Fiesole.) Hannibal was already threatening his enemy's flank; but the Roman commander made no sign; Hannibal marched rapidly along the left of Flaminius, most probably by Saena, (now Siena), at some distance, and was soon in the valley of the Clanis, not far from Clusium, (now Chiusi.) The flank of the Roman Armies was thus completely turned, (this march of Hannibal may be compared to that by which Napoleon, in 1796, turned Beaulieu at Valenza, by moving on Piacenza), Hannibal stood directly in the rear of Flaminius, interposing between Arretium and Rome; a masterly manoeuvre had utterly foiled the plan of operations made by the senate, and had even brought the invader not far from the capital.

Hannibal now formed one of the most extraordinary designs that have ever been made by a great commander. He had just heard that Flaminius was moving against him; with the intuition, which was one of his choicest gifts, he had divined what manner of man his adversary was, (Polybius dwells with just admiration on this faculty of Hannibal, and makes judicious remarks on the subject); he had learned from chiefs of the Gauls in his camp, how the consul had been in straits on the Oglio, and had narrowly escaped defeat at the hands of the Insubres. He resolved to lure the Roman Army into a deadly ambush, and to annihilate it where resistance would be vain; an opportunity was presented in ground hard by.

The lake of Trasimenus, (now Trasimeno), nestling under the Gualandra hills, was at a distance of a few miles only; it was on the line of a march from Arretium; and the lake, and the lowlands at its base, which spread out into two distinct recesses, divided by cliffs jutting out from the range, combine to form a lair, so to speak, in which even a large army could be concealed, and made ready to fall in force on an unsuspecting enemy.

Hannibal placed his troops in the recess to the south, between where the small towns of Torre and Passignano stand,(I agree with Colonel Dodge, *Hannibal*, in his description of the locality chosen by Hannibal for the ambush, this, too, is the spot chosen by most writers); his heavy cavalry and infantry closed the extreme exit; along the slopes of the plain which runs down to the lake, and the uplands which meet the range above, his light infantry were hidden in folds of the ground, and in thickets and brushwood at hand; the Numidian cavalry, also well screened, were so arrayed as to be able to seize and hold the entrance. The camp of Hannibal could be descried at the exit of the recess; but the whole of the army was kept out of sight, especially at the entrance of the deeply-laid ambush.

★★★★★★★★★★

It has been thought extraordinary that an army could be completely concealed in this manner. But the country around was probably a solitude; there was no one to give information; nor can we forget how the Germans in 1870 repeatedly emerged from woods and took the French by surprise.

★★★★★★★★★★

While Hannibal had been making his way to the Arnus, Flaminius had kept in his camp at Arretium, surrounded by flatterers, looking out for a victory. The impetuous and reckless nature of the man broke out when he heard that his skilful foe had outmanoeuvred him, and stood in the way to Rome; his overmastering thought was fighting and vengeance. It was in vain that experienced soldiers pointed out that he ought to summon his colleague to his aid, and fall on Hannibal with their united armies, (well indicated by Macdougall, *Campaigns of Hannibal*); he threw counsels of prudence to the winds; possibly, too, Servilius did not wish to join him, divided as the men were, in mind and sympathy. Flaminius broke up from his camp and advanced by forced marches to the entrance of the fatal lake from the north; night had fallen; he would fight on the morrow; apparently, he threw out no advanced guard.

The following day was another of the great disasters which befell Rome in her strife with Hannibal. In the first hours of an April morning, the doomed army moved by the edge of the lake and passed safely through the first recess in the hills; a dense fog hung over water and land; not a sign appeared of an enemy near. At last, as the second recess was attained, Hannibal's camp was seen at no great distance; the consul eagerly pressed on his men; they were soon engaged with the foot and horsemen, who threw them back as they endeavoured to advance. The battle had thus began, when the agile Numidians closed on the enemy's rear, and cut off his retreat, and thousands of Africans, Spaniards, and Gauls, suddenly issuing, as it were, out of the ground, burst in irresistible force on the hostile army's flank. The Romans were hopelessly caught in a trap; escape and relief were not to be looked for; but they fought with a desperation worthy of their name; for three long hours they endeavoured to repel the furious assaults made on every side upon them.

At last, their efforts began to slacken; Flaminius fell at the head of his men, slain by a chief of the Insubrian Gauls; and as the dissolving

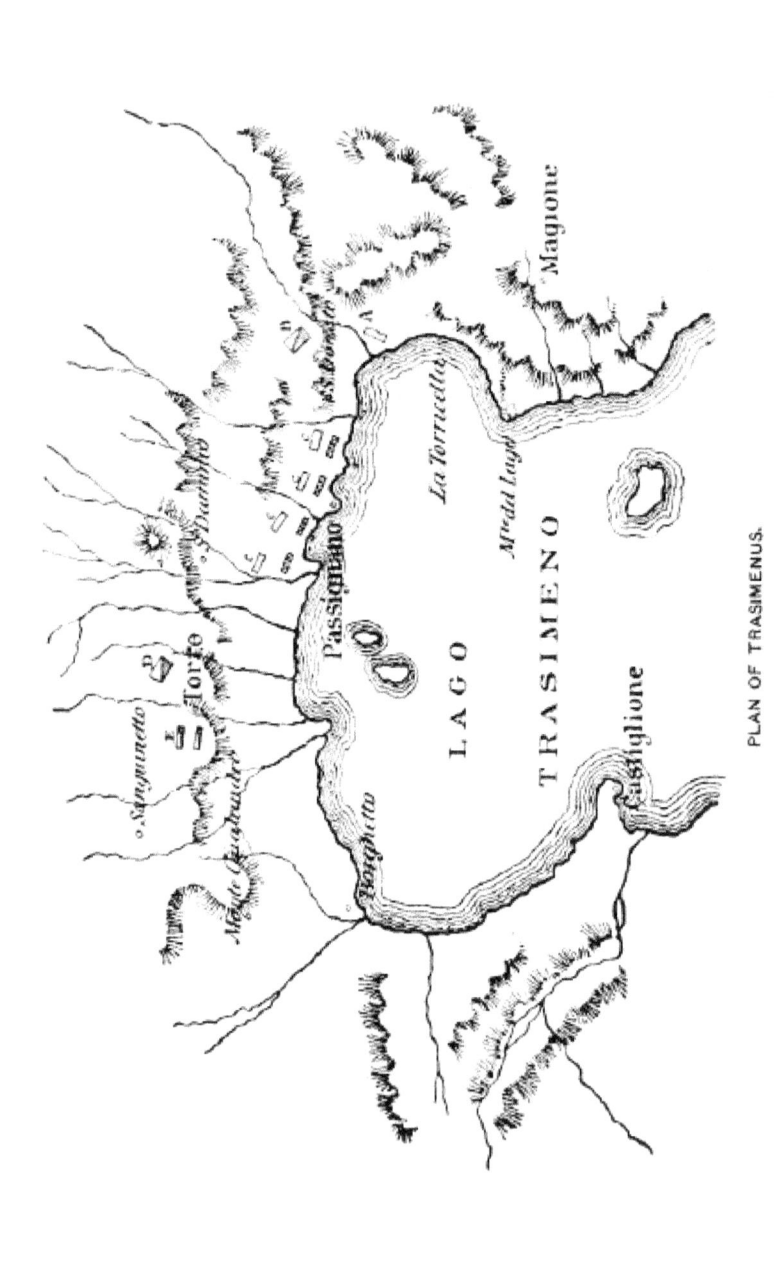

PLAN OF TRASIMENUS.

lines of the legions broke up, thousands of Romans were driven into the devouring lake; thousands were scattered in flight among the hills; thousands perished sternly fighting to the last. It was a horrible scene of pitiless massacre, and the passions of the combatants were, it is said, so intense, that they took no notice of an earthquake that shook the neighbourhood. (Byron notices this strange incident in *Childe Harold*.) Fifteen thousand of the Romans were slain or wounded; 10,000 fled through the Etrurian plains; the victors lost only 1,500 men. Yet Roman steadfastness, as at the Trebia, was again made manifest, 6,000 cut their way through, and moved off in good order.

After this great and decisive victory, Hannibal apparently made a short halt; he tried to find out the dead body of the fallen consul, in order to give it funeral honours. His career proves that he respected the courtesies of war; this, and other examples refute the calumnies heaped upon his memory by Roman libellers. He was not the man, however, to throw away success; he despatched Maharbal, one of his best lieutenants, to pursue the 6,000 men of the enemy who had escaped; these were caught, surrounded, and forced to surrender. (Livy declares that a promise was made by Maharbal that the 6,000 men should be allowed to go home and inveighs against what he calls Hannibal's "Punic Religion," Polybius simply says that their lives would be spared, and that was done.)

He had now about 15,000 prisoners he carried out the policy he had adopted before; he kept the Romans in durance, and set the allies free. (If 15,000 men of the Army of Flaminius were killed and wounded at Trasimenus, 10,000 scattered, and 15,000 made prisoners the consul had evidently fully 40,000 troops. These figures, however, may be exaggerated. Polybius.)

Another disaster ere long overtook the arms of Rome, fated, as it were, to defeat. Servilius had evidently not communicated with his brother consul, though excellent roads lay between their camps; but in time he heard of Trasimenus and its results, he detached a body of some 4,000 horsemen, to reconnoitre, perhaps to assist his colleague. This weak half-measure inevitably failed; Maharbal cut the detachment to pieces, or made it prisoner; the consul was deprived of nearly all his cavalry. Hannibal now marched by Perugia upon Spoletum, (now Spoleto), holding the main road from Ariminum to Rome, the Via Flaminia already made; this was the line of the retreat of Servilius; and it seems not improbable that Hannibal's purpose was to intercept the consul, whose whole army must have been very inferior in

HEAD OF MARCELLUS. STRUCK B. C. 42.
FROM THE BRITISH MUSEUM.

NEGRO HEAD AND ELEPHANT. STRUCK AFTER THE BATTLE OF TRASIMENUS.
FROM THE BRITISH MUSEUM.

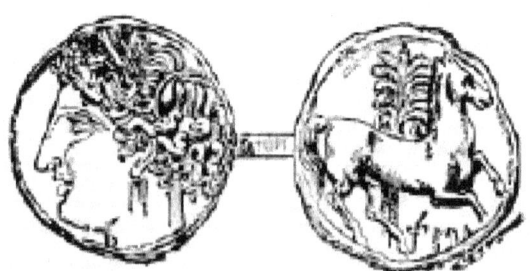

CARTHAGINIAN COIN (ELECTRUM).

strength to his own, to bring him to bay, and to compel him to lay down his arms. (This subject is discussed with much ability, by Hénnébert. The ingenious commentator may be too much under the influence of the Napoleonic strategy; and may without sufficient reason attribute to Hannibal a project which Napoleon certainly would have formed. Still, I agree with him in the main.)

But he was beaten off in an attack on Spoletum; and he abandoned his design if he ever formed it, though, it will be observed, his opportunity seems to have been favourable in the extreme. We can only conjecture, why, as in the case of Scipio before, he did not proceed to strike down his enemy. It is certain that he suffered much loss at Spoletum; his army had been greatly weakened by disease, especially by an epidemic among the horses, (Polybius and Livy); and perhaps Hannibal feared that he might be assailed by a double attack directed from Rome, now at the distance of a few marches only, and by Servilius with the whole of his forces. Still Hannibal stood between divided enemies; the army of Servilius was now perhaps not 20,000 strong; he may possibly, in this instance, have missed a great opportunity.

It is more easy to refute the criticisms, made at this, and another great conjuncture, that Hannibal, after Trasimenus, ought to have marched on Rome. (Hénnébert makes out that Hannibal marched on Narni, and that a council of war was held whether he should march on Rome. But he gives no real authority. Polybius emphatically asserts that Hannibal had no notion of making such an attempt.)

It is certain that he had no siege equipage; the military strength of the republic had not been broken, grave as had been the disasters of the last six months; the city was fortified and extremely strong; not an allied state of Rome had thrown off its allegiance. Hannibal would assuredly have met a terrible reverse had he attempted to attack Rome under conditions like these; his conduct in this point, in fact, was evidently wise. His projects for the war were far-seeing and profound, and offered him the only solid hope of success he could have. He knew that Carthage was much inferior to Rome in military force; nay, any army he could bring into the field, must ultimately be weaker than the Roman Armies.

His purpose, therefore, was not to strike directly at Rome, and to hazard the issue of the contest in a decisive effort against the great city, in which he felt that nearly all the chances would be distinctly adverse. But he had calculated from the first that Macedon and Hellas might come to his aid, and that the communities of Italy might rise

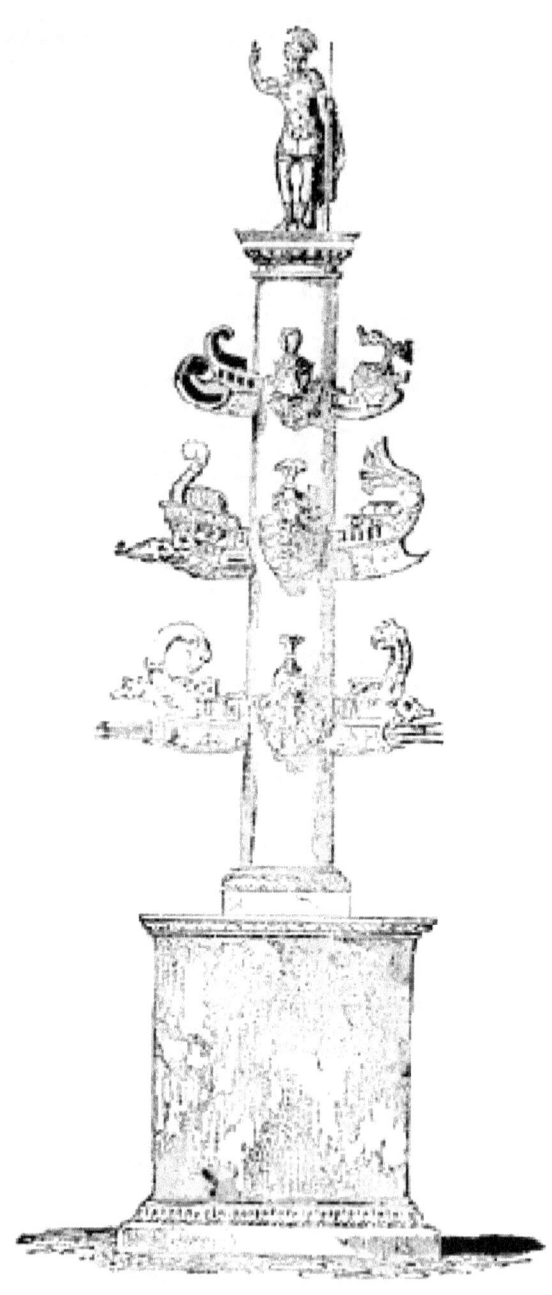

COLUMN OF DUILIUS.

against the dominant power; here were his real prospects of success; he prudently resolved not to advance on Rome, until he had combined a mighty league against her. (The reasons that determined the course of Hannibal are very clearly set forth by Mommsen.) Hannibal marched accordingly across the Apennines; moved probably along their eastern spurs; and descended to the fertile plains of Apulia; his object being, we are told, to obtain news from Carthage, perhaps to stretch a hand towards his expected Greek allies, and, almost certainly, to draw near the Samnites, of all the Italians, the most likely to throw off the yoke of Rome.

He devastated the country through which he passed, in part in order to procure supplies, in part to impress the minds of men with a sense of his power; but we may reject the malicious legend that he put to the sword the Roman and Latin youth of an age to bear arms. (This story is, no doubt, told by Polybius, but it is hardly credible, and Livy does not allude to it.)

He established his headquarters at Luceria, (now Lacera), and gave his sickly and war-worn army a few weeks of repose, which gradually restored it to health and strength. It deserves notice that he armed his African troops with weapons taken from Roman soldiers, (Polybius), clear evidence of their superior excellence; and there is reason to believe that, to some extent at least, he adopted the formations of the Roman legion.

While Hannibal was thus renewing his strength, and maturing his designs against his life-long foe, Rome was again presenting the noble spectacle of a great nation superior to adverse fortune. When the intelligence of Trasimenus arrived, when knots of fugitives announced that all was lost, and that a host of barbarians was even now at hand, advancing by the track of Gallic invasion, terror fell, for a brief space, on the minds of men; the proud city bowed her head in mourning; affrighted crowd, thronged the gates to learn the tale of disaster. But the hours of grief and panic quickly passed away; the senate, with admirable tact, told the whole truth, and bade the citizens to be of good heart; Roman constancy was soon as steadfast as ever.

The walls and ramparts were manned and put in a state of defence, for an immediate attack was expected by all; the bridges on the Tiber were broken down, to retard the approach of the victorious enemy; the country around was wasted for miles, in order to prevent his obtaining supplies. Military preparations were at the same time made, which proved that Rome had no thought of parley or yielding. The

GATE OF SPOLETO.

consul Servilius had slipped past Hannibal, and had arrived with the greatest part of his army intact; two fresh double legions were quickly mustered; and though these were largely composed of recruits, they formed, in numbers at least, a respectable force. (Polybius says four legions. Livy says two. No doubt two double legions, about 20,000 strong, were raised.)

Meanwhile recourse was had to the time-honoured expedient adopted by Rome in grave crises Quintus Fabius Maximus, a scion of the most ancient *noblesse*, and of a house illustrious even in the days of the monarchy, was made dictator, and placed at the head of affairs; his election was characteristic of Roman patriotism and sound sense. The appointment should have been made by the two consuls, but Flaminius was gone, one only survived; the senate referred the selection to the mass of the citizens, and thus probably secured the choice of its own candidate.

It is significant, too, of the Roman nature, that after making provision for the needs of war, the new dictator appealed to religion in this hour of disaster, for religion he knew was a mighty force with his countrymen. The *Sibylline Books*, the oracles of Rome, were solemnly consulted, and made to reveal their mysteries; public prayers were offered up and holy rites performed; magnificent feasts were set forth to appease the gods of Rome. But there were no cowardly sacrifices of human victims; the religion of Rome was not superstitious cruelty.

Fabius was at the head of 40,000 or 50,000 men, a few weeks after the late disaster. He was an aged man, hardly a man of genius, though he had honourably held important commands; but he was gifted with strong common-sense and sagacity, a quality of the Roman patrician. He had perceived the true methods by which Hannibal was to be opposed; he had gauged the dangers which surrounded his enemy, and the weakness of the great Carthaginian, despite his triumphs; and he had thought out a plan of operations which, he felt assured, would in the long run lead to the invaders' defeat, and secure success for the essentially superior power of Rome.

Hannibal was infinitely greater than any Roman general; he owed his wonderful victories to this single cause; but his army was small, chiefly composed of Gauls, left in Italy, without support from home; and the strength of Rome in war had an immense preponderance, especially if the allies remained faithful to her. Hannibal, therefore, was not to be encountered in great pitched battles, in which his skill would almost certainly decide the result, especially as the Roman

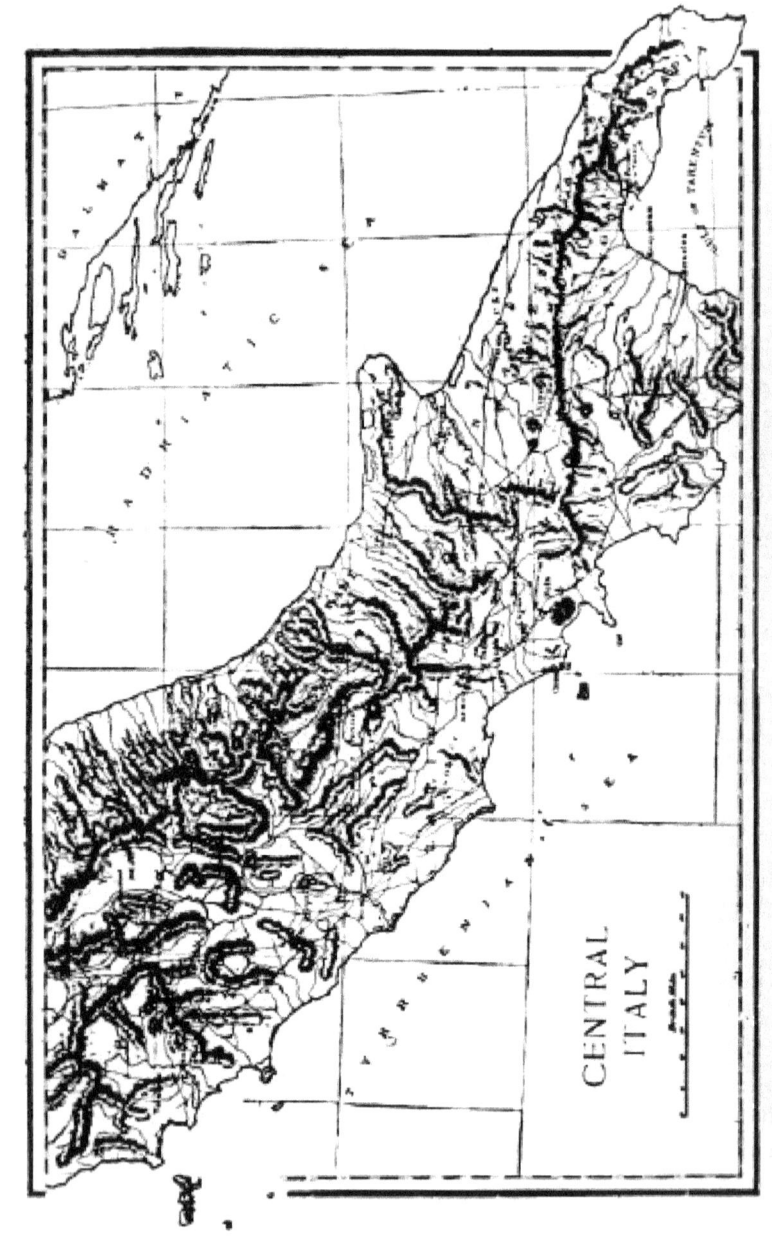

Army was raw and young; but he was to be followed, harassed, struck at in detail, kept, so to speak, in a state of perpetual trouble, and then, when his resources were being lessened and cut off, he was to be assailed when the force of Rome was fully developed, or before, should a good opportunity offer.

Above all, he was to be compelled to live on plunder and devastation; this would make the allies hostile to his cause, and keep them in their allegiance to Rome; he was not to be permitted to form magazines and depots; and this would divide, weaken, and impair his army. "Wear out the enemy by patience," was the whole plan of Fabius; and if we bear in mind that a daring offensive had always been the tradition of Rome in war, these wise and original counsels are almost marked by genius. The command of the dictator, indeed, did not last long, nor did he succeed in all his projects; but he was the first who checked the floodtide of Hannibal's success; and history has confirmed the high estimate his countrymen ultimately formed of his conduct. Rome, doubtless, did not owe her final triumph, in the tremendous contest of the Second Punic War, to the veteran *Cunctator*, or to any single man; this was the result of her invincible constancy, her determined efforts, her admirable government of her subject states, her wise administration of a United Italy. But Fabius was one of her great men; her poetry and her annals have done justice to his name.

Fabius, bent on carrying out his sagacious project, set forth from Rome to cope with his great antagonist. He took a position at Æcae not far from Luceria, and found the hostile army spread over Apulia, as far as Arpi, (probably the modern Foggia), and the surrounding country. The dictator, though carefully husbanding his men, successfully engaged in petty skirmishes, cut off detachments and foraging parties, and gradually contracted the area in which the Carthaginian Army could obtain resources. Hannibal employed in vain insults, stratagems, and wiles, to induce the Roman general to risk a battle; the cautious veteran clung to the spurs of the Apennines, turned his fortified camps to the best advantage, and was not to be drawn into a fatal snare; his adversary, in short, was unable to bring him to bay.

The Carthaginian chief was thus kept exposed for weeks, to a wearying, and even a destructive warfare; and his enemy's army was being largely reinforced, and was provided with an ample store of supplies, (Polybius dwells on this), while his own army was being slowly weakened, and even reduced to straits to exist, for whole districts of Apulia had been eaten up. Hannibal decided on transferring the war to another theatre; a variety of reasons determined his purpose. Rome held the Adriatic and the Ionian seas; he had not received a message from Carthage; he had had no communication from Macedon and the Greeks; the Apulians had shewn no sign of rising; his military situation was even now difficult.

But Samnium lay just across the Apennines; beyond were the fertile plains of Campania, and Capua, a great city unfriendly to Rome, in which he had partisans, who had given him fair words; was it not probable that here he would find allies, in any case he would be more near Carthage? And even if hopes such as these were frustrated, he would pitilessly waste this magnificent region; would not this force his halting enemy to fight, or at least prove to the Italians that Rome had no power to defend them, and make them, in self-protection, turn to his cause? (Polybius emphatically notices this).

Hannibal eluded Fabius, and made his way past him, by means at which we can only guess, (Colonel Dodge, *Hannibal*); and, marching along the great roads to Rome, he moved by Beneventum, the chief town of Samnium, seized Telesia, once an important fortress, and then descended by Allifae, through the Apennine defiles, into the rich Campanian and Falernian land, the garden of Italy, and perhaps of Europe.

The purpose of Hannibal was now effectually carried out; the beautiful tract abounding in corn and wine, rich with olives and flowers, and thriving farms, was turned into a harried and plundered desert. Towns and villages were ruthlessly given to the flames; Numidians and Gauls swept in the harvests; and made booty of the wealth of industrious ages. Hannibal, knowing what the Libyan *fellahs* were, and how oppression would enforce their submission, perhaps thought that the Italians would bow to his will, and at his bidding would abandon Rome, in order to escape such treatment as this; but he made a mistake; Fabius knew them better. The Samnites and Campanians indeed had no affection for Rome, but they had no sympathy with Phoenician invaders carrying devastation and terror in their train; they kept aloof from the belligerents in the field; they did not send a recruit to the Carthaginian Army.

Beneventum had actually shut the gates on Hannibal; his intrigues in Capua had no result; it had become evident that, as yet at least, the subjects of Rome would not rise against her. In truth the wise system of Roman government had weakened the local sentiments of the Italian provinces; Rome now gained the reward due to prudence and justice, (Polybius); in any case, the least well-affected Italians were not ready to welcome their armed deliverers. Meanwhile Hannibal had found himself placed in a military situation of grave peril. Fabius had followed him cautiously in his advance; the dictator, now at the head of a much more numerous army, had first taken care to cover the approaches to Rome; his subsequent operations, very ably conducted, even now promised decisive success.

Hannibal in Campania was enclosed within a broad plain, bounded on the south by the Vulturnus, a wide and deep river, of which Roman garrisons held the fortified passages, on the north by the main avenues to Rome completely barred by the Roman Armies, and on the west by the Mediterranean waters; the "only line of retreat was to the east, on Allifae, by the Apennine pass through which he had entered. Fabius placed his army on the flank of this line, taking care to hold a position of great strength, in which he could not be safely attacked; and he sent forward a body of picked troops to occupy the defile that led to Allifae. Hope beat high in the old general's heart; the defeat of Trasimenus would be avenged; the conqueror would be involved in a similar fate.

Hannibal extricated himself from a very difficult strait with characteristic adroitness and resource. The danger of the situation was that he would be held in check by the Roman detachment stationed in the pass, and that Fabius would then descend, in force, on his flank and rear; this was increased by the circumstance that he was carrying with him a large store of supplies, the spoils of Campania, required for his troops in the coming winter. He endeavoured once more to affront his enemy, who, however, quietly waited in his camp, "hushed in grim repose," and expecting his prey; what force could not achieve was now to be eked out by stratagem. He moved his army on to the lowlands that met the defile; gave orders that his men should hold themselves ready; and took care they should be well fed and rested. (Over and over again we may observe how Hannibal attended to the wants of his men. This, no doubt, was one of the causes of his extraordinary power over them.)

As evening was approaching, he directed Hasdrubal, a most admirable officer we shall soon hear of again, to collect some thousand of the beeves gathered within his camp, and to drive them to the heights on either side of the pass; they were to be accompanied by a body of light troops, whose work had been well explained to them. When the night was advanced, faggots, which had been tied to the horns of the animals, were set on fire; the hillsides seemed to burst out in flame; shouts, wild noises, and a great sound of trampling were heard; it might easily be conceived that this was the movement of the Carthaginian Army in retreat. The Roman detachment was completely deceived; it abandoned the defile in the full belief that Hannibal was moving along the heights; it soon found itself engaged with the hostile infantry in a horrible scene of shifting glare and confusion, making the darkness hideous, and more terrible; and it came to a halt panic-stricken, and awaiting the morrow. (A very similar stratagem was successfully employed by the rebel Irish Army in 1798. It had more than one able leader.)

Meanwhile the whole Carthaginian Army passed rapidly through the now open pass; Fabius put off an attempt to pursue until morning, ignorant probably how matters exactly stood, fearing, doubtless, the craft of his dreaded foe; his hope of a Roman triumph vanished; a great opportunity had been lost, through excess of caution. Hannibal effected his escape with his whole force intact, nay, even with his enormous spoil, he was actually able to disengage his light troops on the hills, and defeated their enemies with great slaughter. In a day or two he was safe at Allifae, and was marching through the Apennines into Apulia again, having baffled and discomfited his aged opponent. (Polybius's account of this admirable *ruse de guerre,* is much the best. Colonel Dodge, *Hannibal,* has also explained it very clearly. Livy, as always, is picturesque but not precise.)

We cannot feel surprise that this signal failure turned opinion in Rome against the veteran chief, who had been invested with the supreme command. The waiting game of Fabius had from the outset been condemned as the feebleness of grey hairs by a large part of his officers; the leader of the malcontents was Minucius Rufus, the dictator's principal lieutenant, or Master of the Horse; the sentiment had pervaded the ranks of the army. It was said:

"What had been gained, but dishonour and shame, unworthy of Rome, by these timid delays; Campania had been ravaged under a dotard's eyes; the Allies had been cruelly wronged; and the army had been just made a laughing stock, entirely through the pusillanimity of its head."

Fabius was denounced as "Hannibal's lackey," and was even charged with treasonable designs against the republic, for Hannibal, with characteristic craft, had taken care not to waste lands which belonged to his adversary in Campania, no doubt in order to throw suspicion on the one Roman general whose judicious counsels and wise conduct he had reason to fear. For though Fabius had not done great things, and had been even foiled by a master of war, he had arrested the march of Hannibal's success—no Trebia or Trasimenus could be laid to his door; he had compelled his antagonist to shift his ground and retreat; had considerably weakened the strength of his army; above all, had indicated the means by which Rome could develop her power by degrees, and might ultimately cripple and wear out her enemy.

Nevertheless, after the late reverse, public feeling in Rome ran against Fabius, as public feeling in England ran against Wellington, after Talavera, and before Torres Vedras; and a marked slight was offered to the old commander. During a brief absence of the dictator from Rome, Minucius had gained insignificant success in skirmishes with the Carthaginian Army—he had followed it as Hannibal had fallen back—and he was appointed by a popular vote a colleague of Fabius, with equal powers, a course without precedent in Roman annals.

The old dictator was ere long to be justified, and his jealous lieutenant to be put to shame. Hannibal had encamped his army, by this time at Geronium, (probably the modern Campobasso near the Tiferno), in the north of Apulia, near the Tifernus; it was here he had suffered the late slight defeats; he had satisfied himself that Minucius was an adversary of the Sempronius and Flaminius type. Fabius, having left Rome, had rejoined his new colleague, too loyal and patriotic to resent an affront; Minucius asked him to follow the consular usage, and to divide the command on alternate days; but fortunately for the army the veteran soldier refused.

Meanwhile Hannibal, with his peculiar skill in divining the character of the enemy in his front, and informed besides, by spies and deserters, had perfectly ascertained the changed state of affairs; he felt, the Roman historian tells us, "a twofold joy," he could make sure of destroying Minucius; the Roman Army "had lost half its strength," since Fabius was not its supreme head, (Livy.) With his perhaps unparalleled power of stratagem, he laid a snare for his rash antagonist; he occupied a hill before the Roman camp, with a small force that seemed to invite attack; but he concealed a body of infantry and Numidians in folds of the ground, with orders to fall on when the right moment had come.

Minucius rushed into the well-laid trap; he tried to sweep away the enemy from the hill; and when he was deeply engaged in the fight, he was assailed on all sides by the troops hidden in the ambush, and was completely defeated with heavy loss. His legions, in fact, would have been routed, had not Fabius come to his aid, requiting ill-will by faithful support, very unlike generals whom history could name. This magnanimity met a fitting response; Minucius gave up his command to Fabius; such was the love of country, and the sense of duty in Rome.

The authority of the dictator soon came to an end; his command devolved for a few months on Servilius, still the consul of the year, and on Atilius Regulus, who had replaced Flaminius. These officers adhered to the Fabian tactics, and reduced the army of Hannibal, still around Geronium, to such distress from want of supplies, that he seriously thought of retreating into northern Italy, (Livy.) The second year of the war, 217 B.C., had come to an end; we can easily see what its incidents really taught, even through the glare of astonishing military success.

Hannibal had been completely victorious in the field; he had utterly destroyed a Roman Army; he had marched, almost as he pleased, through Italy; he had given its fairest region to fire and sword. Yet his success had been checked, and not decisive; for a moment he had been placed in danger; he had not ventured to attack Rome, the mighty power of which he perfectly knew; his great plan of combining a formidable league against the nation he hated had as yet come to nothing. Not a single body of troops had arrived from Carthage; not a single ally of Rome had said God bless him, and sent a man to the Phoenician standards; Macedon and the Greek powers were still keeping back; the Gauls of northern Italy alone recruited his army, and who could rely on these brave, but untrustworthy Celts?

On the other hand, the army of Rome was still making progress in Spain; Publius Scipio had been despatched with a considerable force to conduct the war with his brother Cnaeus; Hasdrubal had been forced to stand on the defensive only; above all, no reinforcements had come to Hannibal along the immense distance from the Ebro to the Po. Rome, too, maintained her absolute dominion of the sea; the consul Servilius, at the head of a fleet, had made a descent on the African coast in the summer; the Mediterranean was in the power of Rome from the shores of Spain to the shores of Dalmatia; and the weak and inactive Carthaginian government—at heart not well inclined to Hannibal—had made no efforts to redress the balance, and to fit out a powerful navy to send him aid, the first, and obvious condition of his ultimate success.

And if Rome had been defeated by a great captain, her resources for war were still enormous. She had already summoned eight double legions to the field, the numbers of the men in the ranks being largely increased, for the campaign of the coming year; she was about to oppose 90,000 men to Hannibal, who had not more than 50,000, three-fourths of them being, perhaps, Gauls; she had prepared an army to march into northern Italy, and to prevent the Gauls from assisting her terrible enemy. Her stern national spirit, too, was as bold as ever; she sent threats to the court of Macedon, and to the Illyrian tribes, warning them they had better remain quiescent; and with admirable wisdom she refused gifts of money offered by Hiero her vassal king in Sicily, and by several of the allied Italian states, accepting, however, their aid for the war. This magnanimous conduct was a striking contrast to the devastation pitilessly wrought by Hannibal, and must have deeply impressed the Mediterranean world.

Noble, however, as were the exertions of Rome, the supreme direction of her military power, for the impending contest, was again unfortunate. The citizens were suffering cruelly from the effects of the war; the agricultural population was thinned and half ruined; the territory of fine provinces had been wasted; some of the allies were uttering complaints, there was great and even natural discontent with the government. For the first time, for many years at least, the spirit of the demagogue and the mob orator had influence on a nation proud of its aristocratic leaders; it was noised abroad that the men in power were incapable; it was even absurdly said that this was the fault of the noblesse, nay, that it was treasonably in league with Hannibal.

The most prominent of these mischief makers was Terentius Varro, a man of the meanest degree, but tongue-valiant; he had certainly filled some civil offices; but he had pushed himself forward by popular arts; and the citizens elected him consul for the new year, in spite, it would appear, of the senate's efforts, and enabled him to preside at the elections of the second consul. Varro had little or no experience of military command; nature had made him a caricature of the brave soldiers who had already succumbed to the blows of Hannibal; he resembled, in fact, one of the noisy braggarts at the head of the French Armies in 1793, but soon replaced by very different men, whose idea of war was to scream at aristocrats, and to throw recklessly away the lives of their soldiers.

The other consul was Lucius Æmilius Paullus, a good soldier, but a very unpopular man, appointed probably through the influence of the noblesse, or perhaps on account of his success at Telamon, and sincerely hating Varro with all his heart. Once more, therefore, the chiefs who were to oppose Hannibal were of different parties, and different views; and while one, as a general, was simply worthless, the other was a mere officer of the ordinary Roman type, and without real capacity for war. (There is no reason to doubt the accuracy of Livy's estimate of Varro. I prefer Mommsen's judgment to Arnold's in this matter.)

It was probably early in May when the Roman Army marched from around the great city to contend with Hannibal. Apart from the discords, and the inferiority of its two chiefs, that army was a fine national force embodying the living strength of the Roman people. The noblesse indignant, perhaps, at the outcry against it, had sent the flower of its order into the field; the consuls of the past year held high command; there was a number of men of senatorial rank; the knights, leaders of the cavalry, made a gallant muster. As for the composition of the army, as usual it was weak in cavalry, not more it appears than 6,000 strong; the soldiers were for the most part young; they were not wholly free from the bad influence of spouters of sedition and class hatred.

But there was a large array of foreign slingers and archers to cope with the Baleares, and to help the *velites*; and the troops were, to a man, fired with patriotic ardour, burning to avenge their allies and their country. The army, too, was perfectly supplied, and moved without fatigue along the great Roman roads, finding all that it wanted provided for by the state or by the contributions of friendly provinces. It reached Apulia nearly 90,000 strong, and had soon spread around Hannibal's camp at Geronium where he had remained during the months of winter. (Including the forces, which had been left at Geronium through the winter to observe Hannibal.)

The Carthaginian Army was very different from the great host which it was ere long to encounter. It was not fully 50,000 men; the ranks of the Phoenician, the Spanish, and the African infantry must by this time have been much thinned; many of the Balearic slingers were gone; the important arm of the elephant was not forthcoming; the Gauls must have formed the mass of the footmen. The army, too, had suffered greatly from cold and privation; and sounds of discontent and ill-will were heard, especially among the mercenaries in the camp, not, however, large in number. But Hannibal had 10,000 excellent horsemen, very superior to the horsemen of his foes; he had lieutenants worthy of him and inured to war; his commanding influence still kept together the elements of which his army was composed; and it was an army flushed with success, and trained in two campaigns, without reckoning the veterans who had served in Spain. And at its head was a consummate warrior, a host in himself, who had never known defeat.

The divisions between the two consuls, and the different characters and sentiments of the men, were, as usual, quickly found out by Hannibal, (Livy); he was again "overjoyed," the Roman historian tells us, (Livy), great as was the superiority in numbers of the enemy in his front. A skirmish in which a Roman division gained partial success, not improbably one of Hannibal's feints, excited Varro's impatient and thoughtless mind; but Æmilius held the command on alternate days—the bad tradition of ages was still followed—and, as he was in command on this occasion, he prevented his colleague from making a general attack. Varro broke out in indignant language; Hannibal made an attempt to profit by the quarrels of his foes; once more he endeavoured to draw the Romans into a trap, which would have enabled him to fight on his own terms.

Varro instantly ordered a general pursuit; it deserves notice that the Roman soldiery, forgetting their discipline amidst the disputes of their chiefs, declared that they "would march against the enemy even without generals", (Livy); but fortunately, superstition held Varro back; the omens were adverse, and he gave ear, reluctantly, to his colleague's advice not to move. Hannibal, it would appear, in great want of supplies, now broke up from Geronium, eluded the consuls by a forced and admirably concealed march; and in a few days he had seized Cannae, a fortified town on the banks of the Aufidus, (now the Ofanto), where the Romans had collected large magazines from the fertile plains of the adjoining country.

★★★★★★★★★★

The operations of the Roman Armies in the weeks before Cannae are obscure. Some writers think that the consuls did not assume command at Geronium at all, and that a large army was at Geronium all the winter. I have followed Livy's narrative—also followed by Hénnébert.

★★★★★★★★★★

The consuls, irritated at being outmanoeuvred and foiled, followed their adversary beyond Canusium, another depot, to positions near Cannae; they had become more than ever at feud; they broke out into mutual reproaches before their officers, (Livy); they studiously kept their legions apart. The Roman Army was then placed in two camps, the larger one, on the southern bank of the Aufidus, the smaller one on the northern bank; this was in accordance with the commands of

Æmilius, who, a friend of Fabius, and true to his counsels, wished to prevent the Carthaginian Army from obtaining supplies, and scouring the country far and wide, and so to compel it to retreat without the risk of a great battle, in which its superior cavalry would have a distinct advantage.

This, however, was not the purpose of Varro, furious "at the pusillanimity and slackness", (Livy), of his companion in arms, and bent on seeking the first opportunity to fight; Hannibal, knowing or divining what was going on, prepared to provoke his reckless enemy to an immediate action. Exactly as had been the case at the Trebia, he sent a detachment of Numidians across the river; the Roman watering parties were scattered in flight, and the daring horsemen pushed forward to the lesser camp, bearding and insulting the enemies within. This was too much for Varro to endure; he would be in supreme command on the next day; against his colleague's emphatic protest, (Polybius comments sharply on the disputes between the consuls), he gave orders for a great general battle.

It was the early morning of a bright day in June, in the year 216 B.C., when the red ensign flying from Varro's tent announced that he was about to meet his mighty enemy. (The Battle of Cannae, by the Roman calendar was fought on the 2nd of August, 216 B.C. But the calendar was several weeks in advance of the true season.) The consul left a division of some 10,000 men in the large camp on the southern bank of the Aufidus, with directions to storm Hannibal's lines; he drew the troops out of the lesser camp; and he moved all the rest of his army across to the northern bank, a singularly false and injudicious step, for. the plains beyond were the very ground for cavalry, Hannibal's strongest and favourite arm.

Many hours must have passed before the legions had got over the river and been arrayed in their positions for the battle at hand; it was doubtless midday before they were ready. They formed a host fully 76,000 strong; young troops, but filled with passion and hope, more than sufficient to defeat the much weaker enemy, had they had chiefs fit to cope with a supreme genius in war. The disposition of the Roman Army was faulty, and revealed a singular ignorance of the military art. The usual order of battle was imprudently changed; the Roman legions were not drawn up in the centre, but placed next the river on the right wing; the allies were in position on the left, probably because this point was of less importance; this change must have caused distrust and confusion. But Varro's tactical arrangements were much

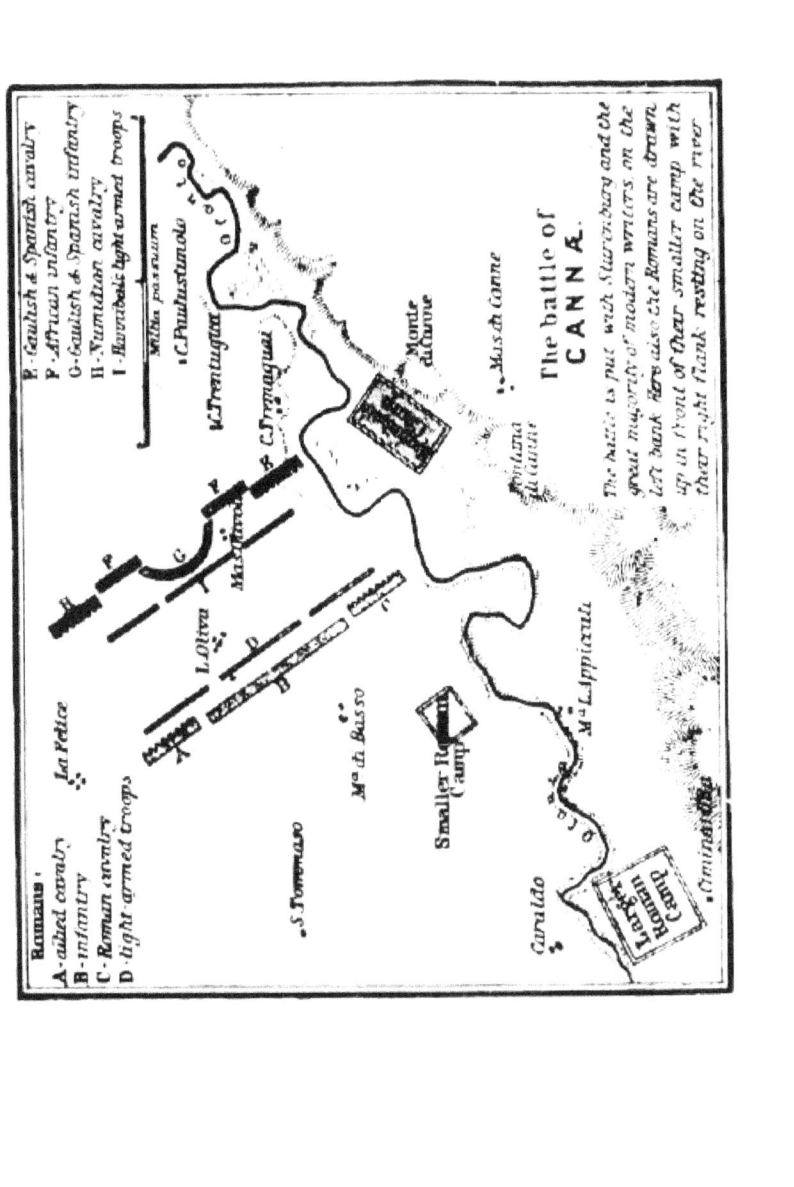

worse; they were such as would lead to disastrous results.

Hannibal had not a single elephant in the field; but the consul, whatever the reason, arrayed his lines as if this arm was to be encountered; the *maniples* of the three lines were made very deep; the gaps between them were almost closed, as on the calamitous day of Tunis; thus, his front presented a line of columns, dense, ill adapted for mutual support, an order, too, that could only hamper the men, and impair the force of their favourite and well-known mode of attack. Still the army offered a noble spectacle; the summer sun lit up the forest of plumes, and threw its brilliant rays on the glittering armour and weapons that marked the front of the Roman battle for miles; the *pilum* and the *gladius* were in nervous hands; the light infantry, backed by their foreign auxiliaries, were in high heart, and eager for the fray. The consul Æmilius was in command on the right, his colleague directed the left wing; the centre was under Servilius the late consul. The Roman cavalry, as usual, weak, stood close to the river on the extreme right; the more numerous allied horse were on the extreme left.

We can picture to ourselves the fierce delight of Hannibal, as he marked his adversary seeking a field, on which he might hope for a decisive victory. He left a small detachment to guard his camp; waited until the Roman Army was crossing the Aufidus; and marched with his own army across in turn, to the northern bank, where he found himself in a plain and open country, a position of the greatest advantage for his powerful cavalry. His whole force was not more than 46,000 strong, certainly 30,000 less than that of the enemy; but he had his 10,000 horsemen in hand; these were to strike the stroke that he hoped would make sure of the issue.

He placed the mass of his heavy cavalry, Spaniards and Gauls, on his left, near the river, confronting the weak Roman squadrons on Varro's right, this was the vulnerable point in the enemy's line; it was here that victory was to be won. He drew up the Numidians upon his right, in the face of the horsemen of the allies; they were to hold their adversaries in check until the proper moment had arrived; they were to wait until their comrades on their left had made the result of the battle well-nigh certain. His Spanish and Gaulish infantry held his centre, arranged in a formation that would now be faulty, but that with the arms of that age would be very strong; they were drawn up on a convex front, very deep, and resembling a half-circular *phalanx*, in order to stem the shock of the legion. But on either flank of this projecting mass, Hannibal had arrayed his best African footmen, armed with Roman weapons, and in long thin lines; his orders were that they were to close on the Romans, from either side, when they were fully engaged with the dense mass before them.

The great warrior and his brother Mago, commanded the centre, probably the weakest spot; Hasdrubal, thoroughly informed of what his work was to be, was at the head of the strong cavalry to the left, an officer of the name of Hanno directed the Numidian horsemen. The appearance of the Carthaginian Army was very different from that of the splendid legions, all of one form and quality. The Spaniards in their white and blue uniform wore the look of fine and disciplined troops; the swarthy Africans were very good soldiers. But the Gauls, formidable warriors as they were, were half-naked and ill-armed barbarians; the army, in short, was a motley assemblage of many races. But it was a trained army in the hands of a great chief; it was animated with the conviction that, under Hannibal, success was certain.

The sun shone with equal light on the hostile armies, (Polybius, this statement is important as regards the site of the battle); but a south-east wind blew in the Romans' faces (Livy, this is also important for the same reason); it raised clouds of dust that proved very annoying. The battle, fought probably in the early afternoon, began with the usual combat between the light troops; the *velites* behaved extremely well; the Balearic slingers were doubtless few; neither side could claim a real advantage. This, however, was but the first scene of the fight; Hasdrubal swept down on the Roman horse in his front; the two bodies of cavalry met in a desperate conflict.

The fury of the combatants was so intense, that some Spaniards and Gauls flung themselves from their horses, and engaged in a savage struggle on foot; but the Roman troopers dismounted in hundreds, by the express order of the consul Æmilius. "I would like to have them prisoners," Hannibal exclaimed. After a brief encounter the Romans were driven from the field, and cut down in their headlong flight; but Hasdrubal in a short time recalled his squadrons—he was evidently an admirable cavalry chief—he crossed the whole field and fell on the allied horsemen, engaged for some time with the Numidians, in an uncertain conflict. The double attack was almost at once decisive; Gauls, Spaniards, and Numidians carried all before them; the allies were routed and completely cut to pieces. The flanks of Varro were thus destroyed; but, meanwhile, in the centre, the course of the battle seemed for a considerable time of high promise for Rome.

The legions, hampered as they were in a new and bad formation, had broken in the convex front of the Gauls and the Spanish footmen; as usual, nothing could withstand that magnificent infantry; they pressed forward, with enthusiastic cheers, bearing Hannibal and his staff backward, the proud light of victory in their joyous faces. Like the great British column at Fontenoy, they made their way into the heart of the enemy's lines; but the wise precautions of Hannibal had now their effect, the Africans fell in force on the enemy's flanks; and assailed the Romans with their own deadly weapons. A murderous conflict followed, perhaps, of hours, men fell in hundreds on both sides; no quarter was given, no prisoners made; but the Roman soldiery, hard pressed as they were, held their ground manfully, with heroic courage, and over and over again threw their enemies back.

The terrible struggle was still at its height, when its issue was determined with appalling results. Hasdrubal, doubtless with the previous orders of his chief, turned away from the pursuit of the beaten allies; like Condé at Rocroy, he again moved with his excellent squadrons along the field; and he bore down with irresistible might on the rear of the legions, left without a body of horse to protect them. One consequence and only one was then possible; the Roman infantry, attacked on all sides, was gradually driven together into a huge weltering mass; the broken ranks of still fiercely fighting men were hemmed in like sheep for the slaughter; for miles along that plain of disaster, the lost battle became a hideous and general butchery, in which the Romans died hard, but perished in thousands, their foes gathering in on the ruined army like vultures on their prey. Of the Consular Armies of 76,000 men, from 40,000 to 70,000 are said to have perished; the loss of Hannibal was only 6,000.

★★★★★★★★★★

> The enormous loss of the Roman Army, probably 50,000 or 60,000 men, is unparalleled in history. But the losses of the armies of the ancients, after a lost battle, were usually very great; no doubt because they fought hand to hand; and there were no firearms to produce their terrible moral effect. But the loss of a square, broken by cavalry, will give some idea of what their losses were. No two ancient writers agree as to the extent of the Roman losses. Polybius says 70,000, but this is an exaggeration. See Hénnébert.

★★★★★★★★★★

The destruction wrought among the Roman generals was also immense; the consul Æmilius, his predecessor Servilius, eighty highplaced soldiers of senatorial rank, and a whole crowd of superior officers left their bodies on the field. Varro escaped with a few hundred horsemen, not ashamed, it has been said, to survive; petty bands of fugitives found safety in Canusium, Venusia, and other Roman fortresses; but the Roman Army was as completely effaced, as if it had been swallowed up in a convulsion of nature. Nor was even this the last tale of disaster; the Roman detachment which had been moved against Hannibal's camp, was defeated and compelled to lay down its arms.

★★★★★★★★★★

With a large majority of the best commentators, I have represented the Battle of Cannae as having been fought on the northern or left bank of the Aufidus, the right of Varro, and the left of Hannibal having rested on the river, and the two armies having extended thence, for miles, into the plains beyond. This seems to me almost fully established: writers, who make the battle to have taken place on the southern or right bank, appear to involve themselves in inconsistencies, nay, impossibilities. I regret to differ on this point from Mr. Strachan Davidson, a great authority.

1. Cannae, in Hannibal's possession, was admittedly on the southern or right bank, Polybius and Livy agree in saying that Varro and Hannibal only crossed the river once; they did not hint that it was recrossed; and if so, the battle must have been fought on the northern or left bank.

2. Livy distinctly asserts that the Roman right was close along the Aufidus; if this is correct, and if the battle took place on the southern or right bank, the Romans, in order to occupy this position, must have marched round Hannibal's front, and fought with their backs to the sea, an idea hardly to be entertained. No doubt Varro was a very bad general; but we cannot suppose he did this; and besides, if the Roman Army fought in this position, the fugitives could not, as they did, have reached Venusia and Canusium; they would have been driven into the sea, or forced to surrender.

3. Hannibal had his choice how and where to give battle; he would not have fought on the southern or right bank, for the ground was not well suited for cavalry, his only reliance; but the northern or left bank was, and this suggests the true inference. I cannot, however, agree with Colonel Dodge, *Hannibal*, that, assuming the battle to have occurred on the northern or left bank the Romans fronted south, and the Carthaginians north; I think they fronted respectively east and west. No doubt Polybius and Livy say they did front south and north; but Polybius and Livy concur in asserting that they had an equal share of sunlight; and as, bearing in mind the time required to effect the passage of the Aufidus, and to place the two armies in line, the battle could hardly have begun before one or two p.m., this almost proves they fronted east and west.

Again, Livy says that the south-east wind blew in the Romans' faces; this certainly points to the same conclusion. The strongest argument, however, is that, on the hypothesis of Colonel Dodge, Hannibal must have given battle with a river close to his back; unquestionably generals of the first order, for example Turenne at Entzheim, have done this; but Hannibal, above everything required free space for his cavalry, and he could not have had this in the state of things put by Colonel Dodge. On the whole, I believe that the Romans fronted east and the Carthaginians west; and this bears out Livy's description that the Roman right and the Carthaginian left were upon the Aufidus. For a fuller analysis of the evidence as to the site of the Battle of Cannae, see another very learned note in Arnold's *Second Punic War*.

****

Another calamity soon befell Rome in this terrible crisis of adverse fortune. An army, we have seen, had been despatched into northern Italy to prevent the Gauls from sending aid to Hannibal; it was decoyed into an ambush and destroyed with its commander Postumius, one of the great nobles. For a moment the republic appeared prostrate; as has been eloquently said, "the statue of Victory in the capitol may well have trembled in every limb on the day of Cannae, and have drooped her wings as if for ever." (Arnold, *Second Punic War*.) In the exultation of a prodigious triumph, Maharbal, the boldest, perhaps, of his officers, entreated Hannibal to march straight upon Rome, and remonstrated with his chief, who quietly refused, saying that "Hannibal can gain, but cannot follow up, a victory." (Livy.)

The tradition of centuries has preserved the legend and charged Hannibal with too great caution, nay with remissness; but this judgment is a complete mistake; the military and political genius of Hannibal was conspicuously seen in his resolve not to assail Rome directly, even after Cannae. (Even Napoleon made this mistake, *Corr*. The emperor's remarks on Hannibal are always worth studying; but his knowledge of the subject was very imperfect. It is remarkable that Cicero, *De Orators*, said the truth.)

We have indicated the reasons of this decision before; they were still, at bottom, as strong as ever; Rome had, doubtless, suffered an appalling reverse; but she had still an ample fund of resources for war; and Hannibal not only had no siege-train to attack a fortress of the greatest strength, but his army was not 40,000 strong and composed in the main of very doubtful elements. A consummate statesman, as well as a soldier—a worthy heir of Hamilcar Barca—the great Carthaginian most wisely determined to bide his time and to see if, after his marvellous success, the league of nations and states, on which his hopes depended, would not ere long be formed against his defeated enemy.

This at present seemed in the highest degree probable; Carthage surely now would employ her vast resources, and put forth her strength to strike down Rome; Macedon, the Greeks, the Illyrians, would seize the occasion to assail the tyrant of the Adriatic sea; the Gauls of the north would send all their tribes to the war; the Italian communities would strike off a comparatively recent yoke, or would take part with a conqueror who need not spare them; Rome would be surrounded by a circle of irresistible foes, and, whatever her might and pride, would necessarily succumb. So, Hannibal reasoned, and not vainly; the chances after Cannae seemed all in his favour, should he persistently carry out his grand scheme of invasion.

And yet even this deep-thinking genius could not understand how pusillanimous and feeble was the government of his native country; how untrustworthy was the coalition on which he had staked his fortunes; above all, how indomitable was the energy of the heroic nation, which he had not even scotched, still less slain; and how well compacted and mighty that power was, "which could be only broken up, like Cyclopean walls, stone by stone." (Mommsen.)

The genius of Hannibal in war was, as always, manifest in the two campaigns of 217 and 216 B.C.. The march to the Arnus, and thence to the Clanis, by which he turned the whole line of the defence of Rome, was a military operation of the very first order; history can shew few marches equally brilliant and daring. Trasimenus was a wonderful example of power in stratagem; in this precious gift of a great captain, we may doubt if Hannibal has had a rival. He may have missed an opportunity in not destroying Servilius, when the consul was cut off from Rome; but there seem to have been reasons why he did not adopt this course; it is scarcely possible to pronounce a decided judgment. His admirable dexterity and craft are again seen in the means he employed to elude and baffle Fabius, and especially in the artful snares he repeatedly laid for the brave but fourth-rate soldiers as yet opposed to him.

His victory at Cannae—unparalleled in war—was largely due to the faults of his enemy; but he turned them to the very best advantage; and in all probability he directed the decisive strokes of Hasdrubal, for evidently, he designed the general plan of his battle. We should specially observe besides, the extraordinary power this mighty master had over his motley and often half-starving army; in this magical influence he has never been surpassed, and it is an influence of supreme importance; and attention should be given to a somewhat kindred quality, his remarkable care and skill in preparing his troops for the field, and in providing for their requirements and wants.

Yet the political genius of Hannibal was not less striking; he rightly abstained from marching upon Rome; he rightly clung to the conception which all along inspired him in invading Italy, that his one great chance of vanquishing Rome was to combine a gigantic league against her. One mistake he certainly made in these years; he misunderstood the nature of the allies of Rome; he could not compel them by cruelties to yield to his will; but, in the case of a ruler of Carthage, the mistake was natural. Hannibal was now at the topmost height of fortune; Rome had been completely defeated in the field; he might, as it seemed, cast his shoe over Italy, and trample her down if she dared to resist. Yet we now see that, even after Cannae, his success was, in a high degree, improbable; should Rome continue to be true to herself, Hannibal could not in the long run subdue her. It has been well written:

> The torrent had swelled into a wide flood, overwhelming the whole valley; but the one rock, now islanded amidst the waters, on which they dash furiously on every side, . . . remains unshaken. (Arnold, *Second Punic War.*)

HANNIBAL. FROM A SILVER MEDAL.

Chapter 7: Rome in a Death Struggle with Hannibal

The second act in the drama of the Second Punic War closes with the appalling disaster of Cannae.

★★★★★★★★★★

The history of Polybius, as a consecutive narrative of the Second Punic War, does not extend beyond the battle of Cannae. Many fragments of his work on the subject nevertheless remain, and these are of great value. The only ancient narrative in existence is that of Livy, picturesque and brilliant but often inaccurate and imperfect, and always unjust to Hannibal. The writings of other classical authors on the war, Appian, Cornelius Nepos, etc., tell us but little, and Plutarch is a mere rhetorician. The feeble poem of Silius Italicus attests the terror Rome felt at the very name of Hannibal and forms a kind of narrative.

★★★★★★★★★★

Steadily carrying out his original plan, though already disappointed in his first hopes, Hannibal had marched from the Trebia to the Clanis, turning the mountain barriers that defend Rome; he had annihilated, at Trasimenus, a consular army; and then, wisely avoiding the mighty city, he had descended to the Apulian plains, and made himself master of part of southern Italy. His progress of conquest is checked for a time by the strenuous efforts of the great republic, and by the insight and wisdom of a single man; but he overruns the fairest of the Roman provinces; he baffles and outmanoeuvres Fabius; and, seizing the occasion given by the errors and the discord of his foes, he strikes down Rome, on the banks of the Aufidus, in the most terrible defeat ever known in war. Yet crushing as the reverse of Cannae was, history marks with astonishment that the gigantic strife assumes before long a new aspect, and is carried on under changed conditions.

Hannibal, indeed, remains invincible in the field, he establishes himself firmly in a large part of Italy; he carries into effect in some measure, his grand scheme of combining a league against Rome; he marches through conquered provinces almost at will; he appears at the very gates of the imperial city. But Rome once more throws off the prostration of defeat, and, taught by adversity, changes her policy in the war; she collects and husbands her immense military strength; she opposes a stern, patient, and incessant resistance to all the efforts of the mighty foe, and though she wins nothing like a real battle, and her resources are strained to the very utmost, and she has to contend against faithless allies, and a threatening coalition of enemies abroad, she succeeds in confining Hannibal within a sphere of operations comparatively small, in preventing him from making the whole peninsula his own, in weakening him, even while he is still victorious. Her exertions dam in the flood of invasion, which, rolling from the Alps, across the Apennines, had seemed, as it were, to efface the landscape; they bring the devouring waters, within narrowing bounds in Italy.

But the designs of Hannibal against his undaunted enemy, though not accomplished as he had had reason to expect, are, nevertheless, by no means abortive; outside her dominions, Rome is beset by a sea of troubles gathering menacingly in from all parts of the Mediterranean world; she has to guard against its waves and its tempests, in Spain, in Sicily, in Sardinia, and across the Adriatic. The great conflict with the victor of Cannae, if gradually limited in its main theatre, is thus extended to other lands, and assumes ampler, if less imposing proportions. It embraces almost every race and state from the Ægean sea to the Pillars of Hercules. And such was the force of Hannibal's genius that, baffled as he repeatedly was in his aims, and deprived of the support on which he had set his trust, and prodigious as were the efforts of Rome, the issue was for a long time uncertain—nay, more than once was of high hope for him.

Hannibal, we have said, had prudently abstained from marching on Rome, even after Cannae. His motley army was small and had been much weakened; he had not the means to attack the city; his one great chance of success, we must ever bear in mind, was to form a league of many nations and powers against his mighty enemy. At this conjuncture there seemed the fairest promise of the accomplishment of his profound designs. The maritime resources of Carthage were still immense; had she done what Rome had done twice in the First Punic War, quickly equipped a really formidable fleet, she could have wrested the command of the sea from a rival for the present almost in the grasp of a conqueror, and whose navy depended mainly on allies in Italy; and, in that event, she might have probably combined an irresistible coalition against Rome.

A Carthaginian Army, leaving the coasts of Spain, could have crossed the Mediterranean, and landed in northern Italy; it would have drawn in its wake the mass of the Gaulish tribes; and Hasdrubal might have appeared on the Tiber, to second Hannibal advancing from the south, and to overpower Rome with their united forces. And even if the republic had repelled this attack, hosts of other enemies might have arrayed against her. Philip of Macedon, urged by Demetrius of Pharos, once a vassal, now a bitter foe of Rome, had already, we have seen, lent an ear to Hannibal; he was already threatening the Adriatic seaboard, and negotiating with Illyrian tribes; assuredly, if at this crisis, he had obtained the support of a Carthaginian fleet, he would have trod in the steps of Pyrrhus, have invaded Italy at the head of a great army, perhaps have conquered in another Battle of Cannae.

Hellas, too, at this time, was not well disposed to Rome; more than one Greek thinker had denounced her growing ambition, and had even proclaimed the creed of Hellenic unity; in the hour of its misfortune, it would have been not impossible to have induced Athens, Sparta, and other Greek states to declare against the defeated republic. Yet the gravest perhaps of the many dangers which encompassed the ruling power of Italy, at this terrible and most trying moment, was to be found in the state of Italy itself. Not one of the allied or the subject communities had, as yet, openly fallen away from Rome; the Latin cities especially had remained loyal.

But Capua, we have seen, had dealt with Hannibal; the sufferings of the Italians had been cruel; and after the frightful bloodshed of Cannae, loud sounds of discontent were heard everywhere; in the words of the great Greek orator, the war had opened the hidden wounds of the commonwealth, and several states were already thinking of revolt. A really earnest effort, on the part of Carthage, might have fused together these many elements of hostility and ill-will, and combined a league that might have wrought the destruction of Rome; had an Hamilcar appeared in the Carthaginian councils, to give aid to Hannibal in the field, the doom of the republic might have been sealed. (The reader will again observe the extreme importance of the command of the sea, at this crisis of the Second Punic War. He may be referred, in addition to Mahan's *Sea Power*, to Hénnébert.)

An immense calamity, however, was not to befall mankind; Providence saved Rome to fulfil her mission. The victory of Cannae, nevertheless, bore great fruit; the foe of Hannibal was placed in the extreme of peril. The conqueror sent his brother Mago from the field of battle, to convey to Carthage the tale of his triumph, and to seek for reinforcements to make his success decisive; the envoy received an exulting welcome. The peace party, indeed, always opposed to the war, and led by a magnate of the name of Hanno—a successor probably of "Hanno the Great," the reproach of his order in the Libyan rebellion—asked awkward questions and made empty protests, (the speech put by Livy in the mouth of Hanno, is, no doubt, an invention, but probably expresses a true tradition), but pride and national hatred prevailed for the moment; cavalry, elephants, and money were despatched to Italy—Carthage evidently at this crisis partly ruled the sea—and formidable additional support was promised. (Livy, this should be borne in mind.)

Meanwhile Philip had made a regular treaty with Hannibal, (text of the treaty will be found in Polybius), which virtually pledged him to land an army in Italy; the Macedonian and the Carthaginian *phalanx*es were to unite in the Apulian plains; the defeat of Pyrrhus was to be signally avenged. We do not know what passed between the chiefs of the Gauls, and the warrior who had wrought such wonders with his Gaulish levies; but the Celts of the Po, when Cannae was won, swept, in thousands, through the Apennine passes, to enrol themselves under the Phoenician standards, and to take part in the impending struggle, which, they dreamed, was to renew the day of the Allia, and to deliver the enemy of their race into their hands.

From Spain alone, which Hannibal had made the base of his operations for his great enterprise, and from which he expected his chief support, no aid or promise of aid was forthcoming. The arms of Rome had, we have seen, been making progress in the peninsula; the two Scipios, with their fleet and their army, had not only secured the line of the Ebro, but had advanced into the regions behind, and Hasdrubal was still prevented from sending help to his brother across the Pyrenees and the Alps.

While Rome, bleeding from the wounds of Cannae, was thus being threatened by enemies from abroad, she was to feel the presence of enemies at home; a large part of Italy ere long had pronounced against her. The colonies she had established throughout the peninsula, from the valley of the Po to the verge of Sicily, and the Latin states still upheld her cause; her rule remained unshaken in the region between the Liris, the Tiber, and the course of the Anio. But northern Italy, for the moment, was in the hands of the Celts, whose hordes swarmed round the Italian cities; and in southern Italy most of the people of the Umbrian and the Sabellian stocks, besides the Campanians and other communities, renounced their allegiance to their sovereign state, and within a few months had thrown in their lot with Hannibal.

The Lucanians, the Bruttians, the Apulians, above all, the Samnites, next to Rome the most warlike of the Italian races, had quickly made terms with the Carthaginian leader, and even sent contingents to aid him in the field; and though most of the Greek cities on the coast were still true to Rome, Tarentum, remembering the days of Pyrrhus, was already plotting against the republic. Five-sixths of the southern provinces rose, in a word, in revolt; in some instances, the revolt found leaders in nobles deprived of their old authority, and in priests driven from their old altars; but it was usually supported by the populace of the towns, and by the men it had placed at its head, (Livy), for the aristocratic rule of the senate and of the Roman noblesse was widely disliked.

Hannibal, as may be supposed, encouraged the movement, with characteristic adroitness and skill. As had always been his wont, he had, after Cannae, drawn a distinction between the Roman and the allied prisoners; he had sent these last free and with honour, to their homes. And, as before, he took care to announce, as a conqueror, that he had come to Italy as a deliverer only, as a champion of a nation oppressed by Rome; and in the treaties he made with the revolted states, he gave ample and liberal guaranties, in fact consented generally to the terms they propounded. (There is a marked, if only general, resemblance between Hannibal's conduct to the revolted Italian subjects of Rome, and Napoleon's conduct to the revolted Italian subjects of Austria in 1796-97.)

Rome, however, as always, remained undismayed; the last and the greatest disaster which had befallen her arms, the dangers surrounding her on every side could not break her noble and imperial spirit. History can hardly shew a second example of such heroic constancy, such resolute daring, above all, such a union of every class in the state, as was exhibited at this time by the Roman people. For weeks after Cannae messengers flocked in, from all parts of Italy, with fresh tales of woe; two great armies had perished beside the Aufidus; another army had been destroyed by the Gauls; southern Italy had risen in arms against Rome; foreign invaders would soon land on the coast; Hannibal, like a king of terrors, was not far from the city.

There was a moment of panic as there had been when the news

of the Trebia and of Trasimenus arrived; crowds of citizens appeared in the streets in despair, the voices of women weeping for those they had loved and lost, were heard far and near, and caused general sorrow. But lamentation and weakness soon gave place to steadfast resolution and unflinching courage; the conduct and the purpose of Rome were never doubtful. Fabius was not in office, but his pious spirit and his wisdom guided the councils of the state; and these were worthy of a nation that no trial could subdue.

A solemn embassy was sent to the shrine of Delphi, the gods were propitiated by continued rites; and if, as in the agony of the Gaulish war, human sacrifices were again offered up, (Livy), this was the single lapse from the masculine faith of Rome. At the same time the walls of the city were carefully manned; disordered multitudes were not allowed to gather; a brief season was permitted for a national mourning; but it was soon to be followed by the round of ordinary duty and work; Rome was to maintain her attitude, and not to give way to grief. And in this terrible crisis of adverse fortune, the people to a man rallied around the government. The voice of the demagogue, the folly of the mob, which had wrought such mischief, were reduced to silence; the senate and the nobles were given the freest hand to act; they acquitted themselves nobly of their arduous task.

It was resolved at all hazards to continue the war; proof was soon given how firm was this purpose. Hannibal had, after Cannae, sent an envoy to Rome, to treat for the ransom of his Roman captives, and if possible, to make a pacific overture; but the envoy was not even given a hearing; the captives were sternly let know they would not be held to ransom; Rome, as in the days of Pyrrhus, refused to parley with an envoy within her own domain of Italy. The spirit, however, that informed the whole Roman commonwealth was most conspicuously shewn in another striking instance.

Varro had been suspended in his command; he had lost Cannae through his reckless want of judgment; he had been summoned to Rome, a beaten, nay, a disgraced soldier. But he had succeeded in rallying a few thousand fugitives; and the fathers of the city met him at the gates, to tell the enemy of the nobles, the darling of the mob, the defeated commander, that "he was to be thanked, because he had not despaired of his country." As the Roman historian has truly remarked, a Carthaginian general, in such a case, would have had only one end, the cross, (Livy); but the act of the senate was perhaps one of deep policy—"this was no empty phraseology—no bitter mockery over a poor wretch; it was the conclusion of peace between the government and the governed." (Mommsen.)

Meantime nothing had been left undone to maintain the tremendous struggle with Hannibal. Rome had been again taken by surprise at Cannae; immense as was her real military force, it had not been fully developed as yet; more than a fifth part of her youth fit for war had fallen; she had, at this moment, few soldiers to send to the field; many of the allies had become her enemies. But she gathered herself up for a fresh great effort; messages were sent to the loyal Italian peoples to prepare their contingents as quickly as possible; the two *legions*, which in ordinary times, were employed for the defence of the city, were ordered to set out upon active service; some troops were collected in the north and the east; a single legion which was about to embark, at Ostia, was detached from the fleet, and marched southwards in hot haste; and the wrecks of the army of Cannae, which by this time numbered from 8,000 to 10,000 men, were removed from the towns where they had found a refuge, into Campania, the scene of immediate danger.

Some 25,000 or 35,000 men were thus soon mustered; but this force was not sufficient to withstand Hannibal; another and strange expedient was devised to produce an extraordinary levy for the state. Slaves, debtors in prison, even criminals, were enrolled in the ranks of a separate army, and promised freedom and forgiveness if they did their duty; by these means 25,000 recruits were, it is said, added to the troops in the field; and arms and weapons, the trophies of fortunate wars, were taken down from the walls of the temples to make up for a deficient supply. The choice of commanders, too, was speedily made; Fabius remained in the city, to direct the government, but a veteran soldier, Marcus Junius Pera, was placed, as dictator, at the head of military affairs; another veteran, Tiberius Sempronius Gracchus, being made his lieutenant, as master of the horse.

At this crisis, however, the eyes of the Romans were chiefly turned on Marcus Claudius Marcellus, a well-proved warrior, who held the rank of *praetor*. Marcellus had already won renown as a consul; he had slain a prince of the Insubres in the Gaulish War; he had distinguished himself greatly in the First Punic War, in Sicily, when opposed to Hamilcar; though advanced in years he had still the energy of youth; and though he was never, in a real sense, a great captain, and dark and evil stains disfigure his career, his countrymen, as the event was to shew, are not wholly in error when they deemed that he was an adversary not unfitting to cross swords with Hannibal. He had been placed for some time in command of the remains of the army which had fought at Cannae.

Seventy or eighty thousand men were thus brought into the field, within four months probably of the day of Cannae. The dictator took a position at Teanum in Campania, covering the main roads to Rome; Marcellus, who had marched from Apulia, through the Apennines, had, after joining his colleague, moved to Suessula in the north-east of the province. By this time the Campanians were in general revolt; and Capua, the second city of Italy, the partisans of Carthage becoming supreme after Cannae, had with apparent enthusiasm declared for Hannibal. The great Carthaginian had meanwhile been negotiating with Philip, restoring his army, forming his new levies, in a word, making his arrangements to carry on the war; he evidently did not contemplate, as affairs stood, anything like a decisive attack on Rome.

We do not know what the strength of his force was; but he had been obliged to employ many thousand men, in watching Roman garrisons, in obtaining supplies, and especially in giving aid to his Italian allies, who had joined him, indeed, but with hesitation and fear; at this moment he could have hardly had forty thousand men under his immediate orders. He advanced, however, into Campania, hoping perhaps that he would be able to surprise the enemy, but if this was his hope, it was completely frustrated. He found himself beset by two armies, each not much inferior in numbers to his own; the example of Fabius was steadily followed; the Romans, avoiding a pitched battle, wasted the country, hung on the invaders' flanks, pursued and annoyed him whenever a chance offered; and Hannibal's operations were to little purpose.

He took, indeed, two or three small towns and he laid siege to Casilinum (it fell after a stubborn, resistance of many months), in order to master the passages of the Vulturnus and to possess the means of moving through Campania, on either bank of the river. But he failed in attempts to seize Cumae and Neapolis, large Greek towns on the coast, which remained true to the Roman cause; he had thought to occupy these, no doubt, in. the hope that he would obtain assistance from Carthage at these points by the sea;—this may indeed have been one of his chief objects. (Livy dwells on this with emphasis.) It is very remarkable that at this juncture, Capua, a city which it is said possessed an army of 30,000 foot and 4,000 horsemen, did not give Hannibal active aid; like most of the other revolted cities, disaffected as it certainly was to Rome, it had little genuine devotion to the Phoenician cause.

★★★★★★★★★★

It is scarcely necessary to refer to the idle and malicious tale, adopted however by Arnold, *Second Punic War*, that Hannibal treated his Roman prisoners with hideous and refined barbarity when he learned that they were not to be ransomed; the story is not to be found in Livy or Polybius and may be at once dismissed as false.

★★★★★★★★★★

The war had now taken a turn which, after Cannae, might have been deemed impossible. Ere long an incident occurred, not in itself important, but which marked the first change in the tide of misfortune which had well-nigh overwhelmed Rome. Marcellus had been true to the Fabian system; but he was a determined and skilful soldier; he knew the value of moral power in war, (see the remarkable words put by Livy in the mouth of Marcellus, in reply to the timid caution of Fabius); he had resolved to seize the first chance that offered to fight with success, and to efface the memory of a long train of disasters. He found the opportunity round the walls of Nola, a fortress on the northern verge of Campania, against which Hannibal had directed his efforts.

The aristocratic party in Nola, as usually happened, was still loyal to Rome; but the people, led by a young noble, who had been released after Cannae with special marks of favour, had pronounced for the invader's cause; and Hannibal expected an easy triumph. Marcellus, however, threw himself into the place, apparently with a considerable force; and having won over the popular chief, addressed himself to the defence of Nola, and to taking his adversary at disadvantage, as now appeared possible. His dispositions shew skill in stratagem, and resource; he placed his best troops at the middle gate of the town, and the rest of his men, at the gates on each side; he forbade the citizens to appear on the walls, and he arrayed his invalided soldiers and camp followers in a body collected behind the ramparts.

Hannibal advanced on Nola, for once off his guard; he waited, outside, for some hours, with his army, convinced that a surrender was certain, and deceived by the sight of the deserted walls, but ultimately, he made a demonstration of attack, it would seem with a part of his men only, being confident that the town would rise in his favour. The gates were then suddenly thrown open; and the Romans, issuing in full force, loud cheers marking their exulting onset, and shouts arising from the crowd behind the ramparts, fell on their enemies in front and both flanks and drove them away defeated and baffled.

It was the first real check Hannibal had received for months, and curiously enough it was one of the first instances in which we see the Romans, taught by their great adversary, attempt flanking attacks and turning movements. The effect of the success of Marcellus was immense; a weight was lifted up from the heart of Rome; the historian has remarked:

> Whether the victory was great or not, it was, perhaps, the most memorable event of the war, for not to be conquered by Hannibal was then more difficult than it was afterwards to conquer him. (Livy.)

Marcellus was thenceforward greeted as "the sword" of Rome, as the aged Fabius had been called "her shield"; this was, no doubt, the origin of his extraordinary renown, not undeserved but unduly magnified.

The memorable year of Cannae had now ended; the astonishing, the magnificent efforts of Rome had suddenly arrested the march of the conqueror, had saved her when she seemed at his mercy. Hannibal and his army passed the winter at Capua; the destructive effects which the vice and the pleasures of a great city had on his war-worn men have been exaggerated by false rhetoric; but we may readily believe that the order and discipline of a motley assemblage of troops of many races, and especially of the barbarian Celts, were, to some extent, relaxed for a time. We must pass rapidly over the events of the contest, in Italy, during the next three years, 215, 214, 213, B.C., for they were marked by the same general character, and the accounts we possess are confused and imperfect.

We remain in the dark as regards the extent and even the quality of Hannibal's forces; but we do know that he did not obtain the reinforcements he had the fullest reason to expect. A short time probably after Cannae, Hasdrubal had made an attempt to cross the Ebro, to reach the Pyrenees, and, no doubt, to try to join his illustrious brother; but he had been defeated by the Scipios with heavy loss, and the Roman standards were carried beyond the Tagus. The Carthaginian empire in Spain was shaken; and the Carthaginian government, never well inclined to Hannibal, sent Mago to Spain with the large contingent which it had promised to land in Italy, neglecting the decisive point on the theatre of war and sacrificing the principal to a subordinate interest. (Livy dwells on this.)

Philip, alarmed at the presence of a Roman fleet at Brundusium, and at the energy of Rome, broke the faith he had pledged to his

CAMP OF HANNIBAL AT ROCCA DI PAPA.
FROM TROLLOPE'S "ITALY."

great ally; he did not despatch a man to Hannibal's camp, and turned aside to raid on the Adriatic cities. No assistance, of course, could arrive from Spain; and, strange as it may appear, the Gaulish chiefs in northern Italy seem, at this period, to have become lukewarm in the Phoenician cause, and made no effort to give it general support. Whether this was owing to their feuds with each other, or to the effects of Roman statecraft, which tried to conciliate them at this crisis, or to fear of Roman vengeance, or to distrust of Hannibal—as soon as the excitement of Cannae died away, the Celts certainly ceased to descend into southern Italy, in any large numbers, or to enrol themselves under the Carthaginian standards.

The armed assistance, too, which the revolted states gave to Hannibal, was comparatively small; the military strength of some had decayed, and this was especially the case with Samnium; some were jealous, suspicious, nearly all divided. And we must bear in mind that the wear and tear of Hannibal's army must have been very great; it was gradually losing its best elements, the Phoenician and Spanish soldiers, and the Numidian horsemen; it was being filled with levies of a very inferior kind.

For these reasons, we may rest assured that Hannibal's army, in these years, was never 100,000 strong; and as large deductions must be made from this force for secondary services, such as procuring supplies, holding points of vantage, observing Roman fortresses, he was no doubt, inferior even in numbers, to the enemies he opposed. This inferiority, however, was but a small part of the difficulties and dangers which beset his path. His invasion was still in the nature of a huge raid; he had no base of operation, no great stores of supplies; his communications with Carthage were scarcely ever open, those with Spain and even northern Italy were closed.

He was isolated, in a word, in a country still largely hostile, in which Rome was the mistress of armed strongholds, the garrisons of which could harass him from many points, attack his foraging parties, cut off his detachments; and he was almost shut out from the sea, whence alone he could look for powerful support. His relations, too, with the revolted subjects of Rome, were, we have seen, even from the first not cordial, and this growing estrangement rapidly increased as it became evident that Rome had been in no sense conquered. The Italian states had insisted, when they treated with him, that they should be independent and have their own governments; they rather sought to compel him to give them aid, than sent cheerfully their troops to the

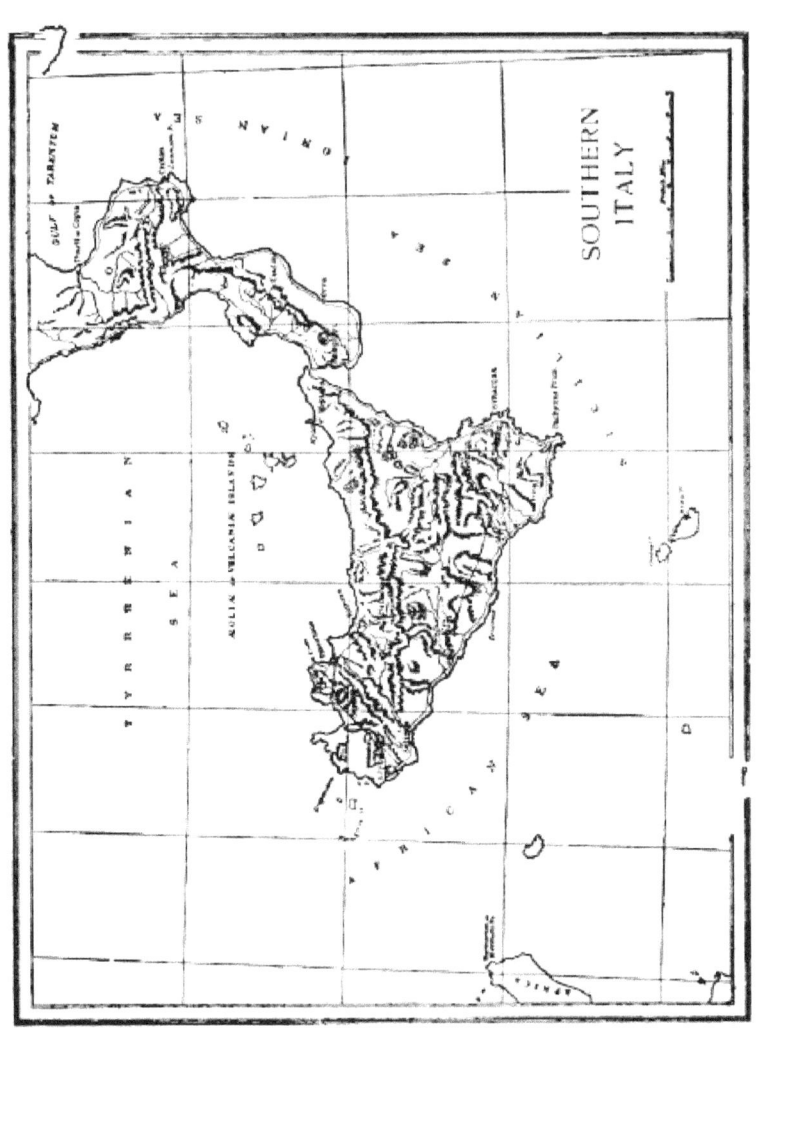

field; they hampered him with their complaints and their murmurs, more than once they impeded, nay opposed his projects.

They became, by degrees, a hindrance rather than a support; and nothing but his consummate diplomatic art could have kept them even as nominal allies together, in the face of the great people of their own race, whose power they dreaded, and even revered. Hannibal's authority over the Italian league was thus, to a great extent, paralysed; and it must be borne in mind that in almost every state, there remained a Roman party, more or less powerful, which was continually acting and plotting against him. It is certain, too, that even in the land he had seemed to have made his own, Hannibal had foes of which history has made little mention.

> We cannot calculate the numbers of guerilla bands which were on foot in Lucania, Bruttium, and possibly in Samnium, and which, hindered Hannibal from having the whole resources of those countries at his disposal. The Roman party was nowhere probably altogether extinct; wealthy Lucanians, who were attached to Rome, would muster their slaves and peasantry, and either by themselves, or getting some Roman officer to lead them, would ravage the lands of the Carthaginian party, and carry on a continued harassing warfare against the towns and districts which had joined Hannibal. Thus, the whole centre of Italy was one wide flood of war, the waters everywhere dashing and eddying and running in cross currents innumerable; while the regular armies, like the channels of the river, held on their way, distinguishable amidst the chaos by their greater rapidity and power. (Arnold, *Second Punic War*.)

Spite, however, of foes superior in numbers, and of obstacles and disappointments of every kind, Hannibal maintained, by his overmastering genius, the hold he had taken of southern Italy. He remained in military possession of the great tract from the Vulturnus to the range of Garganus, (now Gargano), northwards, down to the extreme verge of Calabria, comprising Apulia, Samnium, Campania, Lucania, Bruttium, most of the Greek cities being still excepted; but two of these, Locri and Croton, fell into his hands. Within this region, more than a fourth part of Italy, he controlled nearly all the operations in the field; no enemy ventured to fight a pitched battle with him; he marched through intricate, often hostile, countries, amidst armies whose leaders avoided his presence, with all but complete mastery of the theatre of war.

His position, in fact, bore a kind of resemblance to that of Frederick the Great in the Seven Years' War, when the king kept moving from the Elbe to the Oder, and making head against Austria, France, and Russia; but if Hannibal won no Rossbach or Leuthen he had to contend, not with a league of divided allies, but with the formidable power of united Rome, and his exploits were certainly more wonderful in the complicated, shifting, and repeated marches we behold him making at this period. Nothing is as astonishing as the perfect ease with which he appears to have flitted from point to point, surprising, eluding, brushing aside his enemies; this can be accounted for only by the Roman strategy, and by the ascendency of his still overpowering success.

In these operations he met two slight reverses, undoubtedly made too much of by the flatterers of Rome, at the hands of the brilliant and able Marcellus; and his lieutenant Hanno was defeated with heavy loss by the extraordinary levy of slaves and outcasts, under the command of Gracchus, before referred to, a victory which set them free from bondage, (Livy's description of this scene of liberation is picturesque and spirited), and was welcomed with exulting delight at Rome.

★★★★★★★★★★

There were skirmishes at Nola, which Livy enlarges into victories. The last of these is memorable for the first appearance in the field and for the failure of Cains Claudius Nero, the greatest Roman general in the Second Punic War

★★★★★★★★★★

But Hanno had his revenge in turn; and, as a rule, the Roman generals in the field, like the allies in the great struggle of 1813, took care not to attack the master of war they feared. Hannibal, nevertheless, though his military skill was perhaps never more clearly displayed, was kept by his enemies on the defensive; he was restricted within well-defined limits; and if his defence was always offensive, like that of every general of the first order, he was never given a chance of bringing his adversaries to bay. Once or twice, we see him trying to strike at the armies around him, and to beat them in detail, but he was even then resisted by superior numbers; and his efforts, it deserves special notice, appear to have been more than once baffled by that admirable bulwark of an army, the Roman camp.

Hannibal, in his lair, in the south of Italy, was thus like the mighty lord of the forest, surrounded by angry beasts of prey, which hem him in, yet will not abide his onset. Yet the Trebia, Trasimenus, and Cannae were things of the past; he was never to win such triumphs again;

Rome, taught by awful lessons she had well laid to heart, had learned how to cope with her gigantic foe, and was steadily employing her best military force in a method of warfare that promised success at last. During these years Fabius was her most prominent leader, he was twice consul, his son, once; and though Marcellus and Gracchus were his colleagues, he evidently had the supreme direction of the war with Hannibal.

He carried out cautiously, persistently, and with a stern purpose, the plan of operations which he had seen from the first was the best adapted to wear out the great enemy of Rome; and, at the same time, the senate, the nobles, and the citizens as a whole, spared no efforts to add to the armed strength of the state, and to make its forces effective for the contest in the south of Italy. Year after year the legions arrayed against Hannibal became more numerous, or of augmented strength; year after year they were more inured to war; and, simultaneously, the vicious system of short and divided commands and of discordant counsels, was, in the presence of the national peril, changed.

Taught by a fearful experience, the Romans adopted a more judicious system of conducting the war, appointed none but experienced generals to the charge of their armies, and left them at least where it was necessary, for a longer time in command. (Mommsen).

Throughout this period Fabius was the real general in chief opposed to Hannibal, though he wisely allowed his lieutenants much freedom of action.

This system of war was not grand, it was even a confession of weakness; it contrasts strikingly with Hannibal's fine movements; it wasted the resources and the power of Rome, for, it has been truly remarked, that in these years the Roman Armies seem, more than once, to have been strangely inactive in the south of Italy. (Arnold, *Second Punic War*.) But conducted as it was with prudence and skill and backed by superior forces in the field—six or eight legions usually lay around Hannibal, and his army was not nearly equal in strength—it gradually produced the natural results. Hannibal might march from the Samnite hills into Bruttium; he might hold important positions of vantage; he might make brilliant dashes at his foes, might proclaim that Rome was still lying at his feet

But he was kept within a circle of enemies of formidable power; these eluded his efforts to make them fight; and while they carried out on a larger scale the tactics Fabius had adopted from the first, cut off Hannibal's detachments, struck petty blows at the parties he was obliged to send out in many directions, and, above all, wasted and harried the country, they slowly weakened his unaided strength, and imprisoned him within his own conquest. Meanwhile the statecraft of Rome was conspicuously seen in her conduct to the allies in revolt. She appealed to her partisans by every means in her power; she encouraged their attempts to rise in her favour, and to maintain a kind of irregular warfare, she made frequent overtures of reconciliation and peace. But if a revolted city defied her summons, and fell into the hands of one of her armies, the vengeance she exacted was signal and terrible.

Through the obscure and ill-told operations of these years, Hannibal seems to have aimed at two main objects. He was in possession of Capua and held the city in force; he kept on trying to make himself master of Cumae and Neapolis, (Livy), along the coast. He evidently wished to make this part of Campania his base in the south of Italy; from this he might find the means to advance on Rome, if Capua would place her large resources in his hands; from this Carthage could send him aid by sea, if she chose really to support her glorious champion. But the Roman commanders, doubtless, perceived all this also; they always had a large army around Capua, guarding the Via Appia and the Via Latina, the two principal approaches to Rome; and Cumae and Neapolis were never taken. Hannibal was more successful in his second purpose, though ultimately his partial success was fruitless.

Tarentum, we have seen, had had a party hostile to Rome; hostages had been taken to secure their allegiance; and these had been cruelly slain by the Roman government, in an unfortunate attempt they had made to escape. A conspiracy was formed in the city against Rome; the conspirators applied to Hannibal to come to their relief. The great warrior wished for nothing better; Tarentum is one of the finest ports in Italy, it would afford a Macedonian Army a strong position, and make its communications well-nigh secure, should Philip at last keep faith with him; it had often sheltered Carthaginian fleets; it could be made a great military and naval Carthaginian station; in a word it would form a new and formidable base of operations against Rome.

Partly through a movement skilfully planned by himself, and partly through a device of the conspirators within, the city fell into the power of Hannibal, and, with characteristic diplomatic art, he had soon made arrangements which at once conciliated the population and his partisans, and yet gave him the lion's share of power. (With, the majority of commentators, I think Tarentum was taken by Hannibal in 213 B.C., not 212 B.C.)

A notable instance was now seen of the extraordinary resource in war of this great master. The citadel of Tarentum was placed on a rocky height commanding the approaches to the city landwards, and closing the passage from the Mediterranean into the main harbour, still known by the name of the "little sea," (Mare Piccolo), in which the powerful Tarentine fleet was moored. This important work, though the town had fallen, was still occupied by a Roman garrison, which bravely rejected a Carthaginian summons; and its defenders certainly threatened the place, for the fleet in the harbour being locked in, while a Roman squadron held the sea outside, they intercepted the course of supplies, and, in fact, effected a kind of blockade. (Livy).

Hannibal took a position outside Tarentum, drew lines round the citadel on the land side, and thus deprived the garrison of help from without; and then, by one of his "Punic" devices, lured out the Romans from the walls and drove them back with great slaughter. Rome, however, sent reinforcements by sea, assisted by Metapontum, a Greek city, (now Torre di Mare); Tarentum was being almost invested, when it was saved by Hannibal's inventive genius. He constructed a kind of way, made as easy as possible, by smoothing the ground and laying down a course of planks, greased and covered with hides; the Tarentine fleet, drawn out of the main harbour, was placed on this strange improvised road, and dragged by beasts of burden and other means, across the land, to the open sea, where, it would appear, it drove the enemy away, kept the garrison in along that front, and enabled the city to obtain its regular store of supplies. Tarentum was thus won by Hannibal for a time; this conquest was before long followed by the defection of Thurii and other Greek towns from Rome.

★★★★★★★★★★

Some writers have denied that the expedient adopted by Hannibal was possible; but exactly the same thing was done at the great siege of Constantinople, 1453. Gibbon, gives this account; "A level way was covered with a broad platform of strong and solid planks, and to render them more slippery and smooth, they were anointed with the fat of sheep and oxen. Four score light galleys and brigantines of fifty and thirty oars were disembarked on the Bosporus shore, arranged successively on rollers, and drawn forward by the force of men and pulleys; two guides or pilots were stationed at the helm and the prow of each vessel, the sails were unfurled to the winds; and the labour was cheered by song and acclamation. In the course of a single night, this Turkish fleet painfully climbed the hill, streamed over the plain and was launched from the declivity into the shallow waters of the harbour,"

★★★★★★★★★★

While Rome was thus in a struggle of life and death with Hannibal, she had to withstand a host of enemies beyond her own borders. The great coalition of states and races, which Hannibal sought to array against her, was never, in any true sense, perfected; but she was threatened far and near, and on every side by warfare, here intermittent, here never ceasing, breaking out in lands where it was not expected, and tasking even her energies to the very utmost—this embracing the chief parts of the Mediterranean world. We must rapidly survey the events of this contest, in which she was involved by her mighty enemy, and which, but for her grand constancy, might have proved fatal, though it did not even nearly fulfil his purpose.

After the diversion of her forces, under Mago, from Italy, the great scene of the struggle, Carthage seems to have sent no aid to Hannibal; with the ingratitude of a partisan government, with the ignorance of a state that never understood war, she left her illustrious hero to his own resources. Her attention, at this time, was chiefly turned to Spain, whence she drew a large part of the revenue, and where her empire was being threatened with ruin. The brothers Scipio, well supported by the men in power at home, had made Tarragona a great naval station; they had recovered Saguntum and taken other towns; and they advanced by degrees with large and increasing forces from the Tagus to the Guadalquivir, and the Andalusian plains.

They seem to have possessed some of the attractive power of Africanus, their renowned kinsman; Celtiberian princes and tribes, flocking to their armies, opposed, in whole provinces, the power of Carthage; indeed her cruel and oppressive yoke was naturally thrown off when compared to the administration of Rome. The Scipios even succeeded in striking at Carthage in her domain in Africa; they stirred up Syphax, a Numidian prince, chief of the peoples of Oran and Algiers, to rise against his Phoenician *suzerain*; and Hasdrubal was compelled to evacuate Spain, and to make head against a far-spreading revolt. Syphax was defeated after a sharp contest, chiefly through the efforts of Massinissa, another Numidian, then friendly to Carthage, and soon to appear prominently on the stage of events; the Libyan rebellion, as had been the case before, was suppressed after horrible deeds of atrocity and blood.

Hasdrubal was enabled to return to Spain, but the work of Hamilcar had been half undone; Carthage had lost territory, authority, and what she thought of most, money; the prospect of sending help to Hannibal, from the peninsula, seemed more than ever hopeless. (Arnold, *Second Punic War*, properly warns the reader against Livy's extravagant account of Roman victories won by the Scipios. This was flattery of Africanus, perhaps a set off to Hannibal's triumphs in Italy.)

The war in Spain, however, compelled Rome to keep a large military and naval force on the spot; this, though very indirectly, gave aid to Hannibal, and was another burden for the hard-pressed republic. The state of affairs beyond the Adriatic was in some respects similar, and was attended by somewhat similar results. Philip of Macedon soon discovered that when he had failed to land an army in Italy at once after Cannae, he had not only lost his best chance of supporting Hannibal, but had to deal with formidable enemies at home. Rome was not content merely to keep watch on the king, from Brundusium, and to abide his attack; with the true genius of a conquering race, she carried the war into his own dominions.

About the time of the fall of Tarentum, in order to parry, perhaps, a blow from Macedon, which, if ever, seemed now impending, she made a league with the half-savage Ætolians; she promised them considerable territory and spoil, and she persuaded them to assist her, with all their forces, in the war she boldly declared against Philip. At the same time, she played on the old jealousy of Macedon, felt by Athens, Sparta, and other states of the Hellas of a better day; she made them her allies in the contest; she stirred up the wild barbarians of Thrace and the Balkans, against her enemy; she even looked to the distant east, and induced Attains of Pergamus to give her assistance.

We have no means of knowing what land forces were employed in the struggle she had almost provoked; but her fleets swept the Ægean waters, and disembarked troops on the eastern coasts of Greece; and this bold, offensive attitude must have made an immense impression on every foreign state, for after Cannae, she had been deemed on the verge of destruction. Philip found himself encompassed by a circle of foes united against him by Roman policy:

> He had to turn against the Ætolians, who, in concert with the Roman fleet, annihilated the unfortunate Acarnanians, and threatened Locris and Thessaly; an invasion of barbarians threatened his northern provinces; the Achaeans solicited his

help against the predatory excursions of Ætolians and Spartans; King Attalus of Pergamus and the Roman admiral, Publius Sulpicius, with their combined fleets, threatened the east coasts, or landed troops in Euboea. (Mommsen.)

The king, in a word, was paralysed, and given more than enough to do; and all the result of his treaty with Hannibal, through which he might have overwhelmed Rome, was to expose his weakness and want of good faith, and to divert a part of the Roman forces—perhaps not a large part—from the seat of the war in Italy. Philip saw, at last, that his best remaining chance was to join Hannibal and to try to land an army in Apulia, or at Tarentum; he began to construct a fleet for this purpose, but the opportunity had passed; he was too late.

The Gauls of northern Italy, during these years, continued in the strange state of inaction to which we have before referred; there was no general rising at least against Rome. But five-sixths of the country was in their hands; Rome was on her guard against the treacherous Celts, and kept an eye on her loyal colonies; rumours of discontent were heard in Etruria, once the seat of a formidable independent power; the republic was obliged to place two or three double legions to watch the line of her northern frontier, and to bar the approach of Gaulish levies to Hannibal. Sardinia, too, which Rome, we have seen, had acquired just after the First Punic War, had broken out in general revolt. Rome had extended her rule over the whole island, beyond the Phoenician settlements on the coast; she had placed it under tribute and Roman governors; she had lately extorted a contribution she had called a free gift.

The half-tamed populations flew to arms; applied to their old *suzerain* Carthage, whose heavy hand they had probably hardly felt; Carthage, ever true to her bad instincts, sent the assistance she ought to have sent elsewhere, a squadron (it is evident that for some time after Cannae, Carthage had again, to some extent, the command of the sea; her conduct to Hannibal is all the more to be condemned), and a considerable body of troops; a wild guerilla war spread through the plains and the hills. But Rome acted with her wonted decision; two, perhaps double, legions were engaged in Sardinia; Titus Manlius Torquatus, a distinguished soldier, routed the Carthaginian and the native forces; reduced the towns, laying heavy charges on them; in a word, made the restored authority of Rome absolute. The island was, without difficulty, held down; but it was necessary to provide against fresh risings, and especially against Carthaginian descents; and one or two legions were kept throughout the war in Sardinia, another drain on the military resources of Rome.

At this juncture, however, the severest strain on the energies of the republic, outside Italy, and the most formidable difficulty that beset it abroad, arose in a quarter where the trial appeared to be least probable. Rome had been dominant in Sicily for many years; the great city of Syracuse, its leading state, had practically become a Roman stronghold; Hiero, the vassal king, had through a long life been a most loyal and devoted ally. One of the latest acts of Hiero, we have seen, had been to offer aid to his *suzerain*, before Cannae; soon after that disaster, he had given valuable help, in corn and other stores, to the Roman fleet stationed in the east to hold Philip of Macedon in check.

On the death of Hiero, however, his crown had devolved on a grandson, Hieronymus, a foolish and licentious youth, but second in descent from the renowned Pyrrhus, (the mother of Hieronymus was a daughter of Pyrrhus), and Hieronymus, giving ear to bad and artful flatterers, began to dream of repeating the great deeds of his ancestor, of defying Rome, of making himself the lord of a united and an independent Sicily. These tales reached Hannibal soon after Cannae; the great Carthaginian, ever intent on raising up enemies to strike at Rome, sent two envoys of mixed Greek and Carthaginian blood, to fan the flame of ambition and hate; and Hippocrates and Epicydes—these were their names—expatiated on their mighty leader's triumphs, befooled the stripling to the top of his bent, said that he would succeed where Pyrrhus had failed, and held out bright prospects of Carthaginian support.

The bait dexterously laid by Hannibal was seized; the Roman officer in command at Syracuse, remonstrated and made angry threats; but the young king, with the sanction of elder kinsmen, and doubtless of many partisans at his court, gave an answer that could be only deemed an insult to the majesty of Rome, and sent ambassadors to treat with Carthage. The Carthaginian government, as usual, turning away from Hannibal, but eager to recover a magnificent domain it had lost, promised to send an army and fleet to Sicily, and even to recognise Hieronymus, and his claims to the sovereignty of the whole island; if it could once expel the Romans, it well knew it could easily get rid of a weak, fickle, and worthless boy.

Syracuse was soon virtually at war with Rome, and many of the Sicilian cities took part in the revolt. Though Hieronymus may have set the example, this was, no doubt, a general movement; in Sicily, as in Italy, the multitude of the towns and their leaders were not well disposed to Rome, and turned to Hannibal and Carthage, perhaps in the hope that Sicilian independence would be the result.

As might have been expected, however, Syracuse contained a strong aristocratic or Roman party; it was comprised, in part, of the following of the old king; and, doubtless with the connivance of the Roman officials in the place, it conspired against Hieronymus and the revolution he had made. The cry of the tyrant—a name justly abhorred in Sicily—was cunningly raised against the unfortunate youth; Hieronymus and the kinsmen who had led him astray were cruelly murdered by savage partisans, and the whole family of Hiero was afterwards involved in the same proscription and pitilessly slain.

A counter revolution ere long followed; the popular leaders, now the declared friends of Hannibal and Carthage, got the upper hand; and Hippocrates and Epicydes—a remarkable tribute to the genius of the victor of Cannae—were placed at the head of affairs at Syracuse, and invested with the supreme power of government. A great Roman fleet, however, had soon reached Syracuse and made a formidable display of power; the party of Rome again triumphed; the old league with Hiero was renewed; and though a Carthaginian squadron appeared off the coast, the city remained in the hands of its aristocratic masters, whose only hope now was in the Roman alliance. Trouble, confusion, and civil war prevailed, during the succeeding months, throughout the large provinces, which Syracuse had brought under her rule, but many of the cities which were in a sense her subjects refused to follow her lead in what had just taken place, and declared against her sovereignty and their allegiance to Rome.

Leontini, a town of some importance, became the centre and the rallying point of the league of these revolted states; Hippocrates and Epicydes were again made rulers, and the chiefs of the popular party, who had been driven out of Syracuse, found refuge in the place, and endeavoured to spread the insurrectionary movement far and wide. A considerable armed force was placed in the field; it is a most significant fact that it was partly composed of a large body of deserters from the Roman fleet, manned, to a great extent, by reluctant allies.

This state of affairs became so menacing, that notwithstanding his brilliant feats against Hannibal, Marcellas was removed from the scene of the war in Italy and was sent to Sicily in supreme command. The "sword of Rome" cut sharply into the revolt; but it was too fiercely wielded and with evil results. After negotiations which came to nothing—Hippocrates and Epicydes were to be banished—Marcellas fell on Leontini in force; the city was ruthlessly stormed and sacked, the Roman deserters were sent to a cruel death; a considerable number of the townsmen perished. The government of Rome in Sicily had been harsh; these deeds quickened the growing rebellion; a cry went forth that the Greek name in the island had been marked down for vengeance; an incident occurred which completely changed the situation at Syracuse, gave a new turn to the contest, and severely tasked the energies of Rome for years.

The chiefs of the aristocratic faction in Syracuse were leading out an army to assist Marcellus, which contained a body of Cretan bowmen, once the prisoners of Hannibal, but released by him, in accordance with his systematic policy; these men refused to take arms against his envoys, and when the massacre at Leontini had been noised abroad, the whole Syracusan Army arose in revolt. The partisans of Rome and the nobles were overpowered; and a revolution took place in the city; the ascendency of the populace and its chiefs was restored; Hippocrates and Epicydes were made its chief magistrates once more.

The numbers of the army were swelled by other Roman deserters, by mercenary soldiers of many races, perhaps by a few Carthaginian troops; and Syracuse addressed herself to resist the might of Rome, and to defend herself to the last extremity amidst terrible scenes of blood and popular passion. (Livy gives an elaborate and striking account of these revolutions in Syracuse, so characteristic of Greek cities. But his Roman sympathies are palpable, and he carefully screens the conduct of Marcellus.) Marcellus, indignant at what had occurred, marched against Syracuse and laid siege to the place with an army perhaps 30,000 strong, and a fleet of 100 large war-ships.

The city, under the prosperous rule of Hiero, had expanded beyond its old limits; it was the most magnificent of Greek cities, it overflowed with the wealth of commerce, it was adorned with fine temples, and beautiful works of art. It was now divided into five quarters, Achradina and Ortygia, the ancient fortified town, with its citadel and its great harbour overlooking the Mediterranean waters, Epipolae, Tyche, and Neapolis, modern suburbs extending to heights landwards, the whole circumference being strongly walled and covered at one point by a large outwork, the Hexapylum or six main gates. The *praetor* Appius Claudius directed the attack by land, but the principal attack was made by sea; Marcellus directed this in person.

It was the third great siege Syracuse had resisted, and this, in some respects, was the most remarkable. Marcellus did not attack the Great Harbour—a scene of some passages of the Athenian siege; he moored his fleet against the sea front of Achradina, and he made vehement efforts, probably for weeks, to storm the walls from his ships, and to carry the town by assault. But the defence had been committed to Archimedes, the first mathematician and engineer of the age, who had long made preparations against an attack; it was then seen, by a notable instance, what science and skill could effect against even Roman courage.

Archimedes had supplied the ramparts with an artillery so powerful that it overwhelmed the Romans before they could get within the range which their missiles could reach; and when they came close, they found that all the lower part of the wall was loopholed, and their men struck down with fatal aim by an enemy whom they could not see, and who shot his arrows in perfect security. If they still persevered and attempted to fix their ladders, on a sudden they saw long poles thrust out from the top of the wall like the arms of a giant, and enormous stones or huge masses of lead were dropped from these upon them, by which their ladders were crushed to pieces and their ships almost sunk.

At other times machines like cranes were thrust out over the wall, and the end of the lever, with an iron grapple affixed to it, was lowered upon the Roman ships. As soon as the grapple had taken hold, the other end of the lever was lowered down by heavy weights and the ship raised out of the water until it was made almost to stand upon its stern; then the grapple was suddenly let go, and the ship dropped into the sea with a violence which either upset it or filled it with water. With equal power was the assault on the land side repelled; and the Roman soldiers, bold as they were, were so daunted by these strange and irresistible devices, that if they saw so much as a rope or a stick hanging or projecting from a wall, they would turn about and run away crying that 'Archimedes is going to set one of his engines at work against us.'" (Arnold's *Second Punic War.* There has been no Thucydides to describe this memorable siege of Syracuse; but the accounts of Polybius, and of Livy, are clear, even graphic.)

The attack by sea was abandoned in despair; the siege was turned into a loose blockade continued with intermissions during many months. But the defence of Syracuse had important results; many of the cities declared against Rome, Sicily became a theatre of general revolt, the authority of the republic was upheld in a few districts only, and in the strong fortresses chiefly along the coast. The Carthaginian Government, it has been said, with the advice of Hannibal, (this, however, seems doubtful, see Mommsen), made a real effort to restore its power; a large fleet and army were sent to the island; Hippocrates joined a commander, of the name of Himilco, in the attempt at reconquest.

Rome was forced to employ probably 40,000 or 50,000 men in the defence of her imperilled domain; a curious example was then witnessed of her hard military discipline, and politic statecraft. The few thousand troops, who had escaped after Cannae, had, we have seen, been moved into Campania in the agony of the state; but as its strength was renewed, they were banished to Sicily in disgrace. They now entreated that they might be allowed to serve in the field; they were sternly told they might do work in garrisons; the stigma was left, but other soldiers were set free. At Syracuse events took at last a turn which almost secured the ultimate success of the siege.

The aristocratic party had never ceased to conspire; an accident enabled a Roman soldier to discover a vulnerable point in the ramparts. The night of a great festival was chosen for an attack; the Romans marched to the spot in silence, slew and drove away the scanty and drunken guards and having scaled the walls, with deserters and spies as guides, seized the Hexapylum, the key of the land front of the city. Epipolae, Tyche, and Neapolis were now in their hands; Marcellus shed tears, we are told, at the sight, but the thought of compassion quickly passed away; the lives of the townsmen of these quarters were spared; but the fierce old warrior allowed Roman vengeance and licence to revel in plunder and crime.

Achradina and Ortygia, however, were not yet taken; Epicydes, alone in command for some time, sent messengers to the Carthaginian leaders in Sicily; an attempt was made to raise the siege by sea and by land. The Romans, however, were not to be conquered, especially within their fortified lines; Marcellus tenaciously clung to his prey; he obtained possession of a fort by a bribe; faction within the city encouraged his hopes. The Carthaginian Army and fleet remained around Syracuse for several months; but pestilence, as had happened in other sieges, destroyed thousands of men in the marshy flats of the

Anapus, in which their camps were placed; the Roman troops on uplands suffered much less, and a large Carthaginian squadron, which had received orders to land reinforcements and stores of supplies, perhaps owing to treachery, set off for Tarentum.

The place, nevertheless, or rather all that remained of it, held out long, with desperate courage; it fell at last, indeed, by the hands of its own defenders, and of plotters within in the interest of Rome. Epicydes, from whatever reason, took his departure; he was probably endeavouring to obtain succour, but the city was soon given up to anarchy; frightful scenes of violence and blood were witnessed in the savage strife of furious partisans; and the men who represented the government were brutally slain. Syracuse had soon fallen into the power of its armed forces; but these were divided among themselves; the regular army tried to make terms with Marcellus, the Roman deserters effected their escape; the mercenaries thought only of booty and their lives.

Syracuse was betrayed by a leader of these dangerous men; the Romans, baffled as they had been perhaps for two years, (the duration of the siege of Syracuse, and the dates of its successive events cannot be precisely ascertained, as Arnold has remarked, *Second Punic War*), were in no mood for moderation or pity. Marcellus forbade a general massacre, but a crowd of innocent victims perished, the illustrious Archimedes being among these; the magnificent city was ruthlessly sacked, and while the soldiery were given a free hand to plunder, the treasures of art with which the place was filled were taken by their conquering leader to Rome. The fall of Syracuse, however, did not bring the insurrection in Sicily to an end; many cities and parts of the country remained in arms, and the genius of Hannibal, as we shall see, succeeded, even from his camp in Italy, in keeping the flame alive for a considerable time.

While Rome was struggling with Hannibal for her existence, she was thus engaged in war, with many changes of fortune, in Spain, in Hellas, in Sardinia, above all in Sicily—in fact from the straits of Gibraltar to the Dardanelles—and she had to keep watch in force on the Gauls, from the Alps to the Apennines. The efforts she made to sustain and increase her military and naval force, at this juncture, were extraordinary and almost surpass belief. She kept from sixteen to twenty-two double legions on foot—each at this period at least 10,000 strong—she had a fleet of one hundred and fifty, even two hundred quinqueremes, manned probably by 40,000 or 50,000 seamen, besides the troops, like marines, who were held on board.

Her regular forces, on land and sea, must have been not less than from 200,000 to 300,000 men, but she also employed thousands of veterans and recruits in garrisons, seaports, and other points of vantage; she had probably 400,000 men in arms, apart from her guerilla levies. And if we bear in mind that she had lost three tremendous battles, followed by a slaughter unknown in modern warfare, that a large part of Italy was in Hannibal's grasp; that many of her allies were still in revolt, and that, in these terrible years she could only rely on her own citizens and the Latin states, it may safely be said that history can shew no grander example of a national defence.

Nothing could have saved Rome but her dogged constancy, her patriotism, her wise and tenacious government, marked not by genius, but by resolution and craft—but above all was the continued union of orders and classes in the state, which no sufferings or reverses could break or lessen. There was no passionate or wild excitement, no spasmodic efforts, no strife of opinion; the commonwealth placed its gigantic strength with calm reliance in fitting hands.

The senate and the aristocracy all through these years were allowed to do almost as they pleased; to appoint the generals to command in the field, to recruit, supply and distribute the armies on the many points of the theatre of war, to arrange expeditions however distant, to levy the imposts required to maintain the contest, to provide for the necessary wants of the people; and nothing was more admirable than the steadfast trust, the sterling devotion, the self-denying patience exhibited by the nation to its true leaders. The spirit that animated the great republic was made manifest in two striking instances. The citizens were about to give their votes for an untried general, when old Fabius rebuked them, saying, "Such a man is not fit to contend with Hannibal"; the aged *Cunctator* was elected himself, (Livy.)

On another occasion, Titus Manlius, a veteran soldier of the highest merit, but who was half blind and had done his work, had actually been named for the second time consul. "I am unfit to command," the old warrior said, "for I can only see through the eyes of others, this is no time for incapable leaders,"(Livy), and he insisted on Rome making another choice.

The distress and sufferings caused by the strain of the war, as may be supposed, were severe in the extreme. The population of Rome and Latium was being rapidly thinned; the poor husbandman, even the slave was sent off to the armies; the fields were tilled far and nearby women and children. Whole tracts of land were left barren and waste; the necessaries of life, especially corn, increased two and threefold in price, notably during the ruinous war in Sicily, even then, in some measure, a granary of Rome; the misery of the humbler classes was extreme. The pressure of taxation, too, became cruel; the taxes were doubled more than once; and though the state attempted measures of relief, these could only be a very partial remedy. (Arnold, *Second Punic War*, conjectures that the relief was the payment of taxes in kind.)

The condition of part of the domain of Rome, during this period, began to be greatly changed; the small farms of the hardy tiller of the soil became fewer; large pasture lands and slave farms multiplied; the germs, so to speak, of grave ills in the future. Yet the patriotism and the devotion of the ruling orders, and indeed, of all classes, overcame the trial. A graduated property tax was cheerfully paid by the rich, a tax like ship-money was levied to support the fleets, which had been objects of special care since the naval strength of Carthage had seemed to rise. (Livy.)

Examples of loyal unselfishness, too, were noble and frequent; the masters of the slave army, which had been set free, refused to accept compensation for their slaves; contributions of arms and horses flowed into the treasury; trustees were permitted to advance to the state trust-monies; loans without interest were made with little reluctance, (Livy.) Yet all these expedients could not suffice to meet the stress on the over-burdened finances; Rome had to suspend her cash payments; she had her assignats, her bank-restriction, her "green-backs," like other great nations in supreme crises. (Livy.)

Still, even in Rome signs of terror and weakness, of demoralisation, selfishness, and cowardice were not wanting. As has always happened in great national troubles, superstition laid hold of faint hearts; the sky blazed with awful portents and signs; the gods of the great city had forsaken Rome, and gave her no more their benign influence; men, and especially women, turned to strange gods, neglected the honoured rites of religion, sought out soothsayers and false prophets. (Livy.) Vestal Virgins broke too often their vows; matrons were not ashamed to indulge in licence; vice rioted to an extent never known before. The shopkeeping spirit did not prevail in Rome; but even in the hour of the peril of the state, and of the general performance of the noblest duties, merchants were found to haggle and drive hard bargains; contractors wickedly cheated the army; a patrician was guilty of this odious fraud.

Nor were instances of an unmanly and craven spirit unknown; noble youths, after Cannae, had thought of flying their country; hundreds of able-bodied men had tried to escape enlistment; there was much desertion, we have seen, from the fleets. The government and the nation, nevertheless, did much to suppress the symptoms of failing energy; and indeed, they were but as spots on the surface. The observance of the religion of the state was strictly enforced; the worship of gods, save those who protected Rome, was prohibited under severe penalties; teachers of strange faiths were proscribed and banished.

Licentiousness, too, was denounced and punished; efforts were made to restore the old moral discipline; the erring Vestals and their paramours met an awful fate. Frauds and crimes against the state were also treated as they deserved; the would-be fugitives, high as was their rank, were degraded; all who shirked military service were pronounced infamous, and dealt with as the worst kind of criminals. Rome, indeed, "rose to the height of circumstances," not after the fashion of the terrorists of half-mad France, but of a great, stern, practical, and united nation.

In the first months of the year 212 B.C., the prospect for Rome had distinctly brightened. Tarentum, indeed, had been won by Hannibal, (probably taken in 213 B.C., not 212, as some writers have said), and some Greek towns had gone over to him; but the Roman arms outside Italy had made progress everywhere; and Syracuse was on the point of falling. (It seems to have fallen in the Spring of 212 B.C.) It was resolved to make a great effort to take Capua. The city still defiantly held out; but it had not given real aid to Hannibal; it still contained, like most of the rebel cities, an aristocratic party attached to Rome. Twenty-three double legions were set on foot, the largest force Rome had as yet placed in the field; and while thirteen of these were sent to other points of the immense theatre of war, ten were employed against Capua and to oppose Hannibal, who, at this time, was around Tarentum, still engaged in the attempt to reduce the citadel.

The consuls of the year were Quintus Fulvius Flaccus, a stout old soldier, already twice consul, and Appius Claudius, whom we have met at Syracuse; these commanded two Consular Armies of four double legions, the one in Apulia, the other in Campania. Nero, unfortunate as yet, but to become renowned, had two legions, at Suessula near Capua; two were in Apulia, probably near Herdonea, (now Ordona), under Caius Fulvius, a brother of the consul; and two were led by Gracchus, still the chief of the liberated slave army, who held Lucania.

Five armies, fully one hundred thousand strong, were thus to attack Capua, and to confront Hannibal, who had probably not more than fifty thousand men, in addition to a small force under his lieutenant, Hanno, at this moment far to the south in Bruttium.

The war now assumed a grander aspect; the Roman generals had become less timid; ample scope was given to Hannibal's manoeuvring genius, and to his extraordinary skill in the field. The consuls united their armies at Bovianum, a fortress in Samnium, not far from Capua, and from which they could observe Hannibal by the main roads from Tarentum. Capua, in terror, sought Carthaginian aid; and Hanno, by Hannibal's orders, advanced from Bruttium, and, eluding Gracchus on his flank, in a very rapid march, (it seems probable that the Roman Armies were changing their positions at this moment; Arnold, *Second Punic War*), reached Beneventum in safety, and sent word to the Capuans that he was at a short distance, and that they should make haste to secure the supplies, which they could gather in, under his protection, on the spot.

But Beneventum was a loyal Roman colony. Information was despatched to the consuls; Capua hesitated and lost precious time, and Hanno, having been defeated in a well fought battle, was compelled hastily to retreat into Bruttium.

The campaign had opened auspiciously for Rome; but Capua was a place of the first importance; and Hannibal, answering another prayer for relief, succeeded in throwing a body of Numidian horsemen into the already imperilled city. These troops routed a hostile detachment; but the consuls ere long had closed around Capua; they were supported by Nero's forces, a few miles away; by Caius Fulvius and by Gracchus, who seemed to bar an advance of Hannibal; and they doubtless imagined they had nothing to fear. But their mighty adversary baulked their hopes; he threaded his way from Tarentum through all the enemies in his path, who ought to have attacked him on both his flanks, by one of those marches which we cannot trace, but the ability of which cannot be questioned.

He suddenly appeared on the heights of Tifata, (now San Angelos); and he thence looked down, with his army in hand, on Capua and the Roman camps and lines. The effect was extraordinary, almost magical; the Roman commanders had not thrown off the terror the presence of Hannibal inspired; they felt, it has been happily said, (Arnold, *Second Punic War*), as the allies felt when they beheld Napoleon advancing against them around Dresden; and Fulvius and Claudius, good soldiers as they were, drew away from Capua in precipitate retreat. Hannibal entered the joyous city in triumph; he was hailed as a deliverer by hearts for the time grateful; he probably left reinforcements behind; but he was soon in pursuit of the consul Claudius, who, it is said, had marched towards Lucania, while his colleague had found refuge in Cumae.

Hannibal was unable to reach his immediate enemy, who had had a start, doubtless of some days, and who made his escape into the depths of Samnium; but he was master of the country around, and he closed these fine operations with brilliant success in the field. An unexpected disaster had, a short time before, overtaken the arms of Rome in Lucania. Gracchus had been treacherously led into a trap by a Lucanian noble and author of the revolt; he met, as became him, a Roman's death, (the speech which Livy puts into the mouth of Gracchus, is really fine), but the slave army which he had led during five trying years, with continuous success, and which had felt the ascendency of a real chief disbanded suddenly after his fall, and simply, went to pieces.

The senate endeavoured to retrieve this defeat; it hastily put together and sent into Lucania a motley assemblage of some 16,000 men, largely composed of volunteers and recruits; and it incautiously placed it in the hands of Marcus Centenius, a stout *centurion*, but a noisy boaster, and wholly unequal to high command. Hannibal, with an army superior even in numbers, pounced down on the ill-ordered array; it made a fierce and tenacious resistance, but it was surrounded and cut completely to pieces; the historian admits that only a thousand fugitives escaped, (Livy).

Rome had now suffered another great defeat, resembling in some measure the first great defeats of the war. When her generals abandoned the Fabian system, and attempted bolder operations in the field, the genius of Hannibal in offensive movements became, in fact, at once grandly manifest. The consuls and Nero were, for the present, far off; the Roman Army in Lucania had been blotted out; Cnaeus Fulvius was in Apulia isolated and alone. He was an incapable officer, who had done little throughout the campaign but lay in supplies; and—sure mark of incapacity—he had let his troops out of hand, and had lost the authority necessary for a chief. He had laid siege to Herdonia, a revolted town, with two legions and auxiliaries, 22,000 strong.

Hannibal, having got rid of every other enemy, without losing a moment, marched against him. He adopted the tactics which had secured decisive success in his many battles. He drew near with the mass of his infantry in front, but he sent an officer, Mago, with a body of horsemen, to seek an ambush, and fall on the Roman flanks and rear; these dispositions were made at night, and completely escaped his enemy's notice. (I do not think this could have been Hannibal's brother Mago; he had been sent to Spain.) Fulvius, advancing hastily, offered battle next day, but his lines had been unduly extended against the protests of his own officers; his men had become insubordinate, and had lost all discipline; they seem to have insisted on taking their order of battle as they pleased. (Livy's account of the battle is very graphic. He dwells especially on the bad arrangements of Fulvius, on the demoralisation of his troops, and on the skill of Hannibal. It is extraordinary to read these words about Roman infantry.) The contest was over in a short time; the Romans gave way at the first shock, and when they were charged by Mago on both flanks their army was surrounded and utterly destroyed. Of 22,000 men 21,000 fell, Fulvius fled with only 200 horsemen. (Livy.)

The military strength of Rome had, by this time, been developed; she stood aghast for a moment at these reverses, but she had, none the less, twenty-three legions again in the field in the next year of the war, 211 B.C.. In Italy the interest of the contest centred around Capua and the operations that ensued. Little seems to have occurred in the southern provinces. Fulvius and Claudius were not blamed for their inglorious retreat; they were continued in command as proconsuls; the consuls of the year were ordinary men.

The proconsuls, seconded by Nero as before, undertook regularly the siege of Capua; they laid in immense magazines of supplies; drew lines around the place of imposing strength—their camps, it is said, resembled a city; had 60,000 men to complete the investment; and systematically wasted the country for miles in order to keep away the ever dreaded Hannibal. Capua, in affright, sent to her champion once more; he had wintered in Apulia and had moved on to Bruttium in order, probably, to obtain recruits; but he advanced again to the relief of the city with an army perhaps 30,000 strong, supported this time by thirty-three elephants. He took up his former position on Mount Tifata; directed the Capuans to combine their operations with his own; a fierce and well contested encounter followed. The Capuan Army, aided by the reinforcements within, made a formidable onset on the Roman lines; the walls, filled with citizens on their ramparts, rang with shouts; but Claudius forced back the assailants with ease; they were driven into the streets of Capua, beaten.

Meanwhile Hannibal had fallen in force on the entrenchments of the enemy from without; his Spanish infantry did great things; three of his elephants reached the external ditch; one of the legions began to give way; the lines were very nearly stormed and carried. The battle, however, was restored; a gigantic *centurion* behaved like a hero; the elephants were slain as they were driven onward; but the assailants forced the ditch across their dead bodies; and the defence was only maintained by the most persistent efforts. At last Hannibal's troops fell back; they were boldly pursued as they drew sullenly away.

The wise measures of the pro-consuls had now good results; Hannibal was unable to remain in a ruined country. His resolution was at once formed. He sent a Numidian—who threaded the enemy's lines—to let the Capuans know that relief was at hand; and he set off by forced marches on Rome, believing that by this grand and daring movement, he would compel the Roman commanders to break up from Capua, and to hasten to the defence of the threatened capital. (The resemblance between this march and that of Napoleon on the communications of the allies, in 1814, in order to draw them away from Paris, is obvious.) He seems to have crossed the Vulturnus high up the river; he then moved through Samnium, still for the most part friendly; and having passed the great lake of Fucinus, he descended by the Allia into the Roman domain, here following the old track of the Gaulish invasion. (With the best commentators I have described Hannibal as marching through Samnium. Polybius particularly says so; and though Livy makes Hannibal march through Latium, this is very improbable. Latium was still bitterly hostile to Hannibal.)

At the approach of the invincible giant of war, Rome, high as was her purpose, again trembled; she had lost three armies a few months before; assuredly Capua was now lost; the cry went forth that Hannibal was at the gates. The scenes after Cannae were for a moment repeated, but it was for a moment only; order and unanimity were soon restored. (Livy describes the attitude of Rome in his usual graphic manner.) Fabius stood out again the master of the state; an extraordinary levy was made; the walls were manned, the public peace preserved; and a message was despatched to the pro-consul Fulvius—his colleague had been severely wounded—on no account to raise the siege of Capua, but to advance on Rome with 16,000 men only. Accidents added to the city's resources; the two legions employed every year for the defence of Rome happened to be fully mustered and upon the spot; and the Latin colony of Alba, having been informed of Hannibal's march, nobly sent its whole forces to join in protecting its

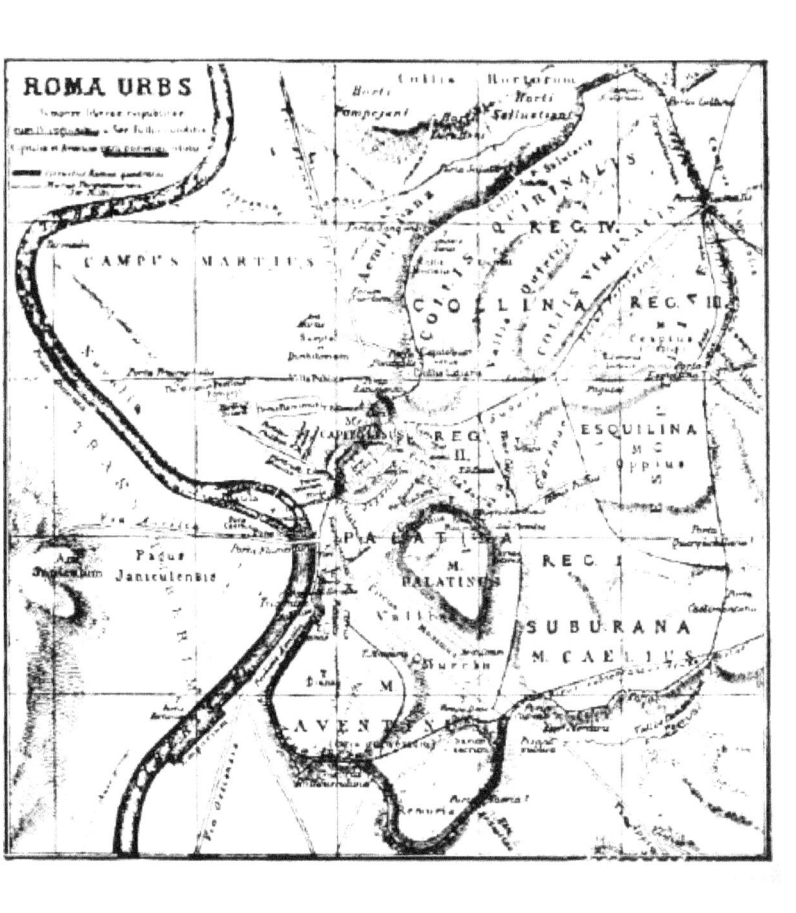

sovereign state. Within a few days Rome was in a condition to defy any efforts her great enemy could make.

Hannibal, meanwhile, had encamped before Rome; he had ridden, with a body of horsemen, to the gates of the capital. We may imagine what may have been the warrior's thoughts, as he beheld the fortified seat of that mighty power, which he had endeavoured in vain, through long years, to crush, defeated as it had been, over and over again; as he gazed on the strong walls of the ancient king, and on the towers and temples rising from the famous hills which he well knew he could not hope to master! He flung, the legend runs, a javelin against one of the gates, (the poetic legends about Hannibal's appearance at Rome are numerous), but he had not contemplated attacking Rome; he was soon on the march with his army southwards, in the belief that his great manoeuvre had been attended with success.

Fabius had, not improbably, accelerated his retreat, the veteran had continued to hold him in check; his apparition was a tale of woe in the annals of Rome for centuries; an altar to a god was placed on the site of his camp; his departure, commemorated in exulting verse, was hailed through long years as a great deliverance. He marched rapidly by the way he had advanced, pursued cautiously by one of the consuls; but he eluded his pursuers until the news arrived that the Roman armies were still around Capua, and that his recent effort had been frustrated; he then turned back fiercely upon his enemy, and defeated the consul with considerable loss. The fate of Capua was, however, now certain; Hannibal gave up an impossible task, and marched as quickly as he could into Bruttium. He had hoped to seize and surprise Rhegium, an important point of vantage by sea; but in this attempt he was also foiled.

The siege of Capua had been going on all this time. A terrible fate ere long overtook the fairest, perhaps, of the great towns of Italy. Since the recent defeat no attempt had been made to force the lines, daily increasing in strength; there was no hope of an army of relief; Numidians, sent out to convey a message to Hannibal, were mutilated and driven back by the enemy. The sufferings of the city became intense; Capua had been a queen of pleasure and riches, the glory of the golden Campanian land; we may conceive what its people felt as they were sinking into the fell grasp of famine. The incidents of that agony are little known; but the popular party seem to have become masters; the nobles ceased to rule or to conspire; some took poison, others sank into silence, awaiting a doom they had too much reason to fear.

A show of inert resistance was prolonged; but Capua was compelled at last to throw open her gates; the Romans entered a place in despair and starved out.

It was the stern, but not unrighteous policy of Rome to lay a heavy hand on her revolted allies; Capua was marked out for pitiless vengeance. Fulvius scourged and beheaded many of the leading men, confiscated the lands and goods of a number of citizens, and carried off an enormous spoil to Rome. A fire in the capital was soon made the occasion for involving the wretched city in a general charge of treason; the senate pronounced an appalling sentence. The remaining nobles were sold as slaves or ruined; the citizens were deported to different parts of Italy; a mixed population was placed in its stead; and Capua was deprived of its civil rights and franchises—it had possessed the coveted citizenship of Rome—and was made a mere thrall of the Roman Government, like the Libyan cities subject to Carthage.

> The city of Capua, bereaved of all its citizens, was left to be inhabited by that mixed multitude of resident foreigners, freedmen and half citizens, who, as shopkeepers and mechanics, had always formed a large part of the population, but all political organisation was strictly denied to them, as they were placed under the government of a prefect sent thither every year from Rome. (Arnold, *Second Punic War*.)

The fall of Capua terrified the rebellious states, and weakened the Phoenician cause throughout southern Italy. The success, however, of the arms of Rome, was balanced by dangers threatening the republic close to its own domain. Etruria, we have seen, had begun to stir, the Latin cities had suffered cruelly, during a struggle protracted for seven years; the appearance of Hannibal before the sovereign capital had spread alarm, even discontent, round the Anio and the Liris. Beyond Italy the strife with Philip had quickened; it was maintained from the Corinthian Gulf to the Strymon; and though Rome never had a great land force engaged, the pressure on her fleets had become extreme, and detached them from the Mediterranean, their chief station, where it was necessary to hold in check the fleets of Carthage.

In Sicily, too, a most trying contest had assumed even more ample proportions. Hippocrates had perished at the siege of Syracuse, but his colleague Epicydes remained; Carthage had sent another great fleet and army to stimulate the insurrection in her own ambitious interests. The cruelties of Marcellus had borne the worst fruits; sixty-six towns had joined the revolt; Marcellus had been compelled to take the field to put down an almost universal rising.

The opportunity was not lost by Hannibal; he despatched a half-caste Numidian, of the name of Mutines, to Sicily to keep up and extend the contest, and this officer, a very able man, justified his great chief's choice, and really accomplished wonders. He carried on the war as Hamilcar had done; seized Agrigentum and defeated Marcellus, at the head of devoted Numidian horsemen; swooped down on the few cities still loyal to Rome; and, in fact, occupied or overcame many parts of the island. It seemed not improbable that Rome would be forced to reconquer Sicily by a great effort of her power.

Just at this time an immense disaster, of which, however, the record is very imperfect, nearly effaced the dominion of Rome in Spain. (I have, with Arnold and the best commentators, made the date of this disaster 211 B.C., not 212 B.C.) The brothers Scipio, we have seen, had carried their arms in triumph, almost to the Pillars of Hercules; they had won over many of the Celtiberian tribes; a great and decisive effort, they thought, would bring the war to an end. (Livy is my only authority here.) They divided their forces into two main bodies,—there were 20,000 auxiliaries of the Celtiberian warriors,—they seem to have marched from the Tagus to the Guadiana, and to have reached, with little opposition, the southern hills of Portugal. (Hénnébert has examined the events of the campaign with great care and thinks the Scipios reached Portugal.)

But Hasdrubal, we have said, had returned to Spain; Carthage had evidently given him large military aid; and Mago, Hannibal's brother, and another Hasdrubal, known as the son of Gisco, were at the head of two armies co-operating with his own. The name of Hamilcar and the great empire he had created at Carthage were still remembered in Spain; Hasdrubal came up with the army of Cnaeus Scipio, and induced the fickle Celts by a bribe to assist him; the treacherous barbarians hastened off to their homes, and the Roman general made a precipitate retreat. Hasdrubal, it would appear, soon joined his lieutenants, and, in a short time, the Roman arms suffered a fatal defeat. Massinissa, still an ally of Carthage, was serving under Hasdrubal in Spain; he had a considerable force of Numidian cavalry; and he succeeded in reaching Publius Scipio, evidently isolated and far away from his brother.

A fierce and doubtful encounter followed; but the Numidian horsemen in their wonted fashion, had contrived to fall upon the enemy's flanks, when the main Carthaginian Armies appeared on the field and utterly routed a greatly outnumbered enemy. (Livy.) Publius Scipio fell fighting bravely with his men; the victors instantly pursued the other Roman Army; it was surrounded in a camp it had formed on a height, and it was slaughtered with its commander almost to a man. (Livy.) The two generals, who had upheld the arms of Rome with such skill and success during seven long years, were thus suddenly removed from the scene; the wrecks of their forces fled beyond the Ebro; many of the Celtiberians declared for Carthage again; the power of Rome in the peninsula appeared in ruin. (Livy.)

To a careful observer the wonderful power of Hannibal as a soldier and statesman appears strikingly in this, his death-struggle with Rome. The time of his grand manoeuvres has, indeed, passed away; he has to contend against the power of Rome at its height; he cannot master more than a part of Italy. But though infinitely inferior in military strength, he defeats Rome in more than one battle, and overwhelms several hostile armies; he is invincible when he appears in the field; his enemies recoil from his dreaded presence. Nothing is more extraordinary than his complete control over the theatre of war in Italy at the time; he moves through hosts of enemies, almost at will; nothing crosses him when he advances on Rome.

This was doubtless largely due to the Roman modes of warfare, but it is a proof also of his pre-eminent skill; it deserves the highest admiration by the student of his art. His resource, too, his power of stratagem, his faculty of command, in a word, his best gifts are, as always, manifest; and if he was less successful than other great chiefs have been in striking at and beating divided enemies, this was largely due to their immense superiority in force, and to the peculiar value in war of the Roman camp. His genius as a politician is not less conspicuous; he does not unite his great league; but he stirs up enemies against Rome wherever a chance offers; this is especially seen in the long war in Sicily, and even' to a certain extent, in the war in Greece.

Yet the wonderful exertions made by Rome, her grand patriotism, and the cooperation of all classes in the state do not less claim the highest praise of History; these have, perhaps, never been equalled, certainly never surpassed; these, we repeat, alone enabled her to cope with Hannibal. The final issue of the contest was still uncertain; if the scales of destiny were on the incline, they were still nearly on an even balance. Hannibal had been, no doubt, on the whole, weakened; Carthage and his allies had done little for him; but Rome, even of late, had been defeated in the field; her energies had been strained to the very utmost; a quarter of Italy was in her enemy's hands; the peninsula she deemed her own was still in a critical state; the power of Carthage at sea had probably increased; the influence of Rome in Spain seemed suddenly blotted out. Might not Carthage yet second her great hero; might not Hasdrubal advance from the Pyrenees, and join hands with his invincible kinsman; might not a great coalition yet strike down Rome?

Scipio

Buckler of Scopio

Chapter 8: The Struggle Slackens—the Metaurus

The ninth year of the Second Punic War had come; the year 210 before the Christian Era. The result of the struggle between Hannibal and Rome, if we survey the position of affairs as a whole, was, we repeat, as yet altogether doubtful. The great Carthaginian had been weakened in the south of Italy, but he was still supreme in operations on the field; he was master of Tarentum, except the citadel. In northern Italy, and throughout the valley of the Po, the authority of Rome was gravely threatened; murmurs were frequent even among the Latin cities: Etruria and the Gauls were in a questionable mood.

Abroad the war with Philip had reached its height; it had been difficult to keep up the Roman fleets, owing to the ill-will of disaffected allies; Mutines in Sicily was conducting a great guerilla war; the Scipios, with the mass of their forces, had perished in Spain. The distress, too, of Rome had never before been so great; the means employed to maintain the fleets and the armies had begun to a certain extent to fail; the treasury was being drained, the finances sinking; the sufferings of the poorer classes had become intense. Evidence of this state of things was seen in the partial decline of the still great military power of the nation; it was impossible to fit out twenty-three double legions; twenty-one only—still a formidable force—were at this critical juncture sent into the field.

The distribution, too, of the armaments of Rome shews how hardly the republic was pressed, (Livy significantly remarks on this. The historian's account of the situation is striking and not unfair, except that he keeps out of sight the dangers of Rome arising from her political and social condition.) Four double legions, about 40,000 men, were required to observe Etruria and the Gauls of the north. A force equal in numbers was engaged in Sicily, where it had become necessary to make a great effort; nine double legions were employed in

Spain, in Sardinia, perhaps in Greece, and for the defence of the city. Four legions therefore only remained; these were to confront Hannibal in Apulia and the southern provinces: the weakest force that had been opposed to him after Cannae.

It was divided into the two usual Consular Armies, and one of these was given to Cnaeus Fulvius Centumalus, a pro-consul of consular rank, and the other to Marcellus, the idol of the Roman soldiery, but only too famous for his late deeds in Sicily, who, with some difficulty, had been made consul. The other consul was Laevinus, a very able man, who had distinguished himself in the naval war in Greece; he was sent to Sicily in the place of Marcellus, who had been intended for that command, but had been kept in Italy by the senate, at the piteous request of the injured Sicilian people, which had declared it could not endure his oppression. (Livy. Arnold, *Second Punic War*.) Significant reductions too were made, at the same time, in the allied contingents.

That so weak a force was arrayed against Hannibal, may have been due to a miscalculation in the Roman councils. The fate of Capua, we have seen, had alarmed the revolted cities; they had begun to fall away from the victor of Cannae. This defection began in Apulia, spread through Samnium, and before long became very general, in most parts of the south of Italy. The senate not improbably thought the movement would be fatal to the military force of the enemy; but if so, it was wholly in error. The Italians had given Hannibal little effective help; they had been exacting, even false friends; they had vexed him and often had hampered his movements; their disloyalty did not reduce his immediate strength.

With superior insight and admirable skill in adapting his means to the ends in view, he took in the situation at a glance, and controlled events like a great captain. He drew in his troops from the garrisons he held; razed to the ground strongholds he had no further need of; in this campaign he seems to have been at the head of forces more numerous than he had had for some time in the field. He certainly was master of the theatre of war in the south: he gained one signal triumph at least. His efforts were first directed against Centumalus, (this Cnaeus Fulvius is not to be confounded with Cnaeus Fulvius defeated at Herdonia on another occasion) who had been endeavouring to regain Herdonia, the scene, it will be recollected, of a previous Roman defeat.

The pro-consul was a bold but an incautious leader, as had so often been the case with the generals of Rome; he had his army in camps around the place, it is said, in a bad position and ill-guarded. Hannibal advanced from Bruttium by forced marches with an army probably of superior strength, fell on an imprudent enemy taken by surprise, and routed him by his wonted brilliant attack, turning both the hostile flanks by the Numidian horsemen. The pro-consul's army was practically destroyed, it lost from 7,000 to 13,000 men, (Livy.) Marcellus—he was at this time in Samnium and had not acted in concert with his ill-fated colleague—made haste to try to retrieve the defeat; he encountered Hannibal at Numistro on the northern verge of Lucania.

The battle was stern and long contested; Hannibal had elephants and Balearic slingers in the field, a sign, perhaps, that he had received some troops from Carthage: of these, however, we have no account. Marcellus was not turned or outflanked and both armies suffered heavy losses. (Livy, as always, makes the best case he can for his countrymen.) But Marcellus was in Apulia during the rest of the campaign; his forces had been greatly reduced; Hannibal remained master of the whole adjoining country. The Roman generals in this year were not sufficiently strong to contend with Hannibal, but their operations had been ill-conceived and very unfortunate.

A sudden revolution at this time, however, brought the insurrection in Sicily to an end and restored the tottering domination of Rome. Mutines, we have said, was the soul of the formidable revolt; he had imitated Hamilcar in his admirable skill and resource. But he was detested by Hanno, the Carthaginian general-in-chief—a creature perhaps of the peace party which disliked Hannibal and all his works; and Hanno had ventured to supersede Mutines and to place his own son at the head of the Numidian cavalry. The indignant half-caste warrior resented the affront, dealt treasonably with Laevinus, the lately elected consul, and in command of a great army on the spot; the Numidians, doubtless at the bidding of their old chief, betrayed Agrigentum to their exulting enemy; the Romans became masters of the main seat of the war in Sicily.

The famous town, the second of the Sicilian cities, another centre of commerce and art, was sacked by a force of soldiers let loose to plunder; Hanno and Epicydes—that remarkable man had continued to serve the Carthaginian cause—contrived with difficulty to effect their escape, but a large part of Hanno's army was cut to pieces; the remains were taken off by the Phoenician fleet. Laevinus inflicted a terrible punishment; the leading men of Agrigentum were scourged and beheaded, numbers of the best citizens were sold as slaves; the cruelties of Marcellus at Syracuse were outdone. These severities, however, a systematic policy of the stern republic, crushed the revolt; the cities in arms submitted without resistance; Sicily was ere long prostrate and at the mercy of Rome.

Laevinus gravely informed the senate that the reign of order and law was restored, and that the islanders had returned to the paths of industry; their harvests were gathered in for his countrymen once more, and this in their distress must have been a godsend. Measures of extreme harshness were taken to prevent even the possibility of a future rising. The great cities of Sicily were disfranchised, immense tracts of land were declared forfeited, the free population was removed from them, they were cultivated by slaves for Roman patricians; Sicily was placed under an exacting official government.

From this time the eventful history of the renowned island was almost a blank for many years; there were no revolutions or series of wars, no vicissitudes of tyranny and democratic licence, scarcely a trace of the animation of the rich and free life of Hellas; the conquered people acquiesced in servitude. Sicily was an oppressed province and a slave farm of Rome until the horrors of the great Servile War were seen. (Arnold, *Second Punic War.*)

While Rome had thus unexpectedly regained Sicily, she had escaped the consequences of her late disasters in Spain. The accounts of all that occurred in the Spanish peninsula at this juncture are so meagre, and have been so distorted by the Roman chroniclers, that we find scarcely anything that can be deemed trustworthy; but it appears certain that the Carthaginian generals did not follow up their splendid success, and made no effort to crush the Roman power in the Ebro.

They were divided by jealousies and mutual dislike; Hasdrubal, the son of Gisco, especially became the declared enemy of his greater namesake, the son of Barca; and besides they acted harshly to the Celtiberian tribes and attacked and plundered Celtiberian princes; in a word, they showed to a proud and suspicious race how odious could be the oppressive yoke of Carthage; and this seems to have been the chief reason why they gained no advantage from a decisive victory. (Polybius, a real historian, obviously gives the true reasons of the failure of the Carthaginian generals to make use of their success.) In these circumstances the remains of the defeated armies were given time to recover discipline and strength; they were rallied by an officer of the name of Marcius, of inferior rank, but a capable man; and Marcius even led them against the enemy once more, though we may reject the tale that he won a great battle, in which 37,000 Carthaginian soldiers were slain. (Livy is ashamed to approve of this palpable lie.)

He was, however, evidently a real commander, and was chosen by his army with acclaim as its chief; but as this vote incensed the government at home, he was superseded by Nero, who, after the fall of Capua, was sent to Spain with large reinforcements to restore the arms of Rome. Nero, if a mere legend deserves credit, advanced with little resistance to Andujar, (Hénnébert identifies Illiturgis with Andujar, but the whole story is improbable in the extreme), that is from the Ebro to the Guadalquivir, and he had surrounded Hasdrubal and brought him to bay, when Hasdrubal, with genuine "Punic faith," effected his escape by a cleverly devised stratagem. All that is historically known is that at this time the defeat of the Scipios and of their two armies did not permanently injure the Roman cause in Spain, and that the cause of her enemy made no real progress.

Fortune had favoured Rome beyond her deserts in the year of the war which was now expiring. She had reconquered Sicily through a mere accident; she had maintained her hold on Spain despite grave reverses, mainly owing to the faults of her enemies, but she had failed in Italy in the struggle with Hannibal. About this time a youth was elevated to high command whose destiny it was to overthrow her great enemy, to carry her victorious arms to the far East, where her very name was hardly as yet known, and to be one of the most brilliant and attractive figures on the illustrious roll of her soldiers and statesmen.

Publius Scipio of the great Cornelian house, was the son of one of the generals who had fallen in Spain; he had saved his father, we have seen, in the fight on the Ticinus; he had distinguished himself on the fatal day of Cannae; he had taken an active part in protesting against the base conduct of the beardless patricians who had thought of abandoning their countrymen after that immense disaster. (Livy.) He was now in his twenty-seventh year only; he had hitherto filled but an inferior civil office. But Nero had been unfortunate in Spain, the senate had resolved to appoint a successor to him; young Scipio was elected by the citizens in his stead. (The date of the election was probably the end of 210 B.C. or the beginning of 209 B.C. Arnold, *Second Punic War*. I follow Arnold's dates for Scipio's conduct of the war in Spain.)

We may disregard the legend that he offered himself as a candidate because no other could be found; his father's name probably had much weight; he was nominated pro-consul with consular powers and placed in command of all the Roman Armies in Spain. He set off from Ostia with 11,000 men and thirty large war-ships. It is remarkable that on his first appearance on the stage of events he seems to have had the influence over the hearts of men which was one of his best and most distinctive qualities. (Livy. The historian of course only repeats a tradition, but his language is striking.)

We may pause for a moment to consider the lineaments of this remarkable man at this the beginning of his splendid career. Scipio was not one of those mighty spirits which have given a marked turn to the course of history, or have even permanently affected their own era. In war he was not to be named with Hannibal, though it was his fortune to overcome Hannibal; a brilliant and able soldier, indeed, he was a general of the second order; on one memorable occasion he made a mistake that placed his country in the gravest danger. Nor had he supreme political genius; he was a great citizen in times when the state was well ordered; he could not have moulded, like Caesar, a worn-out republic into an all-powerful empire.

But Scipio was the first and one of the noblest of the famous rulers who drew subject races into allegiance to Rome by wisdom, clemency, and kindly sympathy; who built up the structure of Roman conquest on the solid foundations of good government; who caused Roman civilisation to extend less through the sword than the power of justice. The Greek historian has compared him to Lycurgus, (Polybius), such was his reverence for law and established usage; but he possessed many of the best gifts of a practical statesman, especially that of understanding the views of others, and of adapting his conduct to them.

He was a diplomatist of extraordinary skill; like Marlborough he subjugated those with whom he came in contact. Scipio, too, had the confidence of greatness in itself; he perhaps believed that he had a divine mission; standing aloof from the ordinary herd, in a kind of kingly state, always composed, serene, and, in a sense, inscrutable, he persuaded the great body of his simpleminded countrymen—for the age of sceptical criticism had not come for Rome—that he was a favourite of the gods and could accomplish anything. (Polybius and Livy dwell especially on this.) For the rest he had the charm of the highest culture and of a stately presence:

> Uniting Hellenic letters with the fullest national feeling of a Roman, an accomplished speaker and of graceful manners, Publius Scipio won the 'hearts of soldiers and of women, of his countrymen and of the Spaniards, of his rivals in the senate and

of his greater Carthaginian antagonist. (Mommsen.)

Unquestionably as we survey his career we see that he owed much to fortune; he fell on times exceedingly propitious to him; but fortune, it has been truly said, is only constant steadily and through life to superior men.

Having landed at Tarragona, long a Roman stronghold, Scipio made preparations for the campaign at hand. He singled out the brave Marcius for special honour; the influence of the young commander was soon felt by a devoted soldiery; he skilfully conciliated the Spanish tribes; his growing renown, it is said, reached the ears of his enemies. (Livy.) Meanwhile news of grave impending dangers had arrived at Rome; the officer at the head of a Roman fleet that had made a descent on Utica, had learned from prisoners that Carthage was about to make a great effort not only to restore her empire in Spain, but to enable Hasdrubal to cross the Pyrenees and the Alps and to lead a large army into Italy to assist his brother. The nation felt another hour of stern trial had come, and, as was its wont, rallied loyally around the government.

It was in vain that *tribunes* of the commons said that the same men should not always command the armies, and that this was inconsistent with the welfare of the state (Livy); the citizens entrusted supreme power at the instance of the senate to its former generals; the aged Fabius was made consul for the fifth time, Fulvius, the conqueror of Capua, for the fourth; Marcellus, already often consul, was named proconsul. Immense exertions were also made to send imposing forces into the field; but these shew how heavy was the strain on the state; hardly twenty legions appear to have been raised, and the city legions were required to observe Etruria. (Livy.) The arrangements, however, for the coming contest were in the main well-conceived and prudent. Taught by the severe lesson of the year before, the Roman commanders had determined to combine the mass of their forces against their great enemy; and while detachments were engaged in guarding the north, the chief armies were directed into southern Italy.

The principal objects in view were to regain Tarentum, for the place gave Carthage and Philip a point of vantage, and the citadel—it was still in Roman hands—was repeatedly in danger of being starved out; to subdue towns still in revolt in the south; and at the same time to hold Hannibal steadily in check, and if it was not possible to overthrow him in a great pitched battle—for the Roman generals, with the exception of Marcellus, perhaps, were still afraid of this—to cripple him, to surround him, and at last to crush him by the weight of overwhelming numbers. In this plan of operations, there can be little doubt, we see the wise and cautious but somewhat timid mind of Fabius.

The Roman Armies were in full movement in the early summer of 209 B.C.. Marcellus, with two double legions and an auxiliary force, marched from Venusia against Hannibal, who was at this moment in Apulia not far from Cannae; Fulvius, with his consular army of two legions, entered Lucania and quickly reduced the province—no doubt already turning in all its parts to Rome—by a judicious display of good sense and clemency; Fabius, with his two double legions, and a contingent besides, had reached Tarentum in a short time, and a motley assemblage of levies, drawn for the most part from Sicily, laid siege to Caulon, a seaport town of Bruttium, which seems to have been a point of importance.

Armies, therefore, certainly 100,000 strong, were arrayed against Hannibal, who had not 50,000 men, comprised in a great measure of inferior troops; and as the power of Rome was being rapidly established everywhere, his position became one of extreme danger. He might almost be driven into the sea by Marcellus, who harassed him from a safe distance—at least be cooped up in Apulia and made powerless; and if Tarentum and Caulon were lost and Lucania and Bruttium wholly subdued, he would be cut off from his base in Italy, deprived of support, even of the means of subsistence, and perhaps be compelled to lay down his arms.

But Hannibal's enemies were divided and far from each other; he extricated himself from a most difficult strait by operations that bring out his genius in war, but that required for success a really great captain. He contrived to catch Marcellus at fault, turned fiercely upon him, perhaps near Asculum, the scene of one of the great fights with Pyrrhus, and routed his adversary in a bloody encounter. Marcellus, however, was an heroic soldier; he was superior to fortune, and fell on Hannibal again; a murderous and long doubtful battle was fought; the elephants, still a part of the Carthaginian force, pierced by the terrible Roman *pilum*—the legionaries had learned to deal in this way with the mighty beasts—threw part of the Carthaginian line into confused disorder, and the Roman historian has had the boldness to say that his countrymen gained a decisive victory. (Livy.)

This, however, is a characteristic falsehood; indeed, the historian exposes it himself. Marcellus was compelled to return to Venusia, and was so worsted and enfeebled that he could not appear on the field during the rest of the campaign; his conduct, indeed, so unlike himself, provoked suspicion, nay, indignation, at Rome. (Livy.) Hannibal evidently won a hard-fought battle, and he marched directly from the field into Bruttium, his object having been to shake off Marcellus and to turn against his enemies in the south. Hannibal, as had so often happened, made good his way without opposition through hosts of enemies; he must have crossed their communications and done much damage; yet Fulvius and Fabius did not attempt to unite their armies and to risk an attack.

This timidity, seen over and over again, especially when he was much inferior in force, attests the ascendency he still had in the field and the consternation his presence still produced. He raised the siege of Caulon without striking a blow, the hostile levies taking refuge in flight; he then marched to the relief of Tarentum; he had been informed that the place was quite safe, and could hold out for a considerable time. He arrived on the scene to behold an immense disaster. What he may have felt has been often compared to the anguish and wrath that shook Napoleon when he found Paris in the hands of the allies on his return from his great march eastward in 1814. (Arnold, *Second Punic War*.)

An accident, caused, it is said, by a love intrigue, had made the Romans masters of the great city, the legions had entered the streets in triumph, the Carthaginian commandant and his troops had been slain; Tarentum, a station of supreme importance, the base of the invaders in the south of Italy, opening a communication with Carthage and Greece, and affording stores of supplies by sea, had passed again into to the power of Rome. Hannibal endeavoured to lure Fabius out by a "Punic trick," convinced that he could annihilate the old consul if he had the chance; but the wary *Cunctator* was not to be deceived; "the omens were adverse, he would not stir," an excuse he probably offered to his impatient soldiery.

The scenes that followed the fall of Tarentum were such as had been witnessed often before when a rebel allied city was captured; a free rein was given to slaughter and licence; an enormous store of the choicest booty was sent off to Rome. The spoil was nearly equal to that of Syracuse, but the conduct of the victorious generals was, in one respect, different. All was grist that came to Marcellus's mill; the fierce veteran had stripped the temples of Syracuse of their divine images. Fabius was not less willing to harry and plunder, but "his piety forbade him to deprive Tarentum of its gods." (Livy.)

Tarentum was doubtless a splendid prize; but it was the only prize won by Rome in Italy in this striking and most interesting campaign; her immense efforts in the south had been almost baffled. Marcellus had really been well beaten; Fabius and Fulvius had not dared to attack Hannibal; great as was the superiority of his foes in numbers, the master was still invincible on the main theatre of the war. Murmurs of anger and disappointment—and we cannot be surprised—broke out again from the lips of the citizens; leaders of the populace denounced the nobles once more; the outcry against Marcellus, we have said, was fierce and bitter. A short time previously, too, the great ruling state had been threatened by a danger that might have proved fatal. Latium, we have seen, had been in a dubious, nay, angry mood since Hannibal had marched on Rome; the Latin cities had suffered much from the ravage of war and social distress; many Latin soldiers had fallen in the great defeat of Centumalus only a few months before.

Twelve of the colonies of Rome, among which names of Latin cities certainly appear, refused at this juncture to send contingents or to pay monies to maintain the war; they seemed on the verge of armed rebellion. The courage that had not yielded to Cannae was for a brief time shaken; the cry went forth from Rome "that all was over at last; the colonies and the allies would betray the city to Hannibal." (Livy.) Eighteen colonies, however, remained loyal: the conduct of the government was a model of prudence and statecraft. The consuls remonstrated with the disaffected twelve; these remonstrances were vain, and they held their peace; but they led the deputies of the eighteen into the senate's presence, and that august assembly and that of the citizens thanked their faithful dependents in the name of the state.

This wise and touching appeal may have saved Rome; the twelve returned to their old allegiance, the whole affair was buried in judicious silence. But the extent of the peril in which Rome was placed appears in the historian's significant words. Livy wrote in a subsequent age:

> These eighteen colonies, shall not even now lose their due meed of glory. They were the men of Signia, of Norba, of Saticula, of Brundusium, of Fregellse, of Luceria, of Venusia, of Hadria, of Firmum, and of Ariminum; and from the lower sea the men of Pontia, and of Paestum and of Cora; and from the middle parts of Italy, the men of Beneventum and of Æsernia,

and of Spoletum, and of Placentia and of Cremona.

Meanwhile Scipio had accomplished great things in Spain, which promised decisive success for the arms of Rome, and redressed the balance of adverse fortune in Italy. In the spring of 209 B.C. the Carthaginian generals were far apart from each other, Hasdrubal near Saguntum, Mago in Castille, Hasdrubal Gisco far to the south-west at Cadiz, and they were notoriously at angry feud with each other. Scipio seized his opportunity with boldness and skill; he crossed the Ebro with an army of some 30,000 men; a Roman fleet accompanied it along the coast; the combined military and naval force attacked Cartagena, a creation of the first Hasdrubal, and a principal centre of the power of Carthage.

The garrison, if isolated and small, made a brave resistance; it was repulsed after a fierce sally; but the Romans failed in an effort to scale the walls, their ladders being too short to reach their summit. A salt-water lagoon, however, extended along the western front; this was almost dry at the lowest ebb; the walls on this side were low and ill-guarded. Scipio characteristically let it be known that the god Neptune had promised him aid, (Polybius), and the Roman Army crossing the marsh when the tide had fallen, made itself master of the defences at the vulnerable point, and broke into the captured fortress. Scipio put an end to a massacre which had just begun; he was very different from Marcellus and men of that type; at his command the soldiery ceased to plunder indiscriminately and spared the city in their power.

The spoil taken at Cartagena was immense; a whole fleet fell into Scipio's hands, besides engines of war of many kinds, and a great store of supplies and treasure; the place itself indeed was of the first importance, commanding as it did the Mediterranean towards the east. But the conduct of the young general in this his hour of triumph was of more advantage to Rome than even his brilliant conquest. Scipio gave proof of clemency hitherto unknown; the citizens were allowed to return to their homes; the Carthaginian garrison were made prisoners, but though sent to Rome they were not harshly used; the artisans and workmen of the great arsenal were allowed to do their ordinary work; the best mariners were employed in manning the Roman war-ships. The wise policy too of the Roman commander was made manifest in another direction.

There were 300 Spanish hostages in the place; these were set free, with presents, and permitted to depart; a Spanish princess was treated with delicate courtesy; Spanish women received no harm or insult. The effect on the impressionable Celtiberian people was great; it was noised abroad that "this Roman youth was a god, that he subjugated not by the sword but by kindness." (Livy.) The cause of Rome in Spain made rapid progress again; that of Carthage as rapidly declined. The contrast indeed between the leaders of the contending nations could not fail to strike a race proud and sensitive throughout its history; it was like that which was presented in the Spain of the nineteenth century by Wellington and the rapacious and quarrelling French marshals.

The fall of Cartagena and the increasing weakness of the Carthaginian dominion in Spain may have prevented Hasdrubal at this juncture from endeavouring to join hands with his brother; if so, we can form a just estimate of the enormous importance of these acts of Scipio. It is certain, however, that throughout the year rumours flew that Hasdrubal was about to march; he was probably in communication with the Gaulish tribes of the Po; and Etruria all but broke out into open revolt from Rome. A vigorous demonstration checked the rising, but the senate wisely increased the strength of the Roman fleets, evidently in order to secure the command of the sea, which probably had for some years been doubtful, and to close the Mediterranean to a Carthaginian attack whether made by Hasdrubal or from any other quarter.

Preparations were now made for the campaign of 208 B.C.; twenty-one double legions seem to have been set on foot; Hannibal was once more to be confronted in the south by a powerful combination of armed forces. The outcry against Marcellus had come to nothing; he "silenced clamours," the Roman historian tells us, "by reminding the citizens of his great deeds" (Livy.); he was elected consul for the fifth time; his colleague was Quintus Crispinus, one of his Sicilian officers. Hannibal was at this time in Apulia—his favourite station throughout winter—at the head of probably 40,000 men; he had to oppose the armies of the two consuls, an army of two legions which held Tarentum, a formidable position whether in front or rear, and one legion at least which lay around Capua; he was thus threatened again by overwhelming numbers.

The plan of the Roman operations, in the first instance at least, was faulty against a great captain. Marcellus alone was to engage Hannibal; Crispinus was to lay siege to Locri, a seaport of some value along the coast; the other armies were to remain as they were; and thus the whole Roman forces were once more to be far away from each other.

This dangerous plan, however, seems to have been abandoned; almost as soon as the campaign had opened, Marcellus and Crispinus had united their armies to observe their adversary, perhaps to attack him; a detachment from Sicily and one of the Tarentine legions were told off to conduct the siege of Locri.

An incident had ere long occurred which proves the ascendency which Hannibal had in the field. The two Consular Armies were as numerous as his own, and probably composed of better troops; they had drawn near him between Venusia and Bantia, (near the Bandusian fountain of Horace); they held positions in which a defeat might have been fatal to him, for it would have penned him up in a nook of Apulia. But he had learned that the legion at Tarentum was on its way to Locri; he weakened his army by 5,000 men—nothing but the certainty that he was safe could have justified this; and this detachment, issuing from a dexterously laid ambush, annihilated the ill-fated enemy it assailed.

The operations of the Romans were all but brought to a close by a disaster which deprived them of both the consuls. The hostile armies confronting each other had had a few trifling affairs of outposts; a hill thick with woodland divided their camps; this had been occupied by a body of Numidian horsemen. Marcellus and Crispinus, with a weak escort, rode towards the eminence where not a man was to be seen; the enemies fell on them from the thicket where they had lain hidden, Marcellus was slain on the spot, his colleague wounded to death. As in the case of Flaminius, Hannibal gave his stout old adversary funeral honours; he never failed to respect a noble foeman; it would have been well had Rome meted out the same measure to himself. With Marcellus, one of the most striking figures of the Second Punic War passed away from the scene. The veteran was not a great captain; his cruelties in Sicily did his country much harm.

But he certainly conducted a battle with skill; he was never turned on his flank by Hannibal, as had repeatedly happened to Roman generals, and he had an heroic spirit that rose superior to defeat. He was perhaps the only Roman commander who had not been stricken with fear when Hannibal was present in the field, and he fairly defeated his great antagonist in one instance. In subsequent ages Marcellus was held in higher honour by his countrymen than very superior men, than Fabius, Scipio Africanus, and above all Nero, for he did not despair of Rome in her darkest hour; he was her "sword," never in the scabbard, always ready to strike. (The fine lines of Virgil on Marcellus,

Æneid, vi. are well known.)

After this disaster the two Consular Armies appear to have gone into winter quarters; they had retreated on Capua and Venusia. Hannibal swooped down on Locri and raised the siege, gathered up supplies in Bruttium and Lucania; in a word, was as usual master of the southern provinces. At the same time, memorable events were occurring in Spain, big with great consequences in the near future. The policy of Scipio had had the best results; Celtiberian tribes had entreated him to become their king—he declined the honour with characteristic grace—and had sent their warriors to his standards; Indibilis and Mandonius, two of the chief princes of Spain, became his loyal and powerful allies.

He strengthened his force by a contingent of men from the fleet, and marched with a great Roman and Spanish Army from Tarragona, across the Sierra Morena, hoping that the peninsula would soon be his own. Carthage seems, meanwhile, to have made an effort to restore her declining power in Spain; Massinissa crossed the straits with a mass of light cavalry; he was perhaps followed by Phoenician and Libyan footmen. But the Carthaginian generals were still divided and at odds with each other; they were separated by wide distances as before; above all, Carthaginian tyranny had isolated and weakened them in a country almost to a man hostile. (Polybius makes sensible remarks on the conduct and policy of Carthage in Spain.)

Hasdrubal, at this juncture, stood alone in a strong position near a place called Baecula; his colleagues were many marches away; but he seems to have had his arrangements made to advance at all hazards across the Pyrenees, and then to descend by the Alps into Italy. (Hénnébert identifies Baecula with Cazorla on a branch of the Guadalquivir. Others think the place was Baylen.)

He was attacked by Scipio with superior forces: the Roman historian tells us he suffered a heavy defeat and lost not less than 8,000 men. (Livy.) This assuredly is a pure invention; Hasdrubal left the field with an unbroken army, carrying a number of elephants in his train; he marched northwards nearly through Spain, and having got over the Tagus, probably near Madrid, he made for the Pyrenees at their western verge by the Bidassoa and San Sebastian—scenes of great deeds in the Peninsular War—and was soon unmolested in the depths of Gaul. (With Arnold, Mommsen, and other commentators, I have described Hasdrubal as crossing the Pyrenees by the extreme west. This may be inferred from Livy's narrative.) No enemy had observed his movements or followed in his track.

Why Scipio, after his supposed victory, did not pursue Hasdrubal in his march to the Tagus, bring his enemy to bay, at least hang on his rear, we can only conjecture, for we have no evidence. It is probable that he was beaten, at all events crippled; and as Mago and Hasdrubal Gisco appeared on the scene soon after—too late, however, to assist their colleague, (Livy, this might have been a description of many French operations in the Peninsular War)—Scipio fell back on Tarragona as his principal base, and spent the summer in strengthening his position in Spain, and in bringing the Spanish tribes into alliance with Rome. He seems to have closed the Pyrenean passes in the east, and perhaps as far as the line of the Segre (Livy); but he sent no detachment near the western passes.

Hasdrubal was lost sight of and permitted to escape. This inactivity and slackness—in striking contrast with Roman operations on another theatre of war, to which we shall soon direct attention—proves that Scipio, brilliant soldier as he was, was not a commander of the first rank, (I entirely concur with Colonel Dodge in his estimate of Scipio in these operations, *Hannibal*), nor can we accept the Roman flatterer's excuse, (Livy.) that he feared a great concentration of hostile forces and was compelled to defend the course of the Ebro. He must have known—for the rumour had spread far and wide—that Hasdrubal's object was to leave Spain and to co-operate with his brother in Italy.

The Roman general's first object should therefore have been to take care that Hasdrubal should not elude him; if he was not sufficiently strong to strike his enemy down, he should certainly have dogged his advance to the Pyrenees, and not have let him reach Gaul unobserved and intact. He did nothing of the kind, and made an immense mistake, (Mommsen points this out very clearly); and it is simply untrue that he was obliged to confront the Carthaginians in great force on the Ebro, for Mago and Hasdrubal Gisco, when Hasdrubal had gone, betook themselves, the one to the Balearic Islands, the other to Portugal, hundreds of miles distant; they were evidently unable to face the Romans in Spain. (Livy.) It appears tolerably plain that, as has been often seen where war is not conducted by superior genius, Scipio sacrificed the paramount for secondary ends.

A diplomatist rather than a warrior, his chief thought was to establish the ascendency of Rome in Spain; he stayed in Catalonia for this purpose; he neglected to pursue or even observe Hasdrubal; and as the event was soon to shew, he exposed his country to the gravest peril, which was averted only by the admirable resource and activity of a single man,

Hasdrubal wintered, it would seem, among the hills of Auvergne (Livy); he avoided southern Gaul, and the Greeks of Marseilles, devoted to Rome throughout the contest; he probably wished to conceal his movements as long as possible. Like Hannibal, he had a well-stored war-chest; he induced numbers of the Gauls to follow him in his great venture (Livy); he sent envoys across the Alps; he was promised the support of 8,000 Ligurian warriors. (Livy.) We do not hear that he had much success with the Insubres and the Gauls of northern Italy; these old allies of his brother's had hardly stirred for years—a passage of the war, we have said, that has not been cleared up;—discontented Etruria made no sign.

But he was certainly at the head of a considerable force; and when it was reported from Marseilles that he was approaching the Alps, there was another scene of terror at Rome. (Livy.) The republic, however, made ready to contend against the two sons of Hamilcar on Italian soil; the efforts it made for the coming campaign, that of 207 B.C., were immense. The situation was favourable in many respects; the war in Sicily had come to an end; Sardinia was subdued and quiescent; Scipio was in the ascendant in Spain; Philip of Macedon was thinking of suing for peace; a coalition, always feeble, was all but broken up. It was possible, therefore, to employ in Italy the greatest part of the military power of Rome; that power was again raised to the highest level it had reached in the Second Punic War.

Twenty-three double legions were again set on foot (Livy); of these fifteen—that is, from 150,000 to 160,000 men—were to confront Hannibal and his approaching brother; eight only were sent on foreign service. The difficulties of the state appear distinctly in the means required to collect these great levies. The allies who manned the fleets were compelled to furnish soldiers; no exemption or excuse was allowed; Scipio sent 11,000 men from Spain; a slave army was placed in the field again. (Livy.) The Roman historian significantly remarks that the supply of youth fit for war was beginning to fail, (Livy.)

Much difficulty was found in placing fitting men in command of the forces to be employed in Italy. Fabius had by this time passed his eightieth year; Fulvius, the warrior of Capua, had done his work; the "Sword of Rome"—Marcellus—was gone. For the supreme office of consul, the senate and people chose Nero, hitherto not fortunate, but instinctively felt to be a true soldier, and Marcus Livius, a veteran of the old Illyrian War, but who had not been in the field for years, having been accused indeed of ignoble fraud. Nero and Livius had been declared enemies; but patriotism and the sense of duty reconciled them; and never was colleague more ably seconded than Livius was by Nero in the hour of trial.

Other officers of note also received commands, the *praetor* Lucius Porcius Licinius the most conspicuous; we find among the names that of Varro of Cannae, not impossibly even now a popular favourite. The disposition of the Roman Armies was dictated by the situation on the theatre of war, Nero, with four double legions, was to confront Hannibal in the south, while two double legions threatened the Carthaginians' rear; Livius and the *praetor* Porcius, in the north, were to keep Hasdrubal back with four double legions; Varro, with two double legions, was to observe Etruria; one legion was to guard Capua, two Rome. The principal object was to hold Hannibal in check, and to prevent Hasdrubal from joining hands with him; and their junction would be obviously difficult in the extreme.

For the Roman forces, greatly superior in strength, would be in middle Italy, in a central position, between hostile armies in the south and the north, divided from each other by hundreds of miles; they would possess interior lines on the scene of events; and Hannibal and Hasdrubal, thrown on exterior lines, would find it a most arduous task to unite. The situation, too, was evidently such that one part of the Roman Armies, especially as these were so superior in numbers, might be employed in restraining the isolated enemy in its front, while a second part, moving by the nearer distance, might be brought into line with another Roman Army opposed to the other unsupported enemy, so that he might be defeated and crushed by this concentration of strength. The Roman generals, in a word, were in a position to strike those brilliant strokes against divided foes which no commander, in modern war at least, has struck so decisively as Napoleon.

The campaign of 207 B.C. had come, a memorable passage of the Second Punic War. Hannibal had received no assistance from Carthage, perhaps for years; his old soldiers must have nearly disappeared; his army was largely composed of Italian levies; he could hardly have had 40,000 men to oppose enemies nearly twofold in numbers. He seems to have marched northwards in the first instance in order, no doubt, to learn something about his brother; but he was ere long back, and he moved through Bruttium, gathering in forces from the few strongholds still in his hands.

If we are to follow the Roman historian's account, his levies were defeated by the legions which held Tarentum and lay on his rear; he lost, we are informed, 4,000 men. (Livy.) Meanwhile, Nero, 42,500 strong, (Livy)—and he commanded the flower of the Roman soldiery—had advanced against Hannibal, who had, perhaps, 30,000 bad troops; the hostile armies met at Grumentum, (now Agramonte), on the Aciris, a little stream of Lucania. The battle was remarkable for this feature: Nero, "imitating the arts of his enemy," concealed a detachment behind a hill to fall at the proper moment on the Carthaginian rear; this was one of the very few occasions where a Roman general tried a flanking movement throughout the whole of the great war. (Livy. The historian sneers at this as unworthy of Roman downright fighting.)

The army of Hannibal proved to be raw and unsteady; Nero charged the troops in front before they were formed; but Hannibal's presence and exertions restored the fight (Livy); the result of the day was still uncertain when the Roman detachment, issuing from its hiding place, attacked the enemy. The rout, Livy assures us, was all but complete; Hannibal lost nearly 9,000 men, nine colours and six elephants (Livy); only the wreck of his army effected its escape. Nero seems to have won a hard-bought victory; but his great adversary could not have suffered much; he was evidently still master of his movements in the field; he marched northwards on Canusium in Apulia, in order certainly to draw near Hasdrubal, at least to obtain information about him. The consul hung on his enemy and pitched his camp near him; but he did not venture to attack Hannibal, a circumstance that renders his late success doubtful.

Meanwhile Hasdrubal had made his way through Gaul, had crossed the Alps and descended into the north of Italy. He had avoided, as before, the south of Gaul, and had certainly followed the route of Hannibal from the confluence of the Rhone and the Isère; he had found little difficulty in overcoming the great mountain barrier. (Livy.) The Gaulish tribes, in fact, had learned by this time that their territories were but an avenue for the assailants of Rome, and that their own independence was not threatened (Livy); and parts of the engineering works of Hannibal, facilitating the passage, still existed. (Livy emphatically dwells on this.) Hasdrubal reached the valley of the Po sooner than was expected (Livy); he easily mastered the Stradella Pass; but he lost time in laying siege to Placentia, which defied his efforts, as it had withstood his brother.

In this conduct he has been severely blamed; but Placentia was a fortress of great strength, capable of holding a considerable force; and he may have had good reason to try to reduce it, and not to allow a grave danger to menace his rear, especially as the Celts of the adjoining countries did not generally rise in his favour, and some tribes remained in their allegiance to Rome. Be this as it may, he drew off from Placentia and marched by Ariminum to the eastern seaboard, where the Apennines reach the Umbrian plains; he bore back in retreat the *praetor* Porcius, who had advanced some way into the valley of the Po. We do not know what the strength of his army was; but he had probably 60,000 or 70,000 men—a motley array, however, largely made up of Gauls; he had ten elephants only, and he was very weak in cavalry, the best arm of a general of his race.

Porcius effected his junction with the consul Livius at Sinigaglia, long a thriving Roman settlement; they were at the head of from 40,000 to 50,000 men, Roman troops better than those of their enemy; and Varro and 20,000 men were at no great distance. Hasdrubal ought, perhaps, to have risked a pitched battle, or slipped round the left flank of the consul and *praetor* and hastened as rapidly as possible to join his brother; but he could hardly have hoped for a real victory; his advance through middle Italy would have been through a host of enemies; we can hardly condemn him for adopting a less hazardous course. (I cannot agree with Colonel Dodge, *Hannibal*, in his very unfavourable estimate of Hasdrubal's operations throughout this campaign. Hasdrubal, no doubt, was not Hannibal; but Polybius, an excellent judge, thought him a great general.) He sent several messengers to inform Hannibal that he would soon be on the verge of Umbria, and that he expected Hannibal to join him in the south of the province, about Narnia, only a few marches from Rome.

The position of affairs on the theatre of war had ere long become of extreme interest. Hasdrubal approached the *praetor*'s and consul's armies, which, with Varro on his flank, barred a further advance; Hannibal remained at Canusium, held in check by Nero, and with enemies at Capua and Tarentum on his flank and rear. More than two hundred miles lay between the brothers; hostile forces and garrisons were in their path; the difficulty of effecting their junction was immense; and yet such was the superiority of Hannibal in the field, and such his extraordinary power of manoeuvre, that it was far from insuperable, nay, could have been overcome, if his adversaries made a single false step, even shewed inactivity or remissness.

The situation for Rome had become very critical; what would

be the result if the victor of Cannae passed by or defeated one of the opposing armies, and, meeting Hasdrubal at Narnia, stood at the head of from 90,000 to 100,000 men? An accident and the genius of a single man prevented a junction of forces, which might have proved momentous. The messengers of Hasdrubal were intercepted and made prisoners near Tarentum, having missed Hannibal; Hasdrubal's despatch was forwarded to Nero in his camp; the consul instantly formed a resolve, which was one of the most masterly ever formed in war.

He sent letters to Rome entreating the senate to make all ready for the defence of the city, to close the roads from Narnia, to call in the legion at Capua; and selecting 6,000 footmen and 1,000 horsemen, the best of his army, he set off with this detachment for the north, in order to join Livius and Porcius, and to overpower Hasdrubal. He left a *legatus*, Catius, to resist Hannibal; Catius must have had 35,000 men and a Roman camp to oppose to any attack made by Hannibal, who certainly was not in greater strength; and Hannibal besides had a foe in his rear at Tarentum. The movement of Nero, therefore, was not too hazardous; with all his arrangements it was that of a great captain.

The consul took his departure, doubtless at night; he had concealed his intentions from his own chief officers. But after a forced march, when pursuit was no longer possible, Nero called his wondering soldiers together, and addressed them in confident and impassioned language. Their mission was to come up with and destroy Hasdrubal; he was leading them to a victory he would make certain; Rome had her eyes on them; the glory would be all their own. The legionaries broke out in stern acclaim; their march along the admirable Roman ways was like the sweep of an Apennine torrent. The peasants on their route supplied them with carts and food; the troops hurried on by night and day; all felt that celerity was the first object; veterans and young men in arms flocked to the colours.

On the seventh day, (Arnold's *Second Punic War*), we are told, of this extraordinary march—an average, if the tale be true, of thirty miles a day. (I do not believe Nero could have made thirty miles a day; but the march was one of wonderful rapidity)—the consul had joined his companions in arms; his troops entered the camp in the darkness; precautions were taken that their presence should not be discovered. A council of war was instantly held; Livius and Porcius wished to give the weary men repose; but Nero insisted on an immediate attack; he had to return upon Hannibal after overthrowing Hasdrubal. (Livy's account of Nero's march, is very spirited. He does full justice to the boldness, the energy, and the judgment of the consul.)

The Carthaginian Army was now face to face with the Roman; the two camps were only half a mile from each other; Hasdrubal had ridden out with an escort to observe the enemy. His eye fell on some rusted shields and worn-out horses; the hostile camp seemed very full of men; he was hesitating what to do, when the loud blast of trumpets sounding a double note made him aware that this was a sure sign that he was in the presence of two consuls. Fear came on him, and it is not surprising; his great brother and his army must have succumbed, and Livius and Porcius, with Nero's legions, were close to him in overwhelming numbers. He waited till nightfall and at once decamped; his object was to cross the Metaurus, a river but a few miles distant, flowing in a deep valley between wooded and steep banks; and behind this strong defensive line perhaps to accept battle. But his army lost heart in its hasty retreat; the guides seem to have led him astray; the half-barbarian Gauls had become disordered in wild drunkenness (Polybius dwells on this); his march was retarded by crowds of stragglers.

He knew that the enemy was in pursuit; there was no longer time to get over the stream; he felt that he must fight before he could attempt the passage. He had probably about 60,000 men; he drew up his army along a range of uplands overlooking the valley of the Metaurus at hand. He placed his left wing, the untrustworthy Celts, behind a hill of difficult ascent, hoping that the obstacle would secure them from attack; his best troops, Phoenician, Spanish, and Ligurian warriors, formed his centre and right wing, and were drawn up on lower ground sinking into plains beyond his front. His ten elephants were ranged before his centre; he seems to have had scarcely any cavalry. His position appears to have been strong; but he was cramped in his movements; he had a river far from easy to cross at his back.

The enemy ere long appeared on the field; the consular armies came into line. Their combined force was about 55,000 men, all, but a few auxiliaries, Roman soldiers; they were supported by their ordinary bodies of horsemen. (Arnold, *Second Punic War*, says that the Romans "enormously outnumbered" Hasdrubal. This seems to be incorrect. According to the best authorities Hasdrubal had about 60,000 men; the Romans, two Consular Armies, some auxiliaries, and Nero's contingent reinforced on the march. They could not have been more than 55,000 strong.)

Nero on the right wing confronted the Gauls; Porcius commanded the centre, Livius the left wing, opposed to the other parts of the

Carthaginian Army. The battle was fiercely contested for hours; the hill screened the Celts, who remained motionless; but the Phoenician, Spanish, and Ligurian troops fought with steady constancy and devoted courage. The elephants made some impression on the enemy's line, but maddened by wounds given by the terrible *pilum*, they broke loose, rushing over the field "like ships without rudders," trampling down friend and foe; they were nearly all slain by their own conductors. The result of the day, however, was still uncertain, when it was decided by a magnificent effort of Nero, the very same as that by which Ramillies was won, the most perfect of Marlborough's victories, one of the finest exhibitions of genius on the field. The consul had endeavoured to storm the hill that covered the Gauls, but failing in this, and seeing the Gauls did not stir, he drew a considerable part of his troops from the wing he commanded, moved them behind the line of the Roman battle, and flung them suddenly on the right flank and the rear of the enemy.

All then became disorder in the Carthaginian battle; the usual scenes of butchery and ruin followed; and if we reject the Roman chronicler's account that 56,000 men were slain (Livy)—the true number was probably 10,000 (Polybius)—the army of the invader was not the less destroyed, the Metaurus doubtless swallowing up a panic-stricken crowd of fugitives. Hasdrubal, who had fought to the last moment, rode into the ranks of the Romans when all was lost; he met a soldier's death, the Roman historian admits, "worthy of Hamilcar's son and Hannibal's brother." (Livy.) He unquestionably was a very able man, if not the equal of his immortal kinsman. (Hasdrubal may perhaps be criticised for not having parried Nero's stroke by drawing the Gauls from his left to oppose the forces thrown on his right. But the Gauls were worthless; he had hardly any cavalry; he probably would have been too late. Hasdrubal seems to me to have been unfairly condemned for his conduct in this campaign.)

Nero hastened from the Metaurus to his camp in Apulia, to take charge of his army again; he had left it, he knew, in Hannibal's presence. He sullied his grand achievement by an ignoble deed; the head of Hasdrubal was flung into the Carthaginian lines; when Hannibal was made aware of the ghastly relic, he bowed his head with grief, and "beheld the coming doom of his country." (Livy.) There was no time, however, for hesitation or regret. Hannibal drew off his army and was ere long in Bruttium, having gathered together every available man. Nero, victor as he was, did not venture to follow.

Meanwhile a load had been lifted from the heart of Rome; she had been apprised of her late great deliverance. The city had been in an agony of suspense when it became known that Nero was marching northwards; the intelligence of the battle was at first hardly believed; the minds of men were divided between hope and fear. At last messengers of high rank from the consuls arrived; the despatch was lead in the senate, then in the Forum; "Rome had been saved, the enemy's army destroyed." (Livy.) Amidst the general exultation order was preserved, and religion had the first place in the hearts of the people; a solemn thanksgiving of three days was decreed; the temples of the gods were crowded with reverent worshippers. Ere long Rome betook herself to her daily round of toil; no sentiment was so profoundly felt as that men could now breathe and do their work in liberty; they could buy, sell, and take their ease without the dread of Hannibal.

At the close of the year the consuls obtained a triumph, an honour that Fabius and Marcellus had not received, a sight that had not been seen for many terrible years. Livius rode in the kingly chariot with its four white steeds, for the victory had been won in the consul's province; Nero rode only as a companion by his side. The spectacle was gorgeous with its characteristic pomp, the procession through the decked-out streets, the shouting crowds, the soldiery in their pride, the spoils, the trophies, the lines of the captives, the offerings at the shrine of the supreme god of the Capitol.

But the eyes of all turned on the great soldier to whom it was due that this glory had been achieved for Rome, whose genius and energy, it was felt, had decided the contest. Strange to say, however, Nero was never in high command again; his nature was haughty, fierce, repulsive; the nation was beginning to put its trust in Scipio, in his youth of brilliant exploits, in his attractive qualities. History not the less pronounces that no Roman general was the peer of Nero in the Second Punic War. In these years, as on all occasions, the pre-eminence of Hannibal in war was grandly apparent. He made, indeed, no one such decisive march as that by which the Metaurus was won; but his operations in the campaign of 209, in which he stood between divided enemies, are admirable illustrations of the military art. He certainly defeated and crippled Marcellus; but for an accident he would have saved Tarentum and crowned the finest movements with complete success. How too he continued to keep his hold on the south, and to be master of the situation for years in the midst of hostile armies two and threefold in numbers, is extraordinary and very difficult to explain.

The timidity of the Roman generals must largely account for this. As always, the energy and perseverance of Rome commands the sympathy and praise of history, especially when she was almost sinking under the pressure of distress, and when her twelve colonies and cities threatened revolt; her tenacity alone carried her through the fearful trial. But she had produced besides one general of the first order; Nero made as perfect a use of his interior lines and of his position between adversaries far from each other, as was ever made by Turenne and Napoleon; his march is one of the most wonderful of which we possess a record; his movements at the Metaurus are a masterpiece on the field.

Scipio too emerges upon the scene; and if he made one capital mistake and was a dashing rather than a consummate warrior, his exploits in Spain, his politic wisdom, his natural authority foreshadowed his subsequent career. The war was now turning completely against Hannibal, the great nation was getting the better of the great man. Rome had dissipated the coalition, such as it was, which his genius had endeavoured to form against her; she was victorious from Asia Minor to Andalusia; she had an overwhelming superiority of military force in Italy.

Carthage throughout the war had almost abandoned Hannibal; her base and short-sighted government had never perceived that Italy was the decisive point on the theatre of war, and that her first interest was to support her hero with every available horse and man; she had been hankering of late after her lost empire in Spain; and her generals in that country had ruined her cause by their quarrels. Hannibal was now isolated in the extreme south of Italy with a dwindling and bad military force; he had probably not more than 40,000 men to oppose to 200,000 trained soldiers of Rome. Yet Rome still hesitated to attack the giant of war; she did not attempt to drive him out of Italy; the hunters of the forest still feared the fangs and the spring of the mightiest of the Lion Sons of the Barcae.

Chapter 9: The Struggle Closes—Zama

The men in power at Rome seem to have thought with Hannibal, that the Metaurus had assured the approaching fall of Carthage. The war indeed, they well knew, was not yet over; they did all that they could to confine their foe within the south of Italy where he had taken his stand, and to make it impossible for him to repeat his great marches, or to strike his dazzling strokes in battle. Two Consular Armies were regularly engaged in confronting Hannibal on the verge of Bruttium; one double legion lay in Capua, another in Tarentum; from 60,000 to 70,000 Roman soldiers were thus opposed to less than 40,000 of many races and tongues, to a considerable extent mere rude levies.

But the forces on land and sea were largely reduced; and if a fleet maintained the contest in the East, and the army of Scipio in Spain was reinforced, a great part of the military strength of the state was employed in taking vengeance on the Gauls who had joined Hasdrubal, and on trampling down disaffection in Etruria. Rome began to feel herself mistress in her own land again; the intense strain on her energies in a death struggle of many terrible years, was relaxed; the republic turned its attention, in some measure at least, to relieving the misery and suffering caused by the war, and to re-establishing its authority throughout Italy. Strenuous efforts were made to restore agriculture almost blotted out in many districts; peasants were encouraged to return to their wasted homes and fields; ruined villages were rebuilt in some places, perhaps at the cost of the state.

Measures were adopted too, to uphold the national credit, and to repair the declining finances; parts of the magnificent Campanian land, which had been confiscated after the fall of Capua, were sold to defray the public debt; patriotic loans were paid off, paper money was redeemed. At the same time strict enquiries were held into the maladministration, the frauds, the abuses, which had inevitably arisen, in different ways, amidst the confusion and the stress of the war; and guilty functionaries were disgraced and punished. The domain of the state was also enlarged by the annexation of thousands of acres of forfeited lands, the territories of rebellious allies; these were colonised or fell into the hands of the ruling orders. The last embers of revolt were quenched, Lucania especially was reduced to subjection; and a severe example was made of the twelve communities, which had been faithless at a great crisis of the war. They were compelled to furnish largely increased contingents; special taxes, it seems, were imposed on them. (Livy; Mommsen.)

This policy, intelligible as it was, when the prospect of peace appeared not distant, and Rome was emerging from a fiery ordeal, nevertheless protracted the course of the war, nay made its results uncertain almost to the last. Hannibal still boldly maintained his hold on Bruttium; for four long years the generals of Rome were afraid to attack him; they were satisfied if they kept him within the province.

Not one of them, indeed, was a remarkable man; Nero, the only captain fit to cope with Hannibal, was not sent into the field again, for he belonged to the unpopular Claudian house, and, as we have said, he was a proud unbending noble; Scipio, it is tolerably certain, did not like a contest with the warrior of Cannae, in the extreme south of Italy. Year after year the Roman annals told the same story; nothing decisive was attempted against the great son of Hamilcar; the war languished in Bruttium and had no results (Livy); the terror Hannibal still inspired prevailed at Rome, his very name was equal to a great army. (See the remarkable speech of old Fabius, Livy. It is of course a mere tradition but the veteran *Cunctator* is made to express a fear that Hannibal might even yet advance on Rome.)

During this whole period, opposed as he was to a military state that could have destroyed him had it made an effort to put forth its strength, the great Carthaginian lost only one town, Locri, captured, too, by defection, and from the sea: he fought only one pitched battle, in which he probably was not worsted—for the Roman account is not trustworthy—and his enemies certainly suffered defeat in Bruttium. (Livy.) In these circumstances Hannibal still remained master of the situation in his recess of Italy; his conduct and arrangements once more gave proof of his supreme genius in every kind of warfare. He abandoned all the towns he had held, except the Greek port of Croton which gave him a good harbour, and the means of obtaining aid from Carthage; and while he seems to have retained the command of the whole adjoining region for many leagues, he sought for and found a strong position, where he could stand firmly on the defensive, and defy the attack of enemies very superior in force.

The headland of Lacinium, (now Capo di Nao, near Cotrone the ancient Croton), near Croton, at the extreme verge of the gulf of Tarentum, gave him the point of vantage which was his object; he fortified this with extreme care, as his father had fortified Pellegrino; he made his lines a great entrenched camp, to hold his army still unconquered in the field; and he had the support of a Carthaginian squadron ready to carry his troops and himself away, should they be obliged to embark. In this position Hannibal stood for two years (Polybius, it was here that Hannibal left his record of the march across the Alps), invincible, dreaded, waiting on events; he improved month after month his array of levies; and though these were largely comprised of Bruttian peasants, and probably never formed a thoroughly matured army, they proved that under the inspiration of the mighty master they could fight heroically on his last fatal field.

What was the position, and what the thoughts of Hannibal, while he stood in this Torres Vedras of Italy exposed to the enormous military resources of Rome? He received no assistance from his ungrateful and base government; he must have learned that the power of Carthage in Spain, on which he had mainly relied, was tottering to its fall. (Livy.) Yet he retained his perfect confidence in himself and his cause; he made no overtures of peace to Rome; though the war had evidently gone against him he seems to have proudly hoped to the last.

And nothing is more certain than that he maintained his absolute ascendency over his troops, in adverse as well as in prosperous fortune; he welded together his motley host of European and African races until it became really formidable again; it followed its great chief with implicit trust and obedience. (Livy, though a systematic libeller, cannot withhold his admiration of Hannibal at this conjuncture.) He may have believed that Carthage at the eleventh hour would make a great effort and come to his aid; he may have hoped that succour could yet arrive from Spain; he may only have had that complete faith in his genius and his sword, which great warriors feel; at all events he never gave way to despair. And yet the prospect around him was becoming more and more dark; the great league he had always endeavoured to form against Rome had by this time been completely dissolved.

The war between Philip and Rome had lasted for years; and though Philip had deserted Hannibal and had made no attempt to descend upon Italy, he had evidently assisted the arms of Carthage. But Philip ere this had made peace with Rome, (206, 205, B.C.), and left her free in the East to turn against her enemies elsewhere. The Ætolians, who had been the allies of Rome, and had borne the brunt of the war with Macedon on land, had suffered many and heavy defeats; the Greek states which at first had supported Rome had become indignant at the cruelties which Greek citizens had suffered at Roman and Ætolian hands, and were hostile to the encroaching republic.

The Ætolians patched up a peace with Philip, notwithstanding angry protests made by the senate; the king seized the occasion to come to terms with an enemy he had good reason to dread. Rome, with characteristic statecraft, dissembled her wrath, and made a treaty with the court of Macedon; she made slight concessions, but had really triumphed in the East. The only result of the protracted conflict was to deprive Carthage of hope of much aid from Philip, and to disclose to a conquering and ambitious state, the jealousies, the discords, and the weakness of the Hellenic world. The Second Punic War opened the way for Rome to the East.

Meanwhile the empire of Carthage in Spain had disappeared amidst wars and troubles. These events had a marked bearing on the results of the great contest, and must therefore be glanced at in some detail. Scipio, we have seen, had sent reinforcements from Spain, when Hasdrubal had made his great march into Italy; the Carthaginian government, always intent on recovering its power in the Spanish peninsula, had despatched one of its generals, Hanno, across the straits; and Mago—he had returned from the Balearic Islands—and Hasdrubal Gisco, united for once, attempted to stir up the Celtiberian tribes in the Castilles.

Their efforts, however, came to nothing; Marcus Silvanus, one of Scipio's lieutenants—he had been appointed as a kind of Mentor to the youthful commander, but had soon recognised his proper place—defeated Hanno, and made him prisoner; the rising in the midland provinces was easily quelled; and Lucius, Scipio's brother, closed the campaign by seizing the important place of Oringis, in Andalusia, a Phoenician stronghold. (Oringis has not been identified with any modern town.)

In the following year, 206 B.C., Scipio gained a great victory, which he evidently thought decisive. Carthage made once more a convulsive effort. Mago and Hasdrubal Gisco united their forces, from 50,000 to 70,000 strong, composed mainly perhaps of Celts, but including

4,000 of Massinissa's troops; they marched to the Guadalquivir overrunning the country. Scipio advanced from Tarragona with an army of four Roman legions, and of Spanish auxiliaries, probably, with cavalry, nearly 50,000 men, (Scipio had probably received back the contingent he had sent to Rome in 207 B.C.); the hostile forces met at a place called Silpia, it is not unlikely the Seville of this day. The operations that followed bore witness again to the capacity of Scipio as a great soldier, as contradistinguished from a great master of war.

The armies confronted each other for several days, without making a really forward movement, the Romans, as usual, holding the centre of the line, their Celtiberian allies on either wing; and the Carthaginian generals, in the belief that this would be the order of their enemy's battle, ranged their best troops, the Africans, against the hostile centre, and opposed their Spanish levies to their own countrymen. Scipio, however, changed his dispositions, evidently at night; he placed the Spaniards in the centre, and the Roman horse and foot on his wings; and remembering doubtless the lesson the Trebia had taught, he made his soldiery eat a plentiful meal, and led them at daybreak against the enemy, who was taken by surprise and caught in a trap.

The Roman cavalry and infantry turned the Carthaginian flanks by a double attack very ably directed—Scipio knew how to manoeuvre on the ground—the elephants in front of the Carthaginian line, as was now often happening, threw parts of it into disorder, by trampling upon its broken ranks; the Africans in the centre remained almost motionless, awaiting the Spaniards who did not even charge, and Massinissa's horsemen seem somehow to have been at fault. (The Battle of Silpia, or as some call it of Baecula, is very well described by Polybius and by Livy. Both historians explain Scipio's manoeuvres and arrangements very clearly, and dwell on the fact that the Carthaginians were caught without having had food.)

The Carthaginian Army was almost cut to pieces; the Spaniards forsook a lost cause; Mago fled to Cadiz, Hasdrubal Gisco into Africa; Scipio returned to Tarragona after a brilliant triumph. He reported from his headquarters that the war in Spain was over. Scipio, believing that the peninsula had been subdued, now turned an attentive eye towards Africa. It is hardly probable, as his eulogists have said, that he had already resolved to finish the war, by assailing Carthage within her own domain, and thus compelling Hannibal to leave Italy. But he knew that his father and uncle had, years before, become allies of Syphax, then a foe of Carthage, and though Syphax had suffered a severe reverse, and had returned to his allegiance to the Phoenician state, the Roman general hoped that he would be able to attach the great Numidian prince to the Roman cause.

Scipio sent a lieutenant Laelius to make overtures; but Syphax replied that he would treat only with the representative of Rome on the spot, and Scipio set off from Cartagena to effect his purpose. Fortune favoured the young ambitious commander; he narrowly escaped falling into the hands of Hasdrubal Gisco, at the head of a large squadron; his two war-ships could have made no resistance; they eluded the enemy by a mere accident. The generals of the great belligerent states met under the hospitable tent of Syphax; he entertained them with barbaric pomp; and Hasdrubal Gisco, the Greek historian says, was so struck by the diplomatic arts of Scipio, by the charm of his conversation, by his attractive graces, that he exclaimed, "That man will be more dangerous in peace than in war." (Polybius.)

Syphax perhaps made a treaty with Rome (Livy); but Hasdrubal Gisco gained the amorous king over by giving him Sophonisba, his fair daughter—the heroine of a famous and dark tragedy—and Syphax became a fast friend of Carthage. Scipio, however, ere long succeeded in another quarter; his success was to prove of supreme importance. He had already tampered with Massinissa, sent him presents, set free a kinsman who had been made prisoner; it is not improbable that the apparent remissness of Massinissa's cavalry on the field of Silpia was due to the fact that he had begun to waver in his military faith.

The Numidian—a cavalry chief of a very high order—had an interview with the Roman commander soon after he had returned from Africa; the fascination of Scipio was all powerful; Massinissa joined his arms with those of Rome. The alliance which ultimately gave Scipio the support of thousands of fine horsemen was in the highest degree fortunate; but for Massinissa, Rome would not have conquered at Zama.

Important events, meanwhile, had taken place in Spain; the peninsula was in a state of dangerous ferment. Mago, who, we have seen, had taken refuge at Cadiz, had probably at the instance of Hannibal—he never missed an opportunity in war—stirred up a rising in Andalusia; several towns broke out in revolt from Rome; the excesses perhaps of the Roman soldiery contributed to the far spreading defection. Scipio advanced from the Ebro to the Guadalquivir once more; Illiturgis, or Andujar, was stormed and plundered; Marcius, the brave soldier referred to before, subdued Castulo, now Cazorla; the population of Astapa, a town always true to Carthage, closed a desperate resistance like that of Saragossa, by a horrible immolation of their women and children.

Spain, however, remained for some time disturbed; it exhibited the temper, which made it for ages the most untamed of the provinces of Rome. Scipio fell sick and his death was reported; Indibilis and Mandonius, the two leading chiefs, who had been his submissive allies and friends, after the fashion of the emotional Celt, always attached to persons rather than any cause, rose suddenly in arms against Rome; a host of fierce Celtiberian clansmen appeared in the field against the foreign invaders.

After a struggle of some months, for a time doubtful, the insurrection was quenched with blood; the peninsula passed again under the Roman yoke. But in the interval a much graver danger had threatened the ascendency of Rome in Spain. Scipio had great influence over his soldiery; he could charm, attract, win their hearts in success, but, unlike Hannibal, he could not subjugate and make an army a mere instrument of his will; and he was repeatedly lax in enforcing discipline. A large division of his forces rose in mutiny on the pretext that their pay was withheld; these troops were chiefly composed of Italian allies, who had been hardly treated, and heavily taxed; Mago, not improbably, had taken a secret part in instigating the disloyal revolt.

The mutineers were so bold and insolent, that they actually made two private Latin soldiers their chiefs; for a time affairs in Spain wore a very ominous aspect. Scipio, however, recovered from his illness; he soon brought his army to its allegiance again by combining mercy with a severe example. In the presence of the repentant legions thirty-five ringleaders were scourged and beheaded; an amnesty was then proclaimed for the crime of the past.

It was now the fourteenth year of the contest, the year 205 B.C.; at every point but one, on the theatre of the war, Rome had triumphed over a world of enemies. Hannibal, indeed, remained defiant in Bruttium; but in every other part of the Italian land, in Sardinia, in Sicily, in the East, in Spain, the supremacy of the great republic had been assured. A direct attack on Carthage was now deemed imminent; the peace party, which seems to have been in office, made an attempt to avert this by a feeble expedient. (Mommsen.) Mago was ordered by the Phoenician Government, (Livy states this in the most unequivocal language), to set off from Spain with the remains of his army, perhaps to endeavour to join hands with Hannibal; this diversion might at least prevent invasion at home.

Hannibal had nothing to do with this vain project, (Arnold, *Second Punic War*, is in error in saying that Hannibal approved of Mago's enterprise), he could not hope that Mago with a small force could succeed where Hasdrubal had failed with a great army, or that he would be able himself to move out of Bruttium; he evidently expected that if he was to receive aid it was to be by troops sent from Carthage and landed at Croton. Mago set sail from Cadiz in the first months of the year, even perhaps a few months before; he had a fleet of some warships, and about 14,000 good troops; the expedition is one of no little interest. He made a fruitless descent on Cartagena; but he reached the Balearic Isles in safety; he stayed for a short time at Minorca—its celebrated port still preserves his name (now Port Mahon); he finally disembarked at Genoa, having been reinforced by seven elephants and nearly seven thousand men.

Whether Rome had at this moment lost the command of the sea, or Mago's squadron had slipped through her fleets, or Scipio, who had laid up his ships at Tarragona, (Arnold, *Second Punic War*, seems to me to praise Scipio, as a general, far too highly. It is difficult to excuse him for letting Mago escape from Cadiz, and reach Genoa after staying at Minorca), deserves blame, we cannot tell with the information we possess; but Mago had made a descent on Italy with an armed force sent by sea from Spain; had Hannibal been able to accomplish this, with his original army of 102,000 men, or even Hasdrubal with his smaller army, the destinies of the world might have been changed.

Mago, the brother of Hannibal, we must recollect, a very able and well-tried soldier, gained one of the Ligurian tribes to his side; and he was soon in the lands of the Insubrian Gauls, who, remembering doubtless his brilliant conduct in the great and decisive fight of the Trebia, sent a number of warriors to his camp. He was much too weak, however, to advance southwards; yet Rome made preparations to resist his attack. Six legions were marched to defend the Apennine passes, between Ariminum and Arretium; among these was the old slave army.

Meanwhile Scipio had gone back to Rome bearing the trophies and spoils of many victories. His career had been one of all but unbroken success; the subjugation of Spain was a terrible loss for Carthage; and he had made the one great conquest of the Second Punic War. He was welcomed in the imperial city with joyous acclaim; his youth, his converse, his presence, won the suffrages of all; he was elected consul by an enthusiastic vote. He had soon unfolded his plans to the senate;

he would descend upon Africa, attack Carthage, and thus force Hannibal out of his lair in Italy.

He encountered, however, a steady opposition on the part of the elders in that august assembly; they despised his graces and popular arts; they suspected him of being an aristocratic demagogue; they especially condemned his laxity and softness in military command. (Livy, probably from tradition.) The aged Fabius—he was approaching his ninetieth year—made himself the spokesman of a party of great influence; he denounced in severe but sensible language the project of assailing Carthage before Hannibal had been defeated and destroyed. (Livy, put the words the mouth of Fabius.) It was obviously a difficult strategic question whether Scipio or the *Cunctator* was right; but assuredly, looking at the position of affairs on the whole, if Rome was to attack Carthage in her own territory and so compel her great adversary to return home, the task ought to be undertaken with a very powerful force, and this the republic could easily send into the field.

Carthage, no doubt, was vulnerable in the extreme in Africa; but the disaster of Regulus many years before, proved that she could be formidable in a defensive struggle; and Hannibal, in Bruttium, was not distant, in possession, it would seem, of a great fleet. It was possible, therefore, for the mighty warrior to elude the Consular Armies in his front, to land in Africa, and to combine his forces with those of the Carthaginian government. Besides, Syphax was an ally of Carthage, and could bring into the field thousands of hardy warriors, many of these the celebrated Numidian horsemen.

An immense array of military power, directed by the victor of Cannae, might thus be assembled in the Libyan plains to resist any efforts the invaders should make; and it was essential, for this reason, that the Roman Army should be, as was quite feasible, of imposing strength.

These considerations must have been apparent to Scipio, and to the ruling powers at Rome. But the jealousy and distrust of the senate increased when it learned that the young general had threatened to appeal to the citizens from its decree, should it refuse him the conduct of the war in Africa, (Livy); and the controversy became envenomed and bitter. The party led by Fabius was for a time opposed to giving Scipio any command abroad; but through the interference of the *tribunes*—representing the people—a compromise was ultimately made. Scipio bowed to the will of the supreme power in the commonwealth; he was allowed to carry out his ambitious design; he was to be free to land in Africa, and to attack Carthage. But the consent of the senate was grudgingly given; the arrangement was only a half measure; the expedition was to be attempted with forces much too weak for so vast an enterprise.

It may be affirmed with confidence that 100,000 men were required to place the success of the invaders beyond the reach of probable adverse chances; for, not to speak of Mago, far away in the north, Hannibal and Syphax, we have said, might be able to unite their forces with those of Carthage, and these might be rendered formidable in the extreme. But Scipio was only given the army in Sicily, composed of the two veteran legions which had fought at Cannae, with the addition, perhaps, of a third legion; and though he was allowed to raise volunteers, he could hardly hope to oppose more than 30,000 or 40,000 men to an enemy who might be certainly fourfold in numbers.

We shall not say with the great German historian that he was "sent upon a forlorn hope," (Mommsen), but his military strength was quite inadequate; and the splendid success he finally achieved cannot blind the impartial student of war to the grave strategic mistake that was made, and of which he must partly bear the blame. Rome, infinitely superior to Carthage in power, was actually inferior upon the field on which the fate of the war was decided; and had Hannibal had 5,000 Numidian horsemen, he would have been victorious on the great day of Zama.

The young consul had soon repaired to Sicily, and made preparations for his daring venture. He harangued the survivors of the beaten troops of Cannae, hinted that they had been hardly treated and were not to blame, and promised they should yet have their revenge on Hannibal. He especially conciliated the leading men of Sicily, induced hundreds of the young nobles to enlist—these he afterwards exchanged for Roman horsemen;—his influence in the island became, in a word, absolute. Yet his brilliant career was well-nigh cut short; his adversaries in the senate all but effected his disgrace.

Scipio had conducted the expedition to Locri, where he had crossed hands with Hannibal for the first time; he left a subordinate, Pleminius, in the place, when captured, and this officer, accustomed to the loose discipline of his chief, was guilty of frightful cruelties and odious acts of rapine. Fabius and his adherents threw the blame on Scipio; it was actually proposed that he should be recalled and be deprived of his command. (Livy.) Rome, however, declared for her favourite again; Scipio after the expiration of his year of office was made pro-consul with consular powers, and virtually retained this position until the end of the war. Meanwhile the magic of the renown of the conqueror of Spain had attracted thousands of volunteers from Italy to his camp; even the maritime allies fitted out a fleet for the descent.

All was in readiness towards the close of 204 B.C.; Scipio set sail from Sicily with 40 war-ships and 400 transports; but his army, at the highest computation, was only 35,000 (Livy) strong, an insignificant force to endeavour to subdue Carthage. The progress of the Roman arms seemed at first decisive; Scipio laid siege to the ancient town of Utica, and though the Libyan cities did not rise, as of old, in revolt, the invaders had soon mastered large parts of the country. The feeling at Carthage for a time was that of sheer despair; the community of slave-owning nobles, of wealthy traders, of a city populace, was feeble in itself, and had been enervated by long misgovernment; the ignoble peace party had submission in its mouth.

But a Semitic race has over and over again given proof of heroism when confronted with peril at home; all that was best and worthiest in the great capital flew to arms. A levy hastily raised and led by a great noble, Hanno, was easily defeated by the Roman soldiery, but this was only the first sign of resistance. Hasdrubal Gisco contrived to array something like an army, Syphax joined his kinsman with his Numidian hordes, and Scipio was not only driven back, beaten, but was compelled to abandon the siege of Utica.

The defects of the Roman strategy then became manifest. Had Hannibal, as well might have happened, learned at this conjuncture the actual position of affairs in Africa, he might have embarked his still large force at Croton—there seems to have been nothing to prevent the movement—and had he once landed in the tracts round Carthage and joined Hasdrubal and Syphax in the field, he ought to have been able to annihilate the invading army.

By this time Massinissa had joined Scipio, but as yet with only a small band of horsemen. The Numidian prince had been at war with Syphax and had lost his kingdom after a series of defeats; he was thirsting for revenge, and brought to the Roman camp the experience and the skill of a real cavalry chief. Scipio and his army now went into winter quarters, fortunately not molested by any hostile force; and the Roman commander, with characteristic art, made overtures to Syphax, in the hope of detaching him from the Phoenician alliance.

An incident had ere long occurred which, despite the apologies of Roman eulogists, has thrown a dark shadow on Scipio's fame, but which was followed by momentous results. The camps of Syphax and Hasdrubal Gisco were at hand; they were a huge enclosure of huts made of light wood and reeds. Scipio, while the negotiations were going on, sent spies to observe them and make a report; and then, when made aware how vulnerable the enemy was, he suddenly broke off his parleys with Syphax and gave the hostile camps to the flames, having surrounded them in force on every side at night.

Massinissa was the soul of the enterprise; the slaughter and destruction was immense; assuredly no such instance of "Punic faith" can justly be laid to the charge of Hannibal. This disaster had a terrible effect on the arms of Carthage; Syphax and Hasdrubal Gisco, indeed, still kept the field; but Scipio boldly took the offensive, attacked his weakened and hardly-pressed antagonists, and routed them in a battle fought in the "Great Plains," a short distance only from the Phoenician capital. Syphax hastened to seek reinforcements among his tribes, but he was pursued by Laelius and Massinissa; these lieutenants of Scipio brought him to bay; he was made prisoner and sent off to Rome.

The dark fate of Sophonisba we cannot dwell on. The daughter of Hasdrubal Gisco fell into the hands of Massinissa, an old lover, and took poison rather than grace a Roman triumph. The power of the best ally of Carthage was thus overthrown, his dominions passed into other hands, and his subjects took no part in the subsequent passages of war, though his son appeared for a moment in arms. But Scipio was not forgetful of Massinissa's great deeds: he restored the Numidian prince to his kingdom, and Massinissa was in a few months at the head of thousands of his admirable African horsemen, an indefatigable and trusted ally of Rome.

A fruitless attack made on the Roman fleet of Utica, brought hostilities for the moment to an end. Scipio, after his late victory, had approached Carthage; the subject towns were showing signs of a rising, the government abjectly sued for peace, and sentenced Hasdrubal Gisco to the death of the cross. The Roman commander offered terms which probably he had no authority to propose—*delenda Carthago* was already in the thoughts of Rome—; they were marked by the moderation and large wisdom of view that were his best and perhaps most distinctive qualities. (Mommsen.)

Carthage was to surrender nearly her whole war-fleet, to pay a considerable sum for the charges of the war, to cede Spain and the Balearic Islands, to recognise Massinissa as the lord of the realms of Syphax—an admirable and judicious stroke of policy—; but she was to retain her African empire and to be still an independent, nay, a wealthy state. The peace party accepted the conditions with delight, an armistice was made, and envoys were sent to Rome. Ere long, however, there was a frantic outburst of Semitic indignation and patriotic wrath; the war party, sustained by the mass of the citizens, was suddenly placed at the head of affairs, and resolved to make a last effort to strike for their country.

Messengers were sent to Mago and Hannibal with orders to return home under the protection of the existing truce, and if possible, to drive the invaders away from Africa. The intelligence reached Mago, but too late; he had been mortally wounded, (Livy asserts this. Cornelius Nepos, Hannibal, makes Mago survive; but this is not probable), and his small army had been overthrown by a superior force near Milan in the land of the Insubrian Gauls. The precautions taken by Rome had not been vain; Quintilius Varus and Marcus Cornelius, the officers in command of the legions in the north, had marched against the Carthaginian leader and had defeated him in a hard-fought battle, remarkable chiefly for the boldness of the Roman cavalry and for the destruction of Mago's array of elephants, the huge animals as usual having been unable to endure the wounds of the terrible *pilum*, and having wrought havoc in the Carthaginian ranks. The remains, however, of Mago's forces, Spaniards, Ligurians, and Gauls, made their way to Africa, and were soon to do great deeds under the command of Hannibal.

The great Carthaginian had meanwhile taken his army in safety away from Italy. He carried with him from 20,000 to 25,000 men, (Hénnébert, Dodge); he probably sacrificed his horses and beasts of burden, but we may reject the idle myths that he put to the sword a multitude of his Italian soldiers, and that he broke out in petty displays of ill-humour. (These stories are about as true as that Napoleon murdered Desaix, strangled Pichegru, deliberately sent the army of the Rhine to die at St. Domingo, and was fond of biting and scratching.) The march and the embarkation must have taken many days, but no Roman general dogged his retreat, and Rome could hardly have been restrained by an armistice, had a favourable opportunity to attack occurred. If vanity had been a fault of Hannibal, or the frivolous passion of false glory, he might have found consolation, in some sense at least, for the failure of his gigantic designs in the very events he beheld around him.

Rome still felt awe at his presence in Italy; even now when her legions were within sight of Carthage and victory seemed within their grasp, her leading men dreaded their meeting Hannibal. (Livy thus describes the feeling at Rome.) But the most marked qualities of this great man's nature were apparently love of country and hatred of its foe; and, at this conjuncture, he was doubtless torn by an agony worse than the bitterness of death. He had stricken down Rome in many a famous battle; he had gained triumphs unequalled in war, but his mighty projects had come to nothing, his enemy had overcome his stupendous efforts; the republic, unconquerable and in the fulness of its strength, was about to place its feet on the neck of Carthage.

The tradition is probably not untrue that in the anguish of his soul he ascribed his defeat and the annihilation of his towering hopes not so much to Rome as to his own base government; and history, on the whole, confirms this judgment. All honour is due to the heroic nation which was superior to every stroke of fortune, and fought on with such untiring constancy that at last it weakened and baffled its terrible enemy. But had Carthage been true to her great champion, had she seconded him as was within her power, had her leaders loyally supported Hannibal, there was a period in the contest, after Cannae, when Rome would have not improbably succumbed.

Hannibal landed his army in the bay of Leptis, and moved it to Adrumetum, the modern Susa. Thirty-six years had passed since he had left Carthage; the man had fulfilled the pledges of the boy; he had devoted powers of supreme genius to a mighty effort to destroy Rome; he had returned, aged before his time, to defend his country. He seems to have fortified a great camp; he endeavoured to increase and improve his forces, to procure elephants and a supply of cavalry, an arm in which he was very weak; he obtained the support of levies from Carthage, and a small contingent sent by Philip of Macedon, now alarmed, when it was too late, at the power of Rome; and he sent messengers to Vermina, a son of Syphax, who promised to join him with a mass of Numidian horsemen.

But, in the meanwhile, the ruling men at Carthage had committed an insensate breach of faith; they had winked at an act of piracy against Roman transports, and at the capture of a Roman war-ship with envoys on board. It was an act of folly instigated by the mob of the city; Scipio instantly declared the armistice at an end; he marched with his army over the plains round Carthage, making severe examples of villages and towns, carrying, in a word, ruin and terror in his path. That hostilities were thus precipitated must have wrung Hannibal's heart; but he had no choice but to confront his enemy; he tried to occupy the long mountain range extending from near Cape Bon to Theveste, which affords excellent positions of defence.

He hoped to be able to keep the Roman general in check on this line, perhaps to gain an advantage by superior skill, and especially to await the arrival of the Numidian squadrons, the favourite force on which he had always relied, and which had done such wonders in his master hands. But Scipio had reached the valley of the Mejerda, and apparently held the passes of the hills. Hannibal sought an interview with his youthful rival; it was probably a device to gain time. There is no reason to doubt that the Greek historian has given us the substance of what passed at one of the most memorable scenes of history. (The interview is set forth by Polybius, he was a friend of Laelius, Scipio's lieutenant, Livy's account bears much fewer marks of truth.)

Scipio was evidently touched by Hannibal's language, but quietly reminded him that the terms of peace he proposed were more favourable to Carthage than those agreed to before a solemn truce had been broken; that the senate would now insist on much harsher conditions; that it was hopeless to refer the question to Rome. "Put yourself in my place," the Roman exclaimed, "there is no alternative, the war must go on."

The spreading plains of Zama were but a few miles distant from Naraggara, the scene of the previous interview. (The exact site of the field of Zama is not known. It was probably Zama Regia near Sicca. Hénnébert identifies it with the modern Zouarin.) The hostile armies had been encamped on these; Hannibal and Scipio prepared for a decisive battle. The mistake made by the invaders became now apparent; Rome, gigantic as was her military power, had fewer troops than her worn-out rival on the field where the result of the whole war was involved. The dispositions made by Hannibal, his enemies have allowed, were admirable, and worthy of a great captain. (Livy.) He had eighty elephants, an enormous mass, but composed of young and ill-trained beasts; he ranged these in front of his army to break the fury and weight of the attack of the legions.

His infantry was formed in three deep lines, the army of Mago, (Mago would certainly have been in command had he been alive), about 12,000 strong, with the Macedonians, were the van of the battle; behind these were the Carthaginian levies, not less probably than 15,000 men, from whom he seems to have expected much; in the rear, but thrown back, was his Italian Army, 20,000 good troops, for the most part well trained and proud of the renown of the mighty master. Hannibal placed his cavalry on either wing; but it was not more than 4,000 or 5,000 horsemen; he had lost the arm that so often had upheld his genius; but his whole army was more than 50,000 strong, and though it contained many bad elements, it was very far from a contemptible force.

The Roman Army was composed of about 45,000 men, some 30,000 being Roman infantry, all soldiers of the very best quality. Massinissa had brought 6,000 Numidian horsemen; Laelius commanded 4,000 Italian troopers; the rest were light-armed and foreign auxiliaries. Scipio's army, though inferior in numbers, was certainly, on the whole, the better instrument of war; and it was very superior in the great arm of cavalry. The Roman commander arrayed his legions in lines of columns, the *maniples* placed on the ground in succession, a formation that often had proved vicious, especially against good cavalry.

But Hannibal was evidently weak in this arm. What Scipio had most to fear was the elephant. To guard against this danger, he placed light infantry between his columns, which he had rather widely divided, and these troops had orders either to attack the great beasts or to let them pass down the kind of lanes which had been opened in his order of battle. Scipio drew up his powerful cavalry on both his wings; he knew he could trust Laelius and Massinissa, especially the last, a really able cavalry leader.

It was the seventeenth year of the protracted combat, a bright morning of the African summer. (The date of the Battle of Zama has not been fixed; it was probably fought in April or May, 202 B.C.) The commanders-in-chief rode along the front of their battle and harangued their soldiery through subordinate officers. (Polybius.) Hannibal had different words for his army of different races; he promised booty and pay to Mago's men, all mercenaries from many lands of Europe; he reminded the Carthaginians of their wives and children; he bade his Italians remember the great days of victory. Scipio appealed to Roman patriotism and pride; this day would decide the destinies of the world; but the legions, to a man, must do or die; if beaten they would perish in Phoenician dungeons. (There is no reason to doubt that the report of these speeches made by Polybius, is reasonably correct.)

The belligerent armies, always so unlike, had never before such a dissimilar aspect. The elephants before the Carthaginian lines, with their archers and slingers, looked like armed forts; but the huge animals were even now unsteady. Mago's army was a kind of image of the great league which Hannibal had tried in vain to combine; well-armed Spaniards from the Iberian plains, half-naked Celts from the valley of the Po, Macedonians with the *sarissa* from the Strymon, a motley array assembled in a cause that was not their own.

The Phoenician soldiery, holding the next line, were not the men they had been in the days of Hamilcar; the "sacred band" of Carthage seems to have disappeared; but they had to fight for everything that made life worth having, for hearths, for homes, for family, for the state. Behind these Hannibal's Italian troops were about to join in a fratricidal strife; but they thought only of their beloved leader; they felt assured that with him they would triumph. Hannibal beheld them with legitimate pride and hope; but his feeble wings, with their scanty cavalry, must have caused him misgivings, and his old Numidians were in the array of his enemies. His great lieutenants too were all gone—Mago, (Polybius does not refer to Mago), the Hasdrubal of Cannae, and many others, his companions of arms in better days; he was himself the last of the lion brood of the Barcae.

As for the Roman Army, it extended for miles in its long-drawn and disciplined lines; on either flank were the powerful masses of Massinissa's and Laelius's horsemen; the men were nerved to the highest point of confidence. They had learned how to deal with the once dreaded elephant; they trusted in a leader who had hardly known defeat. They brandished with exultation the *pila* in their hands; they stood in silence but longing for the fight; they looked out eagerly for the sign that was to announce their onset.

The battle, as always, began with loose skirmishing; this seems to have lasted a short time only; both generals wished to come to close quarters. Hannibal, as became the master, took the offensive; his ponderous line of elephants was ordered to advance; it bore down, in imposing majesty, on the unawed legions. The huge beasts, however, raw and untrained, broke, in a few moments, into wild confusion; they were terrified at the sight of the steady Roman lines, and at the sound of the Roman trumpets and horns, prolonged in loud and threatening clangour; they made no impression on Scipio's men; they rushed to the right and the left against the Phoenician wings, or made their way through the openings between Scipio's columns, harassed and slain by a tempest of destructive missiles. (We fortunately possess two very good accounts of the Battle of Zama, that of Polybius and that of Livy. That of the Greek is the more trustworthy and natural, that of the Roman the more brilliant, but they nearly agree.)

Massinissa very skilfully seized the occasion when the elephants had become entangled with his enemy's horse; he charged home with his quick and dexterous Numidians; Laelius followed his example on the opposite flank; the Carthaginian cavalry, weak in numbers and taken at fault, were driven, completely routed, far away from the field. Hannibal was thus deprived, almost from the outset, of his artillery and his cavalry arms, and both his flanks were left bare and exposed (Livy dwells rightly on this); but his genius and energy did not fail him; he pushed his first line forward and boldly attacked. The mercenaries, nearly all veterans and inured to war, fell on and fought with heroic valour; once more the Spanish sword, the Celtic claymore, and the long pike of the Hellenic footman were pitted against the terrible *pilum* and the deadly *gladius*.

The agility and the daring of the assailants prevailed for a time, and had great effect (Polybius); but the stern cheers of the Romans, in a mighty concert, drowned the dissonant clamour and the savage cries of a soldiery of many peoples and arms, and soon became the presage of coming victory. (Livy.) The discipline, the order, and the weapons of the legions told at last (Livy); by degrees the mercenaries were forced back, fighting, on Hannibal's second line, his Carthaginian infantry. These troops had shewn signs of weakness and hesitated to advance, like the Belgians on the great day of Waterloo; and as the dissolving masses of the mercenaries fell back, the infuriated men shouted out "Treachery!" (Polybius dwells on this), and fell savagely on the Phoenician levies. A scene of confusion and bloodshed followed; the two first lines of Hannibal came in conflict; after much loss in a frenzied struggle they were thrown upon Hannibal's last line, his Italian reserve.

It is impossible to say, with our imperfect knowledge, whether Scipio at this crisis, when his adversaries' host was in a state of disorder and trouble, ought not to have made a general advance, and flung the legions at once on to his half-ruined enemy; but the excuses of his eulogists seem very feeble. (Polybius and Livy attribute what they evidently thought want of energy on the part of Scipio to the slaughter which encumbered the field and made an ordinary attack difficult. But this certainly is no real apology.) Hannibal caught at a respite he ought, perhaps, not to have had; he rallied his broken first and second lines, and managed to place them on both his flanks; his third line, the Italians, now formed his centre; once more he restored and renewed the battle. (Hannibal must still have had admirable officers to carry into effect this most difficult and delicate operation.)

Scipio paused for a time to reform his troops (Livy dwells upon this, the pause may have been ill-timed; but it was no light thing to fight Hannibal at bay); his front presented a single and extended line, like that of his renowned antagonist; the hostile armies met in a last and deadly encounter. Hannibal and his staff fought in the ranks like common soldiers; Scipio and his lieutenants and officers did the same; the Bruttian levies desperately held their ground, thinking not of Italy, but of a leader they adored; the Roman deserters—and there were many of these—knew that defeat meant for them an ignominious death; the fierce Roman infantry urged the fight forward with that dogged constancy which was their grand excellence, in better order, and with superior arms. (Livy finely describes this passage of Zama.)

Yet the result of the battle was doubtful for hours; Scipio engaged the *triarii*, his last reserve; it has been thought that fortune inclined to Hannibal for more than a moment with a treacherous smile; the issue was at last determined by an event so often decisive in ancient war. Massinissa and Laelius had pursued the Phoenician cavalry much too far; Scipio had been deprived for a considerable time of an arm that would have been of the greatest use to him. The two chiefs, however, at last returned to the scene; they seized the opportunity they saw at hand; their squadrons, issuing probably from behind folds of the ground, fell in force on the rear of Hannibal's army, already hard-pressed by the Romans in front.

The effect was instantaneous and complete; the Carthaginian lines were broken and cut to pieces; Hannibal with great difficulty escaped from the field. Yet the rout was not equal to that of Cannae; Hannibal lost about 20,000 men; but he had soon rallied a large part of his defeated host.

It is manifest that Hannibal on his last field was not unequal to himself in war. If he had the more numerous, he had the worse army; he was deprived of his elephants and his horsemen by mere accidents, which it was not possible for him to foresee—a loss which nothing perhaps could repair; yet he rallied his troops in circumstances of extreme difficulty with admirable resource and conspicuous skill; he kept fortune in suspense to the last moment. (Polybius closes a fair review of Hannibal's conduct at Zama with words of sympathy and admiration.) The dispositions of Scipio were not remarkable; the result of the battle was due to the Roman infantry, to Massinissa and his horsemen, and in some measure to chance; Scipio's flatterers have significantly abstained from eulogies.

The Roman, in fact, was no more to be compared with Hannibal, than the two commanders who gained Waterloo are to be placed in the same rank as Napoleon. After Zama, as had happened after Cannae, another disaster befell the defeated state; Vermina's cavalry, in an attempt to join Hannibal were surprised, cut to pieces, or scattered in flight. Carthage was now prostrate; she had no army; she was unable to make a further effort; she could be annihilated if Rome put forth her strength. She was compelled to submit to severe terms, more severe than had been proposed before but not more severe than Rome might justly demand; we may believe with the great German historian that they were arranged by Hannibal and Scipio after a second interview, each, as usually is the case with really eminent soldiers, being anxious to bring the war to an end.

★★★★★★★★★★

We quote Mommsen, ii.: "It is much more probable that the two great generals, on whom the decision of the political question now devolved, offered and accepted peace on such terms in order to set just and reasonable bounds on the one hand to the furious vengeance of the victors, on the other to the obstinacy and imprudence of the vanquished. The noble-mindedness and statesmanlike gifts of the great antagonists are no less apparent in Hannibal's magnanimous submission to what was inevitable than in Scipio's wise abstinence from an extravagant and outrageous use of victory."

★★★★★★★★★★

Carthage had to cede the territory agreed to before; but she had to surrender more war-ships; she had to pay a much larger indemnity, extended over a series of years; and if she retained her African empire, she was not to make war without the consent of Rome. She thus became a tributary and vassal state, yet she had still wealth, commerce, and elements of power which might enable her in time to be formidable again. The conduct of some of her leading men and of Hannibal at this crisis of her fortunes was characteristic. The base peace party when treating before the broken armistice had thrown the whole blame of a disastrous war on the hero it had betrayed and abandoned; one of its orators now began to declaim against the "peace of Hannibal," as it is named in history.

The mighty warrior, knowing that such babble was worse than vain, and that a renewal of hostilities simply meant ruin, caught the tongue-valiant creature by the scruff of the neck, pulled him down, and told him to hold his peace. Hannibal's great object at this conjuncture, was not to provoke an implacable enemy, and to husband the resources of Carthage; but like his father he looked forward and still had hopes of vengeance.

Considerable alarm was felt at Rome, when it was known that Hannibal had reached Africa, at the head of a still powerful army; the mistake was again perceived of an expedition undertaken with a force very much too weak. (Livy expresses this sentiment) But all anxiety was dispelled at the news of Zama, and of the negotiations ending in a glorious peace; Scipio was hailed by his soldiers as Africanus, the name by which he is known in history. His return through Italy was a conqueror's progress; he was welcomed in town and village as the finisher of the war (Livy); he was received at Rome with exulting acclaim.

The distrust of the senate, however, was not wholly gone; he obtained the honours of a triumph as was his right; but the scenes after the Metaurus were not repeated; Rome had been saved by Nero, she had only won through Scipio success that must ultimately have been assured. The aged Fabius did not live to witness the consummation, so auspicious for Rome, to which he largely contributed by his wise insight. He had died a few months before the conclusion of peace; but he had received the highest honour the republic could bestow, a wreath of grass presented by soldiers on the spot, a token of a land set free from invasion.

With Fabius passed away one of the greatest men of the generation that had grown grey before the Second Punic War. He loved the gods of Rome and her ancient laws; he thought the nobles should rule the commons; he held to the conservative policy of the Patrician order; he hated innovation and strange ideas; he clung to the simple life of the Roman citizen, and of an agricultural people attached to its old usages. But he was a man of the greatest sagacity and almost of genius (Livy); his energy and prudence after Cannae may have saved Rome; above all he perceived the true methods to cope with, and ultimately to wear out Hannibal. He was not unjustly called "maximus" by his grateful countrymen.

The Second Punic War profoundly affected the two great states which it brought into conflict. It sent forward Carthage, already in decline, on the path which led, before long, to destruction. Its consequences for Rome were less decisive; but they were many, various, distinctly marked; they are manifest in her subsequent history. The losses of the republic had been enormous; 300,000 citizens are said to have perished in the field; disease and misery had probably many more victims. The senate after Cannae was reduced more than half in number; 400 towns and villages in different parts of Italy are said to have been simply blotted out; and, at the same time, vast tracts of land fell, by confiscation, into the hands of the state. The effects on the social condition of Rome, and on the relations of the community, were immense and lasting.

The population, no doubt, grew up again; but the slave system, for years on the increase, especially in agriculture, was much extended; the class of free owners of the soil and of hardy husbandmen was diminished in a considerable degree; the landed possessions of the nobles were largely augmented. A change was wrought in the economy of the state which was to end in the great Servile War, in the reforms and the unhappy fate of the Gracchi, in the furious strife of classes, of which the names of Marius and Sulla were the symbols, in the internal ills that afflicted the later republic. The war, too, had most important effects on the position of Rome as the dominant power in Italy.

It sealed the doom of the fickle and treacherous Gauls, who had never given Hannibal steady and general support, such were their jealousies and intestine broils, but who had incensed their Roman enemies; they were soon a conquered race, under suspicious masters, spread in colonies over the valley of the Po. The ascendency of Rome, too, in middle and southern Italy, was more fully established than it had ever been, and made more severe and oppressive; the peoples of the Umbrian and Sabellian stocks, the Etrurians, the Samnites, above all, the Bruttians, who, in different ways, had taken part with Hannibal, were degraded almost from allies into vassals; and most of the Greek cities were deprived of their franchises.

Roman colonisation besides, was largely extended; Roman settlements kept down the subdued provinces; the Roman soldiery were planted in forfeited tracts of land wherever it was thought necessary for the defence of the state. All this had been going on before; but after the end of the Second Punic War, the comparatively mild and just government which Italy had enjoyed, was changed for the worse; the character of Roman administration was transformed; it became tyrannical, harsh, exacting; and this was to be aggravated as Rome went on from conquest to conquest, over foreign races. The spirit of Verres entered her public men; the evils were produced that made the rule of the great republic too grievous to endure, and that ultimately prepared the way for Caesar.

In this last passage of the Second Punic War, we see Hannibal in a novel position. He had previously retreated into the south of Italy;

but he had retained the power of acting on the offensive; some of his movements in these years were brilliant in the extreme. He was now confined within a recess in Bruttium, he stands on the defensive only, but he makes himself impregnable within his lines; he forms his Italian levies into good soldiers; he prepares himself for any event, having his communications with Carthage, it appears, secure; he still defies the colossal power of Rome. Such constancy and resource are marvels of war; Hannibal is equally supreme in attack and defence, an excellence of which few captains can boast; nothing is more astonishing than the fear in which he is held by a great military state that could have destroyed him.

We have referred to his conduct on the field of Zama; he lost the battle, but he was not the less superior, by many degrees, to his young antagonist. In this phase of the contest Rome does not display the heroic endurance she displayed after Cannae; she seems contented merely to hold her enemy in check; she turns her attention to her internal affairs; and owing to disputes between the senate and Scipio, she invades Africa with very inadequate forces. That she left the issue at Zama to turn on the hazard of the die, when she could have crushed Hannibal and Carthage long before, is a proof that her councils were not well directed; and Scipio, in this matter, is not free from blame.

Still her magnificent energy in other parts of the war is entitled to the very highest praise; nothing like it, perhaps, can be found in history. As for Carthage, her government acted after its kind; but for Hannibal she could never have sustained the contest; she would probably have succumbed at its very outset, as the senate evidently believed would happen. Yet Hannibal, abandoned and betrayed by his country, brought Rome to the verge of ruin, and maintained the unequal struggle for nearly seventeen years; this alone gives him a place in the very first rank of warriors.

Chapter 10: The End of Hannibal

Rome, after she had shaken off the burden of Hannibal, advanced rapidly upon the path of empire, exhausted as she had been by the Second Punic War. Her armies and fleet were largely reduced; six legions only were kept on foot in Italy; they were chiefly composed of allies and volunteers; the wearied citizens were allowed a brief season of repose. The republic, however, had an ample reserve of strength to deal with its enemies at home and abroad. The attention of the government was first directed to the warlike but fickle and treacherous Gauls, for centuries engaged in angry strife with Rome, but who had given Hannibal only fitful support, had been kept quiet, in part, by Roman statecraft, and were divided by the perennial discords of the Celt.

It was resolved effectually to carry out the policy which had been adopted after the First Punic War, and to make northern Italy part of the national domain. The Boii and Insubres were marked down for attack; these tribes defended themselves with barbarian valour; a great Gaulish league was formed for a time; even the Cenomani, vassals of Rome, were among its adherents. But the power and the discipline of the legions gradually prevailed; and the march of the conquerors received support from the dissensions and quarrels of the fickle Celts, never capable of a firm and united purpose. The Boii were deprived of the chief part of their lands; the Insubres were kept in a kind of bondage in the region between the Alps and the Po; the Roman settlements were largely increased; an Italian population filled the whole tract between the Apennines and the cities on the great river.

At the same time the Alps were finally made the boundary in the north; the Gauls beyond the mountains were steadily held back; the Ligures around Genoa were easily subdued; the fortress of Aquileia, in the land of the Veneti, barred attempts to invade or to menace Italy from the east. The peninsula beyond the Apennines was thus made completely Roman; Roman colonisation made steady progress;

Roman civilisation, following the track of the magnificent roads that were constructed everywhere, established itself throughout the valley of the Po, and from the maritime Alps to the Adriatic Sea. The tribal life, the usages, even the blood of the Celt seem to have been gradually effaced by the dominant race; Polybius has described this "region" as almost wholly Italian; there is no trace of the Celt in Livy or Virgil, great writers whose fathers were settlers in lands near the Adige.

Sardinia, Corsica, and the Balearic Islands, were also penetrated and subdued, (Lanfrey, *Napoleon*, states that the Corsicans could never be made slaves by the Romans, the very contrary was the case with the Sardinians). Sardinia especially supplied the slave market of Rome. In Spain the republic kept the great dominion between the Ebro and the Pyrenees which it had long held; and it entered into the possession of the fallen Carthaginian empire. Its territory extended from Tarragona to Cadiz, and inland along the course of the Tagus; it ruled all the cities upon the coast, whether of Greek, Phoenician, or Italian origin; it made the fairest parts of the peninsula its own.

A kind of native civilisation had long existed in the great mining districts of this region; its agriculture had made the population wealthy, and attached in some degree to the arts of peace; the genius of Hamilcar had diffused its influence from Andalusia to Valencia in the east, and had laid the foundations of a prosperous state; and Rome succeeded to this noble heritage. But outside this comparatively settled land, known as the Hither and the Further Provinces, spread the vast tracts of the untamed Celts, extending from the Guadarramas to the Atlantic; here savage tribes, under warrior chiefs, maintained a rude independence of their own, and lived in a state of continual discord. The Romans had to endure for a century and a half the depredations and the attacks of these wild races; occasionally they united under a brilliant leader, and then accomplished really great things; but their loose confederacies were quickly dissolved, and they were driven back to their mountains and dales after suffering cruelly from atrocious deeds of vengeance.

The Roman arms advanced slowly in this debatable land; its complete subjugation was not attempted; it was regarded as a worse than useless possession, to be controlled only because it could not be made the seat of an obedient vassal kingdom. The greater part of the peninsula remained in this state until the republic ceased to exist; it was left to the courtly poet of the Augustan age to boast that the old enemy of the Spanish Pale had been subdued, and that the Iberian Celt had at last felt the bondage of Rome.

The Second Punic War had not long ended when Rome turned her attention to the Hellenic world. The empire of Alexander was a thing of the past; but Macedon was a great military state; in the divisions and decay of the Greek communities, the only bulwark and rallying point of the nation. Its dominions spread beyond the original kingdom, over Thessaly and parts of the adjoining lands; it exercised an ill-defined supremacy over the republics of a better age; its army was still of formidable strength. Rome had not forgotten the league made between Philip and Hannibal after Cannae, nor the years of protracted strife that followed; she had felt indignant that the Macedonian *phalanx* had appeared among her enemies on the field of Zama, though the king had not actually declared war.

The attempts made by this ambitious potentate to attack the Ptolemies, old allies of Rome, to annex provinces of the Egyptian monarchy, and to subdue free cities on the Asiatic seaboard, led to a rupture with the great republic; and a large majority of the states of Greece, especially the fierce and half-mongrel Ætolians, took the side of a power which, if a seeming friend, was really a danger to the whole Hellenic name. The contest was long, and for a time doubtful; it was fought out on land and at sea; Rome did not scruple to employ the arms of the savage tribes that roamed around the Balkans.

Philip defended himself with courage and skill; had he given proof of the same energy and resource when he could reckon upon the support of Hannibal, he might have thrown a decisive weight into the scale of events; he was more than once victorious in the field. He was, however, at last completely overthrown in the great Battle of Cynoscephalae, not far from Pharsalia in the hills of Thessaly; this sealed the fate of the Macedonian monarchy. He accepted a peace like that given to Carthage; his kingdom was reduced to its ancient limits; he was compelled to disband nearly his whole army; he was degraded to the condition of a mere vassal. Rome soon afterwards with ostentatious patronage, but partly too from her Hellenic sympathies, strong in the generation of her rising public men, declared that all the states of Greece were free; but this nominal independence only increased their weakness, and made them ready for the yoke of Italian masters.

While Rome was thus giving a free rein to her power, Carthage was drinking the cup of humiliation to the dregs. The policy of the senate had not yet been matured; but Massinissa was kept as a thorn in the side of its late defeated and despoiled enemy; the Numidian prince was encouraged to make booty of provinces of the fallen Phoenician state; the Libyan cities were allowed, nay incited, to revolt. It was in vain that the abject peace party implored the dominant republic to trace the limits of the territory that remained to Carthage once for all, and to permit open rebellion to be put down; in vain that it sent envoys to Rome with bribes and gifts; in vain that it submitted to affronts and insults.

A revolution of which we know only the results ere long placed the war party in office again; Hannibal was raised to the head of affairs by a popular vote; he was made virtually a dictator, with the old title of *Suffete*. The great Carthaginian, statesman as well as soldier, and, in both capacities, the first man of his time, addressed himself, with his wonted judgment and resource, to restore in some measure his country in decline; we know from his enemies that his success was remarkable. He strengthened the petty army Carthage still possessed, but so that jealous Rome should not take umbrage; he effected a thorough change in the institutions of the state at once beneficent and on the side of liberty. He transformed the narrow and arbitrary governing board which had usurped and cruelly abused supreme power, and made it responsible to the people; he placed the finances on a sound basis; he reformed the whole system of administration with the best results.

Under his wise rule Carthage began to stir with new life; her wealth so increased that she was able to offer to redeem her debt by a single payment; indeed, so admirable was her position as a seat of commerce that Hannibal might have looked forward with hope to a time when she might regain some part of the power she had lost, and when he might be formidable once more in the field. One anecdote of what he was in council remains; it is characteristic of the man, and perhaps authentic. He laughed a bitter laugh when a driveller shed tears that Carthage was compelled to yield tribute to Rome. The great patriot exclaimed in scorn:

> You ought to have wept, when our arms were taken from us and our ships burned and when we were forbidden to make war even in self-defence. (Livy)

It was the cruel fate of the greatest man of his age, that his foes were those of his own order, and that his countrymen were unworthy of him. It was enough to rouse the suspicious anger of Rome that Hannibal was in power at Carthage and that the vanquished state was rising again under his wise government. The defeated oligarchy fanned the smouldering fire; they let the senate know, what was doubtless true, that its enemy and their own was biding his time, and was looking forward to an opportunity to renew the war. A demand for the surrender of Hannibal was despatched from Rome; it is to the honour of Scipio that he made a protest; but the victor of Cannae was shamefully proscribed; the palace of the Barcae was razed to the ground; the warrior and statesman had to fly from his country.

Hannibal sought refuge at the court of Antiochus, fourth in descent from the renowned Seleucus, the founder of the Greek dynasty representing the great kings of the East, Antiochus was the lord of a vast undefined empire spreading from the Hellespont to the Indus and comprising Asia Minor with its Greek settlements, the provinces of the Assyrian and the Persian monarchies, and the lands of the Oxus and the Jaxartes; Oriental flattery had proclaimed him the Great, by the victories he won in revolted *satrapies*.

He was a vain, arrogant, and shortsighted man; he had fallen away from Philip of Macedon, his natural ally in the late contest with Rome, he had waged a long predatory war with the Ptolemies, "the wards," as they were called, of the Roman senate. But he had consolidated, in some measure, his immense dominions, by arms, diplomacy, and well-planned marriages; and he commanded huge armies of many races and tongues, in which the solid Greek *phalanx* appeared combined with Celtic clansmen from the Galatian hills, with swarms of Arabs on their fleet camels, perhaps with the formidable Parthian bowmen, and with the masses of the light horse of the Medes and Persians.

Antiochus had been engaged for some time in attempts to subjugate the Greek cities on the coast of his realm of Asia Minor—the policy which had cost Philip dear; he had been at war with the league of the Greek maritime states, of which Rhodes and Byzantium were the heads, and with the house of Attains enthroned at Pergamos; and he had invaded the Thracian Chersonese and appeared in arms on the verge of Hellas. These enterprises had, in different degrees, caused resentment and ill-feeling at Rome, the professed patron of the Hellenic name; an accident precipitated an impending rupture. Antiochus received Hannibal at Ephesus, with the highest honours; the welcome given to the still-dreaded enemy of Rome, and the evident dangers that might ensue, caused a declaration of war.

Hannibal had long cherished the hope of restoring Carthage, and engaging once more in a death struggle with Rome. With the foresight of genius, he had seen his chances in the immense natural resources of the Phoenician state, in the distracted condition of the Celts of Italy and Spain, in the late difficult war with Philip of Macedon; his opportunity had, he thought, now come. He was given at first a foremost place in the councils of the king; he proposed that hostilities should be delayed until an irresistible league of the West and the East should be formed against the common enemy of all; the Gauls of the Po and the Celts of the Tagus were to join hands with the Greeks of Hellas and Macedon, and with Asiatic races beside the Halys and the Orontes, and to unite in a coalition to strike down Rome.

In himself he would undertake to awaken Carthage; he would be the forerunner of the great avenging hosts; he would descend on Italy and fight another Cannae. (The words put in the mouth of Hannibal by Livy, no doubt contain the substance of all that he advised but in vain.) It is impossible to say whether these gigantic designs had, as affairs stood, a reasonable prospect of success; but Hannibal's plans were always deeply laid; and assuredly he should have had the supreme direction of the war.

But Antiochus was swayed by mean and petty minds, jealous of the ascendency of real greatness, perhaps by warnings of the peace party of Carthage, perhaps by information supplied from Rome; the war was precipitated before it was matured and prepared; Hannibal was relegated to a subordinate's place, and was given only inferior commands, in which his military genius was thrown away and lost. No effort was made to unite the great league which he had declared indispensable to quell Rome; and the contest was waged under the very worst auspices. Carthage under her present rulers remained submissive, and soon sent a contingent to the Roman fleets; the races of the West heard nothing of what was going on, and though the Ætolians, secretly hostile to Rome, furious and irritated at the events of the late war, which had left them without their expected booty, threw in their lot with that of Antiochus, Philip of Macedon, and nearly all the Greek states became allies of the republic and joined its armies.

After a struggle, beginning with a raid from the Asiatic coast, but never doubtful where the legions appeared in the field, in which Hellas was overrun and ravaged, Antiochus was defeated in a decisive battle fought near the immortal pass of Thermopylae; he was driven back into Asia Minor already half-subdued. The Roman armies had soon reduced the few Greek fortresses which still held out; their leaders made preparations to cross the Hellespont, and to carry the war into the unknown regions beyond, with the support of the Roman and allied fleets.

It was no light thing to invade the remote East, as yet untrodden by the feet of the legions, and distant hundreds of miles from Italy. While Rome was making ready for this new effort, war raged at sea, for months, with varying results, between the Roman and Greek squadrons, and those which Antiochus was able to array. As was seen before in the First Punic War, Roman fighting prevailed over skill in seamanship; the mariners of Tyre proved match for the armed Italian sailor. Hannibal commanded one of the Tyrian fleets; he was defeated in an engagement near Aspendus, at the mouth of one of the Pamphylian rivers; the contest at sea was closed by a great Roman victory won at Myonessus, on the coast of Lydia. (Napoleon, *Corr.*, accounts for the superiority of the Romans in naval battles.)

Meantime a Roman Army had landed from the Adriatic; had passed through Macedonia and Thrace, and, under the command of the victor of Zama, had crossed the straits, and reached the confines of Mysia. Antiochus tried in vain to treat; he returned Scipio a son whom he had made prisoner; the Roman thanked him in stately language, and told him to make peace, whatever the terms. The decisive battle took place at Magnesia on the Hermus, not far from Sardis and Ephesus; it made Asia Minor a dependency of Rome. Whether Scipio was at the head of his army is not certain; Hannibal perhaps commanded a small body of troops; but he had no control over the movements of the day.

It is a tradition that he made answer to the Great King proud of his *cohort*s glittering in Oriental pomp, "Yes that is a brave army, and brave show; it will be enough for the Romans, greedy as they are." (Aulus Gellius.) The battle was one of the many instances in which a small but disciplined army of the West has overthrown the multitudinous armies of the East. (Livy gives us a spirited account of the Battle of Magnesia.) Antiochus gained an advantage over the weak Roman cavalry; but the left wing of the king was scattered in flight; the elephants, as at Zama and other fights, proved fatal to the troops they were supposed to protect, and, when the single *phalanx* on the field gave way, the Syrian host was routed and destroyed. (It is remarkable that the Romans often employed the elephant in battle after the Second Punic War. These animals, dangerous as they were, were nevertheless a powerful arm.)

The humbled monarch accepted the conqueror's bidding; Asia Minor west of the Halys became a Roman subject country; the Greek cities on the coast were declared free, that is, placed under Roman protection; and a kingdom was carved out for the house of Attalus, like that of Massinissa, to be a Roman outpost, and to secure the acquisitions of recent conquest. The dynasty of Seleucus was thus overthrown; Antiochus made the shallow jest that he had lost an empire too large for one man to govern. The Celts of Galatia were ere long subdued; the surrender of Hannibal was made one of the conditions of an ignominious peace.

After this last failure of his towering hopes, Hannibal led, for many years, the life of a fugitive. We see his figure in Crete, and again in Armenia; and, as in the case of Alexander, the East abounds in traditions about the master spirit of his age. He seems never to have had much influence at the courts of the kings where he was now received; the vengeance of Rome was always before them; and the legend that he founded Artaxata is probably untrue. (Mommsen.)

He had his last asylum with Prusias, the King of Bithynia; he was greeted with honour, and obtained a grant of lands; but Prusias was a mere *satrap* of Rome; he pledged himself to betray his illustrious guest. At the bidding of Flamininus, a distinguished soldier, who had taken an important part in the affairs of the East, the abode of Hannibal was surrounded by armed assassins; he swallowed poison to escape the fate which befell Jugurtha in another age; his last words breathed scorn and hatred of Rome, (Livy makes Hannibal utter these words as he died.) Libyssa, the modern Gebsah, has been assigned as the place of his sepulture; but this is only an ill-supported tradition; we cannot tell for certain where Hannibal lies.

He had probably passed his seventieth year when he died; he had done all that genius and constancy could do, to annihilate Rome; yet the state, which, in his boyhood, had not conquered Sicily, which, in his manhood, he had well-nigh destroyed, had in his old age become the master of the civilised world, and was supreme from the Pillars of Hercules to the Euphrates. Strangely enough Scipio Africanus passed away nearly at the same time as the far greater man he overthrew. Scipio entered public life when the fate of Rome was trembling in a still doubtful balance; he filled three continents with the renown of his victories; he led the legions to the East for the first time, he was long the favourite of the great body of the Roman people.

Yet his end was unfortunate, and hardly becoming; he was charged with peculation, and defrauding the state; instead of meeting the charge he told his accusers to follow him to the capitol, and to remember Zama; he left Rome, and he died in exile. The greatness of

Scipio cannot be denied; but he was fond of self-assertion and popular arts; he had not the genius, the depth, the power of Hannibal; he is not to be compared, in war or in peace, with his mighty opponent.

We know Hannibal only from the external side; even this knowledge is far from perfect. We possess, we have said, no letter or despatch from his hand; a few lines on a monument, a short treaty, some pithy sayings, marked with the *imperatoria brevitas*, are the only genuine expressions of his mind that remain.

★★★★★★★★★★

We have referred to some of these already. We may add Hannibal's remarks, "Rome has her Hannibal in Fabius," "Marcellus was a good soldier but a rash general," and the well-known comment on the Greek sophist who discoursed on war in his presence, "It is pretty, but all nonsense." Compare Napoleon on a similar work, "*Cet homme peut avoir quelques idees saines, mais il ne sait rien do la guerre*." ("This man may have some sound ideas, but he knows nothing about war.")

★★★★★★★★★★

His achievements, too, and his character have been described by enemies, forced to admire, but unjust and revengeful; Polybius, indeed, clearly sees his genius; but he is under the influence of Roman sympathies. Yet Hannibal's " awful figure," as it has been rightly called, stands out supreme in the whole era of the mighty and protracted Second Punic War; he soars high over all the men of his time; every competent observer, who has followed his career, has placed him in the first rank of the world's great captains, and of statesmen and patriots of the highest order. Even a cursory survey of his glorious deeds shows that he was a consummate master of war.

With an army of many races and tongues, always very inferior in numbers and power, he defies the gigantic military strength of Rome; he baffles the counsels of her statesmen; he confounds her best soldiers by invading Italy, after a march across the Alps of astonishing grandeur; and he strikes her down in three great battles, which bring her to the very verge of destruction. With admirable foresight and judgment he then takes care not to attack prematurely his enemy's capital; he waits for the completion of the league of nations, on which his real hopes of success rest; he establishes himself firmly in central and southern Italy, whence he expects ultimately to advance against Rome, at the head of hosts of irresistible force.

The cowardly policy of Carthage and the weakness of allies, combining with the efforts of the Roman people, frustrate this vast yet perfectly conceived plan; yet Hannibal does not abandon his purpose; he masters the theatre of war he has chosen; such is the force of his genius, such the fear he inspires, such the wonderful skill of his movements in the field, that the exertions of armies three and fourfold in numbers cannot dislodge him from the positions he has made his own, and his boldest adversaries avoid his presence. When at last his military resources dwindle away, he gather's himself and his army within a nook of Bruttium; here he fortifies himself and restores his forces; he is still so formidable, so strong in moral strength, that his opponents are glad to let him depart in safety, after having overrun their country for nearly seventeen years, and bearded Rome at her very gates. Hannibal succumbs at last on the day of Zama, but the study of the battle proves that on his last field he was not inferior to himself in war.

These general considerations are only confirmed by a more searching and complete enquiry. The intellectual and moral faculties of great captains act and react on each other; it is difficult to determine their exact proportions; we judge of them by the results as a whole. Yet they may be analysed to some extent; the attempt to discriminate them is not without profit. Hannibal has been rightly called the "father of strategy"; he was the first great author of scientific warfare. He possessed, in the very highest degree, the excellences of a true strategist, the imagination that can fashion grand designs, the judgment and insight that can carry them into effect. His conception of assailing Rome by crossing the Alps—the Mediterranean was not open to him—is one of the most magnificent ever formed by man; but it was not extravagant, it was perfectly thought out, it was executed with consummate boldness and skill.

Not less remarkable, if less striking, is Hannibal's decision not to advance on Rome even after Trasimenus and Cannae; and the astonishing ability with which, through long years, he succeeds in retaining his hold on Italy, marching through the hosts of his terrified enemies, outmanoeuvring them by his sudden and unforeseen movements, and finally keeping them in check though in overwhelming numbers, remains an admirable specimen of strategic genius, especially in the adaptation of means to ends. In Hannibal's operations, before the shock of battle, we see also the powers of a consummate strategist.

As Napoleon has remarked, he perceives and occupies the decisive points on the theatre of war; he brings his forces to bear on the spot where success is most probable; he takes the initiative, and usually does what his adversaries are convinced he will not do; he disconcerts them by his rapid attacks, and above all by his skill in hiding his purpose; he is master of the result almost from the first moment. In moving against a hostile force, he follows the principles of strategic art; he gathers on his adversary's flank and rear, avoiding, if possible, simply to assail him in front; and he does all this with a fertility of resource and a brilliancy of design which command the highest praise.

Undoubtedly, in one exhibition of strategic skill, striking to the right and left at divided enemies, and beating them in detail, in succession, Hannibal has apparently been surpassed, but his operations in the campaign of 209 B.C. show that he perfectly understood this very method; and we must bear in mind that he was usually so inferior in force, that efforts of this kind would have been extremely perilous, and that he had to encounter the great obstacle of the Roman camp.

The student of war observes with wonder the conduct of Hannibal on the field of battle. As a master of tactics, he has never been surpassed; it is doubtful if he has had an equal. In this province of the art his grand intelligence and his perfect judgment came alike into play, the results were extraordinary, complete, decisive. He had to cope with generals, daring and stout soldiers, but without practice or skill in manoeuvre, accustomed always to attack an enemy in front, and to rely for victory on downright fighting: he was opposed to an army, admirable, indeed, in its organisation and its heroic infantry, but weak in cavalry and in the power of missiles, and the formations of which, in some respects excellent, were nevertheless defective in important points, and dangerous under certain conditions.

Hannibal seems to have grasped these truths at once; his tactical system was adapted to make the most of all that was faulty and weak in Roman command and Roman methods in battle. His cavalry was by far his best arm; he almost always made a free use of this, assailing his enemies in flank or in the rear, outwitting and disconcerting astounded leaders utterly unprepared for attacks of the kind, breaking through with his horse the gaps in the legions, where these had been shaken by his Balearic slingers, or by the weight of the armed elephant, and holding his worst arm, his infantry, in reserve, until success had been well-nigh assured. (Napoleon, Corr.: "*Toutes les batailles d'Annibal furent gagnées par sa cavalerie; s'il eût attendu pour la faire donner la fin de la bataille, il n'aurait pu remployer qu'à faire sa retraite.*"; "All of Hannibal's battles were won by his cavalry; if he had waited to make it until the end of the battle, he could only have resorted to making his retreat.")

We see these features in most of Hannibal's battles; but each of them has varieties of its own; there was no mannerism in his finely conceived tactics. No general has ever made better use of peculiarities of the ground to assist his troops; he knew how to keep his Numidians behind a screen, until they could be let loose with effect; he seized every advantage which woods, streams, and villages could in any way afford; he saw at a glance where his enemy was most vulnerable and made this point the object of his most determined efforts. Yet the supreme excellence perhaps of this great tactician was his marvellous skill in surprise and stratagem. We see this in the course of his strategy; we see it more distinctly in his great battles.

Nothing so terrified the brave but simple-minded Romans as Hannibal's ambushes and unforeseen attacks; their idea of war was to fight it out, on an open field, in a bold and dogged fashion; they were paralysed when they found themselves assailed by enemies issuing out of hidden lairs, and striking them down, as it were, in the dark; the strong but untrained swordsman was smitten with fear, when he was disarmed or pierced through by the perfect fencer. The craft of Hannibal in war was no doubt the origin of the charges of "Punic faith" that have been made against him; and though one or two of his opponents learned something from him, as a tactician he easily surpassed them all.

In the great work of organising armies and preparing them for the field—an inferior, but an important part of the noble art of war—Hannibal stands, also, on the highest eminence. His military chest was usually well filled; if his troops were sometimes in arrears of their pay, he always managed to supply their wants; the care he took of his resources is probably the cause that he was accused of "covetousness" by his Roman detractors. The south of Italy, indeed, was a fertile land, perhaps more fertile in those days than now, and Hannibal was enabled for some years to obtain supplies from the rich Campanian plain; but it is, nevertheless, wonderful how, encamped as he was in an enemy's country, and with, at best, precarious communications on land or by sea, he contrived to support, to clothe, and to pay an army, composed of many races from different parts of Europe, not engaged in a patriotic cause, attached only to one great leader, and therefore very difficult to keep together.

That Hannibal should have accomplished this is another specimen of his extraordinary gifts; the devotion his troops constantly shewed to him was certainly as much due to his admirable care in providing for their needs and daily requirements, as to their confidence in his supremacy in the field. If we pass from the parts of the military art in which the intellect of a great captain is most conspicuous to those in which his moral qualities are chiefly prominent, Hannibal shews, also, the same supreme excellence. If we bear in mind that he was opposed to a great nation of soldiers, and possessing enormous military power, and that his adversaries were commanders who had seldom known defeat, the ascendency he gained and preserved to the very last moment over every enemy and leader that met him in the field is certainly without a parallel in war.

Marcellus was the only Roman general who was not cowed by Hannibal; and Marcellus was taught by Hannibal such severe lessons, that the fear of his colleagues was only increased. Nor less astonishing was the complete supremacy of the great master over his motley arrays of Phoenicians, Africans, Spaniards, Gauls, and Italians; these men of many races were the slaves of his will, and followed him for seventeen years in victory and defeat; a generation of them must have passed away; yet they fought for him to the last when his cause was hopeless. And if we reflect on what Hannibal was in the stress of battle, how admirable was his faculty of command, how extraordinary his resource in moments of danger, above all, how unbending his constancy in adverse fortune, we shall not hesitate to say that history can shew no more noble example of moral grandeur in war.

The traditions of Rome abound in tales of Hannibal's barbarities and deeds of wickedness. The laws of war were severe in that age; he exercised them severely in a few instances; he was compelled to plunder whole districts to support his army. But the generals he fought committed worse acts, notably the unscrupulous and fierce Marcellus; Hannibal was singularly courteous to his opponents; unlike Nero he did not throw the head of a kinsman slain in battle into the enemy's camp; he gave his fallen antagonists funeral honours. He was more magnanimous and less harsh in war—and this was natural—than the men he vanquished; and the charges of cruelty made against him are nearly all calumnies.

Hannibal, like other great men who have been equally denounced, could never have attained his prodigious eminence had he been a monster of perfidy and crime; the conscience of mankind would have turned away from him. It is more to the purpose to consider this mighty spirit as a statesman and a political figure. Hannibal was brought up by an illustrious father; he was trained in government, in diplomacy, in public affairs, from his teens; this partly accounts for the profound wisdom we see in his conduct in matters of state. He failed to combine his great league of nations; but the conception was not the less magnificent; and it would have been carried out had not Carthage been ruled by an oligarchy of a despicable kind, and had Philip of Macedon been worthy of his name.

If Hamilcar had presided in the Phoenician councils, while Hannibal was at the head of the army of Cannae, the world would probably have witnessed the fall of Rome; the destinies of mankind would perhaps have been changed. Nor less admirable was Hannibal's judgment, when, after Zama, he insisted on making peace, and when he addressed himself to restore the state; he worked to save his country for better days, to prevent its destruction by a revengeful enemy. The leading principles of this great man in public life were hatred of Rome, and intense love of Carthage; he was true to them throughout his wonderful career, apparently without one selfish or ambitious thought; and had Carthage been worthy of her glorious son he would probably have made her the first state of Europe.

For the rest we know little of Hannibal's private life; but he was a chaste, religious, and earnest man, without show or theatrical glitter, little moved, it would seem, by human passion. His conversation had a peculiar charm; it was rich in the varied culture of his age; and he evidently possessed a kind of native wit, which expressed itself in sharp, pregnant, and brief sentences.

War, however, was Hannibal's peculiar sphere; his exploits have, in all ages, claimed the attention of competent judges of the military art. There is no more shallow or false notion than that suggested by a school of petty experts, that the conditions of modern war have so completely changed that the grand examples of the past do not require to be studied. The moral faculties of a great captain, resource, energy, craft, constancy, his intellectual faculties, imagination, judgment, quick and clear perception, will certainly play as decisive a part in the huge but short-lived contests of the present day, as they ever did in bygone centuries; the exhibition of these by the warriors of all time, will form matter for careful thought and reflection. (Of the seven great generals held up by Napoleon as the most perfect masters of war, three belonged to antiquity, four only to modern times. *Corr., Alexandre, Annibal, César, Gustave-Adolphe, Turenne, le prince Eugène, et Frédéric.*)

It is a mistake to suppose that the great movements of war, and those which give proof of peculiar excellence, are essentially different in any age. True strategy has but little changed; to occupy the decisive points on the theatre of war, to bring superior forces to bear on them, to turn military strength to the best account, to endeavour to gain an enemy's flank and rear, to operate on his communications, to defeat him in detail—all this has been illustrated far more perfectly in the past than in the last thirty years; and these grand examples, therefore, retain their value. (Napoleon.)

Nor have the material inventions of modern days profoundly modified, as has been alleged, the larger and more important combinations of war; they have made them, indeed, more rapid and complete; but they have not affected their real character; they have not given them a new aspect; and that for this, among other reasons, that they are forces capable of being employed on both sides alike, and capable of producing the same effects for both.

****

> For example, it has been gravely argued that the invention of the field telegraph and the telegraph generally justifies an advance on double and separate lines against an enemy within striking distance, and even annuls the advantage of the possession of interior lines on the theatre of operations. This apology was discovered to excuse the first offensive movements of the campaign of 1866; it has long been given up as hopeless by impartial judges; the field telegraph and the telegraph give equal advantages to the commanders on both sides.

****

The lesser tactics indeed have altogether changed; the formations and the modes of fighting of the last century are nearly as obsolete as those of the days of the legions; and as, owing to the enormous size of the armies of this age, the front of battles has been immensely increased, there must be more independence in separate commands than there was when a general-in-chief could survey the whole scene of action. But the greater tactics are still what they have always been: to make the best use of the arms on the field, to turn advantages of the ground to their uses, to concentrate force on the weakest parts of the enemy, to attack by the flank rather than the front, to do all that feints and stratagems can effect—these should be the objects of a commander of this day, as they were of commanders two thousand years ago.

For these reasons the conduct of Hannibal in war should be studied by those who seek to understand his art. There is, besides, a special reason why it should be considered in this age. The present generation has been a witness of huge armaments prepared for a series of years, and of huge invasions followed by extraordinary success. These operations reveal little genius; they are not marked by originality or grandeur of design; they are characterised by plain and palpable mistakes that gave adversaries many and excellent chances; they ended in not very brilliant triumphs, mainly as the results of the faults of those who opposed them, and of overwhelming superiority of force.

Their real significance is understood by good judges; but they have been exalted to the skies by the worshippers of success; they have powerfully affected military thought; they have spread abroad the false notion that mere numbers and organisation, as contradistinguished from genius, are the most important elements of power in war, and the most certain means to make victory assured. The exploits of Hannibal, prolonged for many years, confute a shallow and dangerous theory; he contended against an enemy sixfold in strength; the Armies of Rome were far better, and far more numerous than his small army; and yet he brought Rome to the very edge of ruin, because he was a captain of extraordinary power. What a great chief can accomplish with a little force is a lesson to be specially learned in our day.

Pallas issued in complete armour from the brain of Zeus; Hannibal, one of the earliest, was one of the greatest of the masters of war. Napoleon, indeed, is the only general of ancient or modern times who can be compared to him; the genius of the two men if alike, was also dissimilar. Both had the imagination that forms mighty conceptions; both carried out these with wonderful energy and skill; but the conceptions of Napoleon seldom reveal the perfect judgment of those of Hannibal; and the plan of assailing Rome more nearly attained success that the projects of marching from the Nile to the Indus, and of descending on England from across the Channel.

Both accomplished marvels in war with very scanty means; the campaign of 1796 may stand beside the campaigns that began on the Trebia, and ended at Cannae; both made genius supply the want of force, one of the best tests of really great captains. Both had in the highest degree the faculty of command, of ruling armies, of terrifying foes, of organising and administering war; both excelled in dexterity, in readiness, in fertility of resource; both had extraordinary powers of stratagem; both could extricate themselves from the extreme of peril, and baffle adversaries who thought they had them in their grasp. Both were strategists of the very first order; both conducted strategy on the same principles; but Napoleon was perhaps the more dazzling strategist of the two, if not as safe, or even as profound as Hannibal.

Both were masters of tactics in the highest sense; but Hannibal was the better tactician; we can scarcely detect a fault in his battles; this certainly cannot be said of Napoleon, often too sanguine and too impetuous on the field. Both had firmness of character and great strength of purpose; but here Hannibal is perhaps superior; no achievements of Napoleon give proof of the tenacity of Hannibal in his lair in Bruttium when he defied the overwhelming forces of Rome. Hannibal, taken altogether, produced greater results considering how inadequate his resources were; Napoleon's ambition and lust of conquest made him the destroyer of the edifice of power he had built up.

As political figures the two men are not to be compared; Hannibal was trained to statesmanship from earliest youth, and exhibited the best gifts of a statesman; Napoleon was a son of the French Revolution; and though mighty as a ruler and in the art of government, and potent as his influence for good was in some respects, he was too extravagant and impulsive to be a perfect statesman. Napoleon's nature, too, had many defects and flaws; we know much less about that of Hannibal; but as far as we can judge he was almost free from selfishness, ostentation, and even ambition. For the rest Napoleon may fill as large a place in history, yet Hannibal was perhaps the greater man; but it has been truly said that master spirits like them can be weighed only in the balances of God. (Thiers, *Consulat et l'Empire*.)

The Second Punic War and the War of the French Revolution illustrate, Arnold has truly said, how a great man may be subdued by a great nation. (*Second Punic War*.) The two periods, however, do not resemble each other; and the careers of Hannibal and of Napoleon were very different. The Second Punic War was merely the conflict of the two leading states of the Mediterranean world; the French Revolutionary War was a mighty struggle between the ideas of the past and of a new era, which, after convulsing Europe from Madrid to Moscow, and making itself felt from the Ganges to the Ohio, has permanently affected the destinies of mankind.

Nor did England play so decisive a part as Rome played, when we look at the two contests; though England was certainly the head of the coalition against France. All honour is due to England for her steady constancy in resisting the armed despot who had overrun the continent; but the efforts of England were trifling compared to the efforts which Rome made after Cannae; and England was never placed in the extreme of peril. The allied powers, too, though without the support of England they would no doubt have succumbed, were prominent actors in the gigantic strife; Rome stood alone when she confronted

Hannibal. Nor had the position of Hannibal much in common with the position of his successor in the nineteenth century. Hannibal was abandoned and betrayed by a base and weak government, and by allies who fell away from him; he was left almost alone to his own resources; when once the war began to turn against him, he had scarcely a prospect of ultimate success.

And yet he maintained an almost hopeless struggle with a pertinacity and a singleness of aim to which history can hardly shew a parallel; and even after Zama he had not lost every chance. Napoleon disposed for years of the vast military forces of France and of many of the chief states of the continent; he was the lord of three-fourths of Europe after Tilsit; had not ambition driven him into wild excesses he would probably have died the head of his immense empire. But he had not the measured judgment and wisdom of the great Carthaginian; he squandered away the power in Russia and in Spain which his enemies could not have subverted themselves; and after Waterloo he was a broken-hearted captive. The two eras and two men were thus far from alike; yet the historian has rightly pointed out one lesson they teach.

In one respect of supreme importance, we see a striking contrast between the two master minds of the ages of the Second Punic War and the French Revolution. Napoleon almost created modern France; what is best and most stable in her institutions was his work; and if his sword carried devastation with it, it effaced feudalism in a large part of Europe. His conquests, if this was not his purpose, tended to fuse divided races together; he was the herald of a United Italy and a United Germany; he spread through many lands the germs of what was most fruitful and beneficent in the French Revolution, the liberation of the soil and equality before the law. Nor is it certain that the complete triumph of his cause would have been an unmixed evil, and without good to mankind.

He never could have subdued England, dream as he might about a second day of Actium; England would have been preserved to fulfil her mission, to unite the past and the present in harmony, to reconcile national order and liberty. But had Napoleon become the undisputed lord of the continent, he probably would have restored Poland; he would have thrust Russia back into the steppes of the North; he would have emancipated Spain from mediaeval bondage; he would have saved Europe from the deadening sceptre of Metternich, from the evil ascendency of the First Nicholas, perhaps from the troubles of 1848-9.

The whole work of Hannibal perished with him; he tried to raise an ignoble state to greatness; and the fall of Carthage soon followed his own. Nor can history contemplate without horror what must have been the results had the victor of Cannae subjugated Rome. The great city would have been blotted out; the Roman people would have been sold in bondage; the principles of enlightened and progressive government which had even then taken root in Italy would have disappeared, perhaps never to flourish again. A tyrannical slave state ruled by a worthless caste would have been imposed on the Aryan races, from the Hellespont to the Atlantic waters; the consequences must have been simply appalling.

Carthage could never have been a great conquering power that makes civilisation attend conquest; the wild tribes from the Oxus and the Jaxartes would probably have destroyed Greek culture in the East; the swarms of the Celts might have overrun Italy; the savage peoples stirring beside the Rhine and the Danube might have anticipated the advance of the Goths of Alaric. Above all, the world would never have been blessed with the "peace of Rome"; the empire would not have arisen to prepare the way for the faith of Christ, for the extension of rational law, for the ideas that spread with the march of the legions; the mould of modern Europe would have never been cast. Hideous idolatry and Phoenician oppression might have maintained, through long centuries, a dread supremacy, in some of the fairest parts of the continent.

Carthage did not survive her greatness for any length of time; her destiny was that of degraded states, which cannot make their independence respected. Massinissa continued to encroach on her borders; her complaints were treated with contempt at Rome; commissions sent by the senate always reported in favour of the unscrupulous Numidian king. Peace, however, increased the wealth of the city; its prosperity, even its power appeared reviving; Rome became jealous of her old enemy, a party of the nobles led by Marcus Cato, a survivor of the great war with Hannibal, began to clamour for the annihilation of the once formidable state, a policy it had always had at heart. Pretexts for hostilities were easily found; two consular armies landed near Utica; the miserable peace party for the moment in office crawled at the feet of the generals of Rome; it actually surrendered the arms and the artillery which formed the defence of the town.

But Rome had resolved that Carthage was to fall; an extraordinary revulsion of feeling was seen when the consuls announced what their orders were; the Semitic fury which blazed out so terribly at Tyre, and in Jerusalem in a subsequent age, burst forth and stirred the citizens to a man; it was resolved, at any risk, to defy the invaders. A truce of a few days was turned to the best advantage; no efforts were spared to man the walls, to replace the engines which had been given up; to empty the arsenals of weapons that remained; and the patriotic party, which had been banished, was induced to return, and to defend the city to the last. A memorable siege of more than two years followed, (the siege of Carthage does not fall within the space of this brief narrative); the strength of the fortifications resisted every attack; it became necessary to invest the place by land and by sea; Carthage was at last reduced by the adopted grandson of Scipio Africanus, a very able soldier, after horrible scenes of carnage and famine.

The great Phoenician city, which had been for centuries a centre of empire and of worldwide commerce, was ruthlessly given to the flames of its conquerors; a thick layer of charred ashes still exists to mark the site of the Carthage of the past. Under the Roman empire, however, a new city arose, not far from the ruins of that which had perished; the plains around the Mejerda became again a region of fine husbandry flourishing to this day; Septimius Severus, one of the emperors, was possibly of Carthaginian descent. (Gibbon; Hénnébert, *Annibal*.) But the Carthage destroyed by Rome is dead; her arts, her letters, her language have disappeared; but for the great deeds of Hamilcar and Hannibal, she would hold but a small place in the pages of history.

We need not dwell on the fortunes of Rome; they connect those of the ancient and the modern world; they will survive until time has come to an end. The republic was to stretch its arms over Hellas, Gaul, and the East; it was to give place to the all-powerful Empire; the empire was to extend from the Nile to the Theiss and the Danube. Under the undisturbed dominion of a long line of Caesars the known world was to enjoy ages of repose; the majesty of Rome was to overawe and protect kings and peoples from the Araxes to the Thames; in the order of things which was then established the foundations of the order of the future were laid.

It was then that Christianity effaced the Paganism of Italy and Greece; that the legions conquered in the sign of the Cross; that the laws and the usages of Imperial Rome united in some measure five-sixths of Europe; that the Gaul, the Spaniard, the Greek, the Italian, felt that all were alike citizens of no mean city. Successive waves of barbarian invasion and conquest overthrew the immense fabric of well-compacted power which many generations had deemed eternal; the Rome of the Tiber and the Rome of the Bosporus ceased to rule by their arms the West and the East.

But out of the wrecks of the perishing empire grew the kingdoms and nations of the Europe of this day; the mediaeval Church, the conception of the state, the feudal system, the organisation of the land, the assemblies and the courts of justice of the Middle Ages—the institutions, in a word, which have been the elements of the government and civilisation of the present time from the Mediterranean to the Pacific—were formed by the union of barbarism with the old order of Rome. Hannibal nearly arrested this grand development, and nearly changed the destinies of the Aryan races; Rome thought of her great enemy with awe for centuries; a reflecting mind cannot even now follow that career of wonders without a sentiment in which admiration is mingled with a feeling of relief.

Hannibal

By Henry William Herbert

HIS CAMPAIGNS, CONDUCT, AND CHARACTER.

It cannot fail, at first sight, to strike even the moat unobservant reader of ancient history with something of wonder, that we know so little distinctly, and, if I may so express myself, individually, of this man, the greatest captain, beyond all question, of antiquity; perhaps—his means and the then state of military science considered—the greatest of all ages.

The causes of this general ignorance are manifold; but the most important arc the entire absence of any Carthaginian narrative of the circumstances of the Punic Wars; and the ignorance or favouritism of the Greek and Roman writers on the subject—Polybius having been a personal friend of Scipio and Loelius; and Livy, writing so long after the occurrence of the facts which he describes, that it was not much easier for him, than it is for us, to arrive at the real troths of what he received as history, or its materials; the legends, namely, of the illustrious Roman houses, and the funeral orations of consulars and senators, which, for the most part, contained as many falsehoods as they counted

It is more remarkable, however, that, until the Colossus Niebuhr came upon the stage, no modern historian was clearsighted enough to discern, through the thick mists which prejudice, blind error, or intentional falsehood, have accumulated over the ages of Roman republicanism, even a glimpse of the transcendent genius, unrivalled military foresight and resource, unwearied perseverance, and indomitable patriotism, of this great captain, this great politician, and, in spite of some defects, which wore those of his age rather than his own, this great man.

Niebuhr, it is true, lived not to bring down the history of that wondrous nation, on whose early ages he first poured the light of intelligence, to the days of the hero, whom I shall endeavour briefly to set before my readers in his true light; but from one passage in his third volume it is clear that, had he lived to write of the Second Punic War, he would have done justice to the incomparable greatness and genius of this much-belied and unappreciated leader. In that passage he speaks of "Scipio as towering above his nation, as much as Hannibal above all nations," and to any person who has carefully studied the career of the great Carthaginian, in the graphic pages of Arnold's magnificent history—alas! like Niebuhr's, left incomplete, by the untimely death of the author—it will be evident that in this phrase there is nothing of hyperbole.

Professing, myself, to adduce no new fact, scarce even theory, concerning this remarkable soldier, it strikes me that a short digest of his campaigns, divested of the dry details which render historical studies displeasing to the superficial reader, and combined with some comparisons of his deeds with those of other greatest soldiers, may prove neither unpalatable nor unuseful to the perusers of ephemeral literature; while it may tend to clear the memory of a much misrepresented hero, from the prejudiced opinions naturally instilled into us by our school readings of Horace's immortal odes, and "Livy's pictured page."

Hannibal was, it would seem, born a general—his father, Hamilcar, was the greatest of his nation and his day; to him succeeded Hasdrubal his son-in-law, to him Hannibal, the greatest of his race, supported by his brothers, Hasdrubal, the younger, and Mago, both generals of extraordinary ability, and with the exception of Scipio alone, both superior in *coup d'oeil,* resource, and strategy, to any Roman leader. Never did one family produce such a galaxy of military splendour.

It must not be understood, however, that they were merely born, for they were constantly bred, soldiers; the camp was their home from their early childhood; the clang of arms and the din of martial music, was the lullaby of their almost cradled sleep; and, when they came to the years of adolescence, the battlefield was alike their playground and their school, and their great father their tutor in the rudiments of strategy, which none could bettor teach. Hannibal was but nine years old, when he accompanied his father to Spain, that father having first made him swear upon the altar that he would never be the friend of Romans, "Hannibal swore, and to his latest hour never forgot his vow." (Arnold II.) The boy swore ignorantly at the time, though he forgot not; but it must not be supposed that the father dictated that vow ignorantly, nor even in the bitterness of blind hatred, or the darkness of political prejudice and passion. The man probably, even then, discovered dimly the future greatness of the child; the patriot assuredly had discovered the inherent and eternal antagonism of Rome and his country, the immutable necessity that one of those two must fall and leave the other the world's mistress.

Rome had just come off conqueror, and humbled Carthage to almost the lowest degradation, after a long and doubtful strife of two-and-twenty years, waged upon sea and land with changeful fortunes. Carthage had lost her wealthiest colonies, and above all the dominion of the seas; for the time she could maintain the conflict no longer, but the genius of Hamilcar saw where her vital energies might be renovated, and whence a mortal blow might be dealt against her now triumphant. To Spain he sailed, and in Spain he laid the plans, and began the system, which his far greater son carried out, and by which he shook Rome to its foundation.

For two-and-twenty years peace lasted between the rival states; and during those two-and-twenty years, thanks to the absence of Carthaginian and the paucity of Roman annals, we know but little of the individual progress of the great Punic family, except that they had conquered and consolidated a vast and wealthy Carthaginian Empire, including almost the whole of Spain south of the Ebro, abounding in rich mines of gold and silver, and swarming with a martial population which formed the very flower of the Punic Armies.

On the death of Hamilcar he was worthily succeeded, by Hasdrubal, his son-in-law, whose progress in farther consolidating the Punic power in Spain, and whose eminent abilities displayed in the foundation of New Carthage, at that time the Gibraltar of the Mediterranean by its commanding and central position, so far alarmed the Romans that even then they would have renewed the war with Carthage, had they not been deterred by the terrors of a Gaulish invasion Three years had elapsed, when Hasdrubal was assassinated in his tent, and by the common voice of the army, ratified by the decree of the Senate, the youthful Hannibal was chosen in his place.

Up to this time we know nothing of the future hero, except his parentage and vow, for the next twenty years he filled the world with his renown, and had his fortunes matched his greatness and his glory, the world today would be no more like that it is, than it would, had the Saracens over-run and subjugated Europe in the day of Charles Martel.

Scarce anyone at all familiar with history can have failed to observe the extraordinary parallelism between the campaigns, the military conduct, and the fortunes of Hannibal and Napoleon. That parallelism is thus strikingly touched upon by Arnold:

"Twice in history has there been witnessed the struggle of the highest individual genius against the resources and institutions of a great nation; and in both cases the nation has been victorious. For seventeen years Hannibal strove against Rome; for sixteen years Napoleon Bonaparte strove against England; the efforts of the first ended in Zama, those of the second in Waterloo."

The extraordinary similitude of the genius, conduct, and military character of these two giants in arms, is far from ending with this general resemblance. Almost from point to point, their destinies are similar. At the age of twenty-six, Hannibal was elected to the supreme command of the Carthaginian Armies, and thenceforth to the close of the war he disposed at his will the resources, and held in the hollow of his hand the councils of his country. At the age of twenty-six, Napoleon assumed the command of the Army of Italy, and from thence his fortunes and his will were those of France. The scenes of the glory of both were the Alps and Italy. Both had the faculty of seeing at a glance where the blow must be planted, which should cripple the enemy; both delivered that blow instantaneously and irresistibly.

Both had the same reliance on their cavalry as an arm of service; Hannibal winning by it all his greatest victories, and Napoleon insisting to the last, that cavalry in equal force, equally led, must conquer infantry. Both vanquished every leader in the field, whom he personally encountered, save the very last; and there is probably no one so prejudiced as to assert at this day that either Hannibal or Napoleon found in his conqueror a superior in strategy or in military genius. Nor does the similarity end even here; for both found their final vanquishers in generals made in Spain by conflicts with their own lieutenants, who were in no wise superior to other eminent leaders of their enemy; and both ultimately perished miserably, in exile, victims to the countries which they had kept so long in awe and perturbation.

In a military point of view, the correctness of their *coup d'oeil*; the lightning speed with which they followed up conception by execution; the power of concentration, by which constantly inferior on the whole, in force, they were ever superior at the point of action; the marvellous foresight, by which they showed seeming rashness to be real prudence; the thunderous crash with which, when they delivered battles, they annihilated, not conquered, their antagonists; nay, the unerring certainty with which they threw themselves on the communications of their enemy, and defeated at a blow the most skilful combinations, were identical in these two mighty captains—none other, in my opinion, ever have possessed the same qualities, or used them with the same effect.

Both were the makers of their own systems, the founders of their own schools; but on the whole, I must consider Hannibal as the greater strategist of the two; because, in the first place, he was the prime originator and inventor, while his great eulogist, and in some points imitator, had the benefit of his example, as well as that of other mighty conquerors; and in the second place, because with means infinitely inferior, against obstacles infinitely greater, and without the aid of modern science, he accomplished, what may be held to have been, in the then condition of the world, results nearly equal.

As men of genuine greatness—I shall observe only, that no single act of Hannibal's life ever subserved to any selfish motive or ministered to his own aggrandisement; and that no single act of Napoleon's did not so. The consideration of self would seem never to have occurred to the one; to have been ever present to the other. Both were fanatics for glory; the one because his own was his country's; the other, because his country's was his own. Both were accused by their enemies of great moral crimes and turpitude; and both, in the main, unjustly. It is one of the sad truths concerning warfare, but no less a truth; that, in playing the game of war, with nations for playthings and the world for a field, expediency must be in a great degree the moral rule; and that, if the game is to be played at all, the sufferings or the lives of individuals, even if those individuals he counted by thousands, must not be considered, where the sufferings or the lives of millions are in question.

The sin lies in the playing the game at all, not in the details or the practice of the play. Both these great men were stern and unrelenting in carrying out the lines which they held it true policy to lay down; neither, so far as history shows, was tainted in the least degree by anything resembling personal cruelty. Both have been accused of faithlessness—a charge never in any case to be much regarded, as brought between nations; for nations are ever prompt to reclaim loudly, when the losers, against deeds, the like of which themselves commit readily, when the winners. In the case of Hannibal, the Romans had all the history-writing to themselves; thence, Punic faith is to this day the proverb for entire faithlessness. Had the French writers atone made the world's annals of the late great struggle, "perfidious Albion" had gone down a byword to all ages. Had the English held the like station, the utter faithlessness of Napoleon would have become proverbial with posterity.

But to return, from this striking parallel, to our immediate hero, we find that he devoted the two first years of his chief command, to completing the subjugation and pacification of Spain; and the third to the conquest of Saguntum, a city allied to the Romans, situate on the River Ebro; a city, therefore, which the Carthaginians were bound by treaties not to disturb; a river which they had no just right to cross. Hence, the sole cause of the charge of perfidy against Hannibal, A treaty was unquestionably violated by Hannibal; as the Romans had violated another treaty far more flagrantly, at the close of the first Punic War; and as they would unquestionably have violated any that existed now, had it been to their interest to do so.

The truth is simply this, that the two nations had been at peace as long as either deemed it very essential to be at peace. Both were preparing for war; Hannibal was ready the first, and therefore struck the first blow. He wished to serve his country; his country deemed that he was serving her, and therefore sustained him; and so well, in truth, did he serve her, that had the genius and character of Carthage borne any relation to those of Rome, such as the genius and character of Hannibal bore to those of the ablest Romans, Rome must have succumbed in the unequal contest; and the world to this day would probably, if not certainly, have been Semitic or Phoenician, and Asiatic, not Roman and European, in its language, its civilization, its religion.

But of this Hannibal thought not; nor, had he thought, would have cared anything. His business was to provoke a war with Rome, and then to deal her one home-stricken blow, that should paralyze her at once and forever. This was his business, as he saw it; and he was one to do that which he saw his business, as thoroughly as Cromwell or Napoleon.

Hannibal's plans were now fully laid, and without further delay he put them into execution. It was already late in May, when he set out from Carthagena for the Ebro, having to cross five degrees and a half of latitude before reaching the Pyrenees, and to conquer the whole half-Romanised territory north of that river, before entering Gaul—then an unknown, unexplored, and barbarous, though highly warlike country, the geography of which was less familiar to the Roman or Carthaginian of those days, than is that of Central Africa to us at this period. His force, on crossing the Ebro, was ninety thousand foot and twelve thousand horse, besides elephants, which was reduced by detachments and losses in the field to fifty thousand foot and nine thousand horse, before he crossed the Pyrenees.

In those days, field artillery there was none, nor its equivalent; but engines for casting huge stones and beams into beleaguered cities—as effective, perhaps, against the imperfect fortifications of those days as our battering artillery—did exist; and of these Hannibal was unable to carry any with him, if he had any in Spain, or even if the Carthaginians knew the use of them, which seems to be doubtful; and to his weakness in this arm, the future of his ultimate attempts against Rome is, I believe, wholly to be attributed. It is a proof of his wonderful power of adapting himself to circumstances, and of his tact in dealing with barbarians, that he actually traversed the whole of Finance, from the Pyrenees to the Rhone—a tract of vast forests and difficult morasses, swarming with fierce and warlike savages—with little loss and no serious opposition.

So rapid had been his motions, and so incredulous were the Romans, though forewarned, of the possibility of such a march, that, although the Consular Armies had time to have disputed the passes of the Pyrenees with him, he had actually crossed the Rhone, and gained three days' march toward the Alps, after a slight skirmish with the Roman light horse, before the Consul Scipio was aware of his arrival in Gaul. That general, finding himself anticipated, did good service to his country, and acted on sound military principles, sending his Consular Army on to Spain by sea, under his lieutenant, while he himself took ship for Pisa, crossed the Apennines, and, having command of the Praetorian Armies of twenty-five thousand men, between Placentia and Cremona, before Hannibal had descended from the mountains, was in readiness to receive him, on his appearance in the plains.

Hannibal, in the meantime, had plunged into the passes of the Alps, in so far as we can judge, by the valley of the Isere, with thirty-seven elephants, in addition to the force of infantry and cavalry as specified above. Now, it appears to me, that to compare Napoleon's passage of the Alp with that of Hannibal, is much aa it would be to compare the voyage of Columbus to the passage of an Atlantic steamer—the former travelled over roads, difficult indeed and dangerous, but still roads, with bridges, depots of provisions, and friendly inhabitants, through a country perfectly known, thoroughly explored, and accurately surveyed for his own purposes by his own incomparable engineers.

The latter forced his way through unknown passes, over bridgeless ravines, with no aid of modern science, no pontoons or devices of engineering, no provisions or forage save what he carried with him, fighting his way, inch by inch, through hordes of hostile barbarians, and that with men and animals from the almost tropical climate of Africa, who perished, in thousands, by the inclemency of weather unendurable ta southern constitutions. Add to this, that it is an undoubted fact, that the limits of eternal snow lay far lower down the mountain sides in those days than now, and that much of the great Carthaginian's line of march lay within and above those limits. Napoleon's celebrated passage was made at the expense, to use his own words, "of a few accidents"—Hannibal's at the cost of thirty-three thousand men out of fifty-nine thousand and all the elephants but eleven. The terrible disparity of loss shows the disparity both of difficulty and audacity The merit of the conception rests incontestably with Hannibal who did what no man had ever dreamed of doing before him and which it might not be possible to do at all. Napoleon did, with splendid ability certainly and prodigious celerity what he well knew had been done before, and *could* therefore unquestionably be done again.

The results in both instances were precisely similar It is now nearly certain that Hannibal crossed the Isere followed the upward course of the Rhone surmounted the Alps by the pass of the little St. Bernard descended the Val d'Aosta and thence marched eastward into the country of the Insubrians, where he expected to find allies, and to raise the Cisalpine Gauls against their old enemies the Romans. Their country lies north of the River Po, in the neighbourhood of Placentia and Cremona—Roman colonies on that great river—and it was on the banks of the Tesino, a northern tributary of that stream, that the two rival nations first came into contact.

This affair of cavalry has been magnified into a battle, though it was but a skirmish, except in the prestige of success, and in the proof, it gave of the superiority, never again doubtful during the whole war, of the African to the Roman cavalry. The Numidians were the Cossacks of that age, mounted on incomparable barbs and Arabs, unequalled as horsemen and lancers; the heavy-armed Carthaginian horse were complete *cuirassiers*, fighting with charged lances and long cutting sabres. The Roman cavalry, never a favourite or successful arm of their service, wore no *cuirasses*, and, for weapons, earned weak, inefficient javelins, and the short stabbing sword of the infantry, which was entirely inefficient as a trooper's weapon.

In this affair of the Ticinus, the heavy Carthaginians met the Roman horse in front with a steady charge, while the wild Numidians broke in upon both their flanks, and routed them in an instant. The country was entirely open and favourable to the movements of cavalry; the Romans, therefore, crippled in that arm, were forced to retreat; recrossed the Tesino, breaking the bridge behind them; crossed the Po also, and posted themselves under the walk of Placentia. Hannibal, without pursuing, passed the Po higher up, by a bridge of boats, and being rapturously received by the Gauls, descended the right bank of the river, and offered battle to the Romans. But they expecting reinforcement by the other Consular Army, of Sempronius, declined it; and in a few days afterward retreated several miles southward, up the valley of the Trebbia, and encamped among the first spurs of the Appenines, where they were comparatively safe from Hannibal's tremendous cavalry, which they had already learned to dread.

The Carthaginian had, in the first instance, taken post to the eastward, in order to intercept the expected approach of Sempronius from Rimini, on the Adriatic; but now, learning, perhaps, that this consul had given, or anticipating that he would give him, the slip, by turning aside into the hill-country to the southward, far below Cremona, he threw himself at once upon the main communications of the Romans, placing himself directly between them and the magazines, on which they were subsisted, at Placentia and on the Upper Po, precisely as Napoleon did by the Austrians at Marengo; thus straitening them of supplies in their camp, while his own cavalry swept the plains in every direction, keeping all his communications open, and the friendly Gauls abundantly supplied him with provision, as he lay on the right bank of the Trebbia.

Meantime, the junction between the two Consular Armies was effected, and by this means the effective force of the Romans was raised to above forty thousand men; while that of Hannibal had been so much swelled by the accession of Gaulish recruits, that he was anxious to deliver battle almost on any terms; the rather, that the subsistence of his army had weighed heavily on the Gauls; who, fickle and treacherous, even beyond the wont of barbarians, were showing symptoms of impatience at his protracted sojourn among them. His great superiority of cavalry, moreover, both as regards quality and numbers, rendered him confident of success in the extensive plains of the Po.

Sempronius was now in command of the whole Roman forces,

Scipio being still *hors de combat* from a wound received in the affair of cavalry on the Tesino; and as this general had no taste as yet of Hannibal's quality, and found himself cut off from his magazines, which the Carthaginians were now beginning to master, and insulted in his very camp, on his own side of the river, by the Numidian horse and Balearic slingers, he merits no reproach for having determined to give battle on fair ground; for with such a force as he commanded, purely homogeneous and Roman; such a force, in a word, as had never within a century encountered an equal foe, he was justified in expecting victory over any troops in the known world. He was falling short of provisions, moreover, and there was great danger of a general Gallic rising, in case the population should be encouraged by the protracted inactivity of the Romans.

To deliver battle, under such circumstances, was therefore soldierly and justifiable on all sound military principles; to do so rashly, however, and hastily, and that, too, on ground and at time of the enemy's choosing—such an enemy too, and so superior in horse—was unpardonable. Yet, just this thing did Sempronius.

It was now mid-winter, for neither of the belligerents had thought of going into winter quartets—Hannibal, from the imminent necessity of striking quickly and decisively, and the Romans, from the impossibility of suffering him to keep the field unwatched. Even now, the climate of the plains at the foot of the Alps, included in the districts of Lombardy and Piedmont, is severe and inclement in the winter season; but in those times, when the country lay in great part uncleared and covered with primitive forest, it was far more tempestuous and cold than at present.

The Trebbia swollen with snow-water, ice-cold from the frozen Apennines, ran now a breast-high torrent, though in the summer droughts its pebbly bed might be crossed almost dry-shod. Across this paralysing stream Sempronius suffered Hannibal to allure him, on a wild morning, with flying sleet storms and snow gusts, by a false attack and feigned retreat, to his own side of the river; and that too without allowing his men to breakfast; while the Carthaginians, expectant of what was to come, had fed heartily, and armed themselves in their tents by blazing fires. In addition to this advantage, an ambuscade of two thousand horse and foot had been concealed, under Mago's command, in an old watercourse covered with brushwood and coppice, which Sempronius, negligently or disdainfully, left in his rear, as he hurried on to attack the enemy, who had drawn out from their camp, and formed line of battle, facing the river, to oppose him.

The order of battle was simple, and on both sides the same; indeed, it was the only order then in use, the centre being formed of the heavy infantry, covered by their light troops and skirmisher, with the cavalry on either flank. So far as I can observe, this form was rarely deviated from by the ancient military nations; the cavalry were invariably directed against cavalry; and, after an equestrian combat which generally terminated in the chase of one party, for miles, perhaps leagues, from the field by the other, a Secord engagement followed between the solid infantry which often led to the occurrence of drawn battle. The same defect of strategy is observable in all Prince Rupert's fighting, during the English Civil War, who, in four or five different pitched battles, had he wheeled on the flanks and rear of the Parliamentarian Foot, after scattering their horse by his headlong charge, would have terminated the war at a blow.

Hannibal, who made more use of his cavalry arm than any other general of antiquity, never appears to have attacked infantry in front with horse, or even in flank, until the enemy's cavalry were in flight; and yet the Roman foot—as foot the best undoubtedly in the world—were from their armature of heavy missile javelins and short stabbing swords, not differing much from the larger bowie knife, peculiarly unfitted to resist the charge of cavalry, which their loose and open order was calculated to invite.

The result of this battle was as must be foreseen from the preceding events which led to it. In the fight itself there was little strategy; the great abilities of Hannibal had been displayed in the manoeuvres by which he compelled the enemy to deliver battle, and then induced him to deliver it, at disadvantage, and on ground selected by his enemy. The rest he left to his soldiers, confident that they would do their work to his satisfaction; nor was his confidence disappointed. He was, moreover, in the open field greatly superior to his enemy, even without taking the exhaustion and ill-plight of the legionaries into consideration, who fought wet to the skin, chilled, and fasting, against men full-fed, fresh, and warm, from their recent campfires.

His cavalry, ten thousand strong, six thousand of whom were incomparable African *cuirassiers* and Numidians, could not be checked by the feeble legionary cavalry of four thousand, for a single instant. The Balearian slingers and African archery were as much superior to the Roman light troops, who fought only with slender javelins; the Italians never having been famous for the use of the bow. The *velites* of

Sempronius, therefore, were driven in upon the legionaries at the first onset, and passed through the intervals of the *Manipules* to the rear, while the cavalry were scattered, as by a thunderbolt, on both wings simultaneously, by the Carthaginian elephants and horsemen.

The soldierly qualities of the Roman foot did not fail them in this emergency—in fact never did fail them throughout the war, for when opposed to foot they were never beaten—for they maintained the fight, exhausted as they were, with advantage, until Maharbal, whom Arnold styles not unjustly "the best cavalry officer of the first cavalry service in the world," leaving the pursuit of the flying horse to his Numidians, unequalled in such operations thundered on both their flanks with his elephants and *cuirassiers,* and to complete the whole Mago, bursting from his ambush broke down upon then rear horse and foot, pell-mell, and pierced them through and through.

The legions of the centre still undismayed and unbroken, cut their way straight through the African foot before them, and reached Placentia in safety, though the whole Carthaginian Army was interposed; the rest were slaughtered ruthlessly and unremittingly, according to the usages of ancient warfare, until the ice-cold waters of the Trebbia checked the pursuit of the victors, and saved the residue from slaughter. During the same night Scipio with the shattered relics of the army, re-crossed the Trebbia and joined his colleague in Placentia; whence in a few days they retreated separately, Scipio on Rimini, Sempronius across the Apennines into Etruria, leaving Hannibal at the close of his first short campaign the master of all Cisalpine Gaul, or, in other words, of all Italy, north of the Apennines.

Hannibal, politic ever, and fearing to distress his new and fickle allies, by wintering among them, and so compelling them to subsist his troops, made an effort to cross the Apennines, but the cold was too severe, and the passes were impracticable to his hot-blooded southern cattle, so that he was forced in his own despite, after losing all his elephants but one, to return and winter among the reluctant and faithless Gauls, from whom he appears to have apprehended even assassination.

In the following year, new consuls having been chosen at Rome, Caius Flaminius and Cneius Servilius Geminius, soldiers were levied very vigorously and an immense force set on foot; two several Consular Armies, each consisting of four Roman legions, or about twenty-four thousand men, besides an equal force of allies of the Latin name, were opposed to Hannibal, covering the two different roads which led to Rome, the Flaminian by the Adriatic coast, and the Emilian through Tuscany, Servilius took the command in lieu of Scipio at Rimini, on the Adriatic, and Flaminius that of Sempronius, at Arezzo, a town of Tuscany, situated among the Apennines on the confines of the states of the church, about a hundred and twenty miles due north of Rome. So that apparently Hannibal could not advance upon Rome, without encountering the one or other of these two powerful hosts.

Many reasons had induced both parties to open this campaign at an early season, and in fact Flaminius was in the field so soon as the 15th of March. Hannibal, however, had no idea of affronting the might of Rome in her own central Latin territory, much less of attacking her walls, when he had no means adequate to the storming of such petty garrison towns as Placentia, Cremona, and the other Roman colonies planted in the half subjugated districts of Cisalpine Gaul. His game was to rekindle the ancient feuds of Samnium and Campania, against their haughty mistress, and, subsisted on the wealth of the rich plains of La Puglia and the Terra di Lavoro, to wear out the patience of the Roman allies by devastating their territories, until he should be able to raise all Southern Italy in one common league against their common mistress; and then, and not until then, to strike a home blow, which should be at once irresistible and decisive.

Skilfully avoiding, therefore, both the main roads he marched almost due south, down the valley of the Serchio, through a tract of almost impassable morasses, among which his army suffered severely, upon the Valdarno, which he entered some twenty miles westward of Florence, and plundered it with extreme severity, compensating his men for their previous toils by the enjoyment of those rich districts. Thence, finding that Flaminius moved not from his post at Arezzo, he advanced rapidly through Tuscany, turning that Consul's left to the west and southward, and passing onward, with Cortona's mountain citadel unmolested on his own left, direct upon the Lake of Perugia—better known as the fatal Thrasymene—which he approached on its northern side, as if it were his intention to strike the waters of the upper Tiber, and so enter the very heart of the Latin country, and descend on Rome itself, leaving both her Consular Armies far to rearward.

To effect this he had made a long and circuitous flank march close under the position of a concentrated enemy; a manoeuvre singularly hazardous if executed in the face of an alert and active foe. It was such a manoeuvre which lost Austerlitz to the Russians, and Salamanca to Marmont; but Hannibal's superior cavalry enabled him to execute it in the plains without fear of molestation from an enemy whom he had now completely outwitted.

Satisfied by this that Hannibal desired to avoid him, Flaminius broke up from Arezzo, and pursued, in hot haste, fearing only that his fugitive enemy, as he vainly imagined him, would have already entered the basin of the Tiber, and commenced the devastation of the especial territory of the city. But Hannibal had foreseen the movement, and prepared a trap, more terrible than that even of the Caudine forks, for his unwary pursuer.

The road, which passes to the northward of the lake Thrasymene, or Perugia, into the Latin country, traverses at first a narrow defile between steep cliffs and the deep waters of the lake, and then turns abruptly to the north, crossing a little lap of land between low hills to the left and right. Within this gorge Hannibal had passed, and crouched like a lion, for his spring. With his Africans and Spaniards he barred the road in front, on the crest of the ridge, where the road wound upward from the lake. His Gauls he posted with his cavalry on the left of the pass, among the low hills; his archery and slingers on the right, while he garnished the tops of the cliffs, above the pass, with light troops and the Gaulish auxiliaries.

Fortune and the weather favoured him, no less than the ground. Flaminius arrived late, after a forced march, at Passignano, just without the passes; encamped, and before daybreak entered the defiles, without reconnoitring or sending forward an advanced guard; thinking only how best he might overtake his flying enemy. A thick mist from the lake covered all the low grounds and defiles, while the heights above were bright in the clear atmosphere; still onward marched the doomed column, crowded in dense array, and marching at their fastest pace, emulous to fall on the rear of the enemy.

Not a sound was heard, not a bowstring was drawn, until the head of the column was ascending the last height, whereon the Africans and Spaniards were posted, and the rear was entangled in the defiles, and overlooked by the Gallic auxiliaries. Then at once, before, behind, and on both flanks, broke on their ears the slogan of the Gauls, the clang and clatter of the Numidian horse, and the fatal whistle of the bullets, slung like hail into their ranks by the fierce barbarians. The van alone cut its way clear through the troops that opposed them, and escaped for a while, six thousand strong, to one of the neighbouring villages. They alone—for of the centre and the rear of that doomed army not one man escaped to tell the tale of the disaster.

The thirsty lance of the Numidian, the claymore of the Gaul, and the deadly missiles of the Balearians did their work thoroughly. Flaminius died like a soldier, in the field which he had lost, and although Hannibal sought for his body, to which he would have given honourable sepulture, it never was discovered whether it was engulfed in the deep waters of the lake, or was confused in some pile of mangled corpses. He slept soundly, and his countrymen forgave his rashness for his valour. It is said, that an earthquake made the soil to reel, unheeded, under the feet of the combatants, so deadly and despairing, on both sides, was the conflict.

Before the sun set, the six thousand men, who had escaped, were prisoners to Maharbal and his indefatigable horse. Of fifty thousand men, fifteen thousand only were left alive, and these prisoners; of whom the Italians were discharged, free and without ransom, while the Romans were kept in strict custody, to be sold as slaves or slain, according to the pleasure of their captors; so, ran the laws of antique warfare.

There was no force between the conqueror and Rome; but no rash impulse, no overweening confidence induced that wise leader to deviate from his preconcerted plan, or to enter the Latin country, in which he well knew that he should find a bare and devastated country, a deadly enemy in every male inhabitant, an impregnable fortress in every Latin town. Even on the day succeeding the defeat, the little borough of Spoleto shut its gates against his horsemen, and he had neither the means nor the inclination to assault it. He devastated, however, the whole rich plain from the Tiber to Perugia and Spoleto; and then, leisurely crossing the Apennines in the direction of Ancona, descended the shores of the Adriatic, through the country of the Abruzzi, into La Puglia, even to the Gulf of Manfredonia; possessing, the whole country, from the Apennines eastward to the Gulf of Venice; and from Ancona southward to the Ofento, in what is now the kingdom of Naples.

During this long excursion, he put to the sword every Latin and Roman who was taken; a policy bloody indeed and cruel, but of which the Romans could not at least complain, since their own practice was the massacre of every living thing, even to domestic animals, in captured cities. Living with his troops on the fat of the land, he recruited his invaluable cavalry with rich herbage of the fertile plains of the south, and so made war feed war, at the greatest cost to the enemy. Still no state joined him; no city opened its gates; nor had he the means of forcing, either by storm or blockade, even the meanest of the Roman colonies:—this is sufficient answer to those empty declaimers who would censure so consummate a master of the art of war as Hannibal, for want of energy in not storming Rome itself.

At this time, though the Romans had no individual man who could be compared for a moment with Hannibal, the spirit of the people was admirable and heroic to the utmost. Not a word was spoken of surrender; not a soldier was withdrawn from any foreign station; only a Dictator was appointed, fresh levies were drawn together, Rome herself was put in a state of defence, and the whole country was ordered to be devastated, the corn destroyed, and every house and hamlet burned to the ground, wherever he should turn his march.

This doubtless, as well as the hope of driving the allies into revolt against Rome, so soon as they should find Rome helpless to protect them, induced him to avoid the Latin country, and to bide his time patiently and with stern perseverance. The people of La Puglia would not join him; therefore, he crossed the Apennines again, into the Samnite country, a hundred years before so deadly hostile to the Romans. But Benevento, its capital, was now a Latin colony, and like all its sister towns, steadily shut its gates against him. Laying its territories waste on every side the terrible invader rolled the tide of devastation onward, ascended the Voltorno till he found it fordable, then crossed it, and rushed down like a torrent of lava, sweeping all before him with pitiless conflagration into the very garden of Italy, the glorious Falernian plain, the pride of Campania.

Summer had scarce yet commenced; a long campaign was still before him; Fabius the Dictator was in the field watching him from the hills where Hannibal could not assail him; for unaided by their invincible horse, the Carthaginian foot could not cope with the legionaries—the rawest levies beating them with ease, when fighting from behind entrenchments. Hannibal, it might be remembered, had no base of operations, no fortified garrisons, no guarded magazines, no hope of reinforcements from the rear; his hospitals, his magazines, were necessarily in his camp; his granaries and store-houses were in the fields of his enemy and her allies.

Thence it became a trial of patience between Fabius, the Delayer, as he delighted to be termed, and Hannibal, who, perhaps, deserved the title better, for prompt as he was to strike when a blow was to be stricken, he never once struck a blow untimely. Hannibal waited patiently the time when the allies should desert Rome as unable to defend them; or when Rome, conscious of their near defection, should descend to fight in a fair field, in order to defend their loyalty. Fabius waited patiently the time when Hannibal should expose a weak point to an attack, or should attack at a disadvantage—but that time never came.

Once Fabius thought that he had taken his great antagonist as in a net, and that he could not escape one more example of the Caudine Forks; but by a simple stratagem his wily enemy baffled his deep laid schemes; extricated himself from the toils, without the loss of one man; and returned into his old quarters, east of the Pyrenees, loaded with plunder, to pass the autumn and winter at his ease, leaving the Dictator and his system, a stumbling-block to his friends, and a laughing-stock to his enemies. So discontented indeed were the people, that a bill was passed at Rome, giving equal power to the master of the horse, Minutius, and the Dictator, and dividing the armies between them; but it soon became apparent that if the system of delaying was ineffective, the system of delivering battle to Hannibal was fatal. For Minutius, venturing to do so, was very severely handled; and a second rout of the Trebbia was prevented only by the timely rescue of the slow Dictator,

No farther action marked that autumn; Hannibal went into winter quarters, well assured that one of two things must occur in the ensuing campaign—either the Romans must deliver battle to retain the fealty of the allies, when he looked forward confidently to an overwhelming rout of their forces, which itself would induce defection of the allies—or they must again abandon them yet another season to plunder and devastation; when they would assuredly rise in revolts unsolicited.

The steadiness with which this great captain adhered to his first system, is worthy of all praise, as a quality of the highest strategical ability; and scarcely second to it, the military observer must rate the care with which he nurtured, cherished, and preserved his great resource, his invaluable cavalry, never to be replaced if once lost. Nor will the tactician fail to remark, in this connexion, the difference between this conduct of the Carthaginian, and that of the great French Emperor; who, by recklessly sacrificing in the morning of the 18th of June, his incomparable *cuirassiers* and dragoons against the immovable English squares, suffered that to be converted into an utter rout, which might have been only a severe check, had his retreating columns been covered at night by the fourteen thousand unrivalled cavalry, the bulk of whom were uselessly expended in vain charges on an impenetrable infantry, and lay cold on the red clay of Waterloo.

At Rome, in the meantime, there was discontent from within and clamour from without. The hot spirits within cried Shame, that Roman Armies should avoid any enemy in the field; the cold spirits without cried Shame, that Rome should see her allies suffer the extremities of war, without striking one blow to aid or deliver them. The crisis, for which Hannibal had been so long waiting, had arrived.

The consuls of the year were elected with a direct reference to the question of giving battle, or no; and the choice decided the question in the affirmative. The Consular Armies had lain during the winter at Canusium, a small town to the south of the Ofanto, deriving their support from a large magazine, which they had established at Cannae.

In this campaign Hannibal took the initiative, and again threw himself suddenly on the communications of the enemy, getting unexpectedly into their rear, and surprising their magazines at Cannae; in the citadel of which, as a place of some strength, he established himself. The campaign had not opened so early as usual in this season, for the corn was already ripening; yet the consuls had not yet reached the camp at Canusium, when the proconsuls sent for instructions from the senate how to act, after their supplies had been thus cut off

The answer was the arrival of the consuls, Terentius Varro, of plebeian, and Lucius Æmilius Paullus, of the highest patrician blood, with reinforcements—raising the Roman force to about ninety thousand men—and orders to risk a battle. On their arrival, they marched upon Hannibal, and found him encamped on the left bank of the Ofento, at about nine miles distant from the sea, on very open ground, highly advantageous to cavalry operations. Perceiving this, the Consul Æmilius was desirous to retreat farther from the sea, into the hill country, where the Carthaginian cavalry would be less efficient, and whither he supposed Hannibal would be compelled to follow him, so soon as the crop on the seaboard should be exhausted.

Varro, however, of a bolder and more sanguine temperament, when his day for command arrived, took steps which must needs bring on an action, by interposing himself between Hannibal and the sea, with his left on the river and his right on the town of Salapia. Hannibal at once marched down upon the Roman camp, and offered battle, which Æmilius, in his turn being in command, declined. Some unimportant manoeuvring followed, in which the Romans were somewhat the sufferers. A few days elapsed, when Varro forded the river and drew out in battle array, on the right bank, upon which his right flank now rested. Hannibal immediately followed his example, and crossing the Ofanto at two points, drew out opposite to him.

This battle is the most worthy, of any in ancient history, unless perhaps it be that of Leuctra, of the attention of both the scholar and the tactician; for it is the prototype, and very counterpart, in its arrangement and results, of those of the greatest pitched battles the world has ever witnessed—Fontenoy, Aspern, and Waterloo. And, if I do not err, the result must ever be the same, where, of two armies, equally matched for courage and strength, and equally well led, the one rushes in solid column of attack into the centre of the other; which, if steady enough to fight in line, must envelop and overwhelm it. Such was the fate of the all but victorious square of the Highlander at Fontenoy; such of the terrible column of Lannes at Aspern; such of the terrific final onslaught of Ney with the young guard on the heights of Mount St. Jean; and such, even more markedly, was the result of the battle now under consideration.

For some inexplicable reason, the Roman Army, which was infinitely superior in numbers and quality of infantry, and the habit of which was to fight ever in line, was crowded into deep, narrow columns, on this occasion.

On the extreme right of the Roman line, next to the river, were the Roman knights, and next to these the legions; on their left the Allied infantry, and on the left again the cavalry of the Latin name.

Opposing these in order, stood, next to the river, the Gaulish and Spanish horse; then half the African foot, armed like the legionaries; then the Gaulish and Spanish foot, and to their left the remainder of the Africans, with their left covered by the Numidian horse.

Thus, for all was even; but Hannibal had purposely arrayed the Carthaginian Army, precisely as the English Army was drawn up at Waterloo owing in the latter instance, to the formation of the ground that is to say, in a great convex line, with the apex toward the enemy.

On the signal being given, the cavalry charged on both sides; and, although the Roman knights fought stubbornly, they could not resist the onslaught of Hasdrubal, who chased them up the river bank, slaughtering them unsparingly, till seeing them utterly dispersed and broken, he wheeled across the whole rear of the Roman host, and falling on the Latin horse, who still held their own against the Numidian skirmishers, scattered them like a thunderbolt.

Meanwhile, the Roman legions, seeing the Carthaginian infantry advancing in a wedge—instead of withdrawing their own centre, as they should have done—rushed in toward the centre from the flanks, till they were all crowded into a vast dense single column, which forced its way onward by the weight and fury of its own desperate charge. Thus, the Gauls and Spaniards in the centre of the Punic line were pushed hack bodily into the rear, so that the Africans on the wings, who had been originally withdrawn, were now in advance; and the whole Carthaginian Army, from being a convex, had become a concave line, overlapping and tearing to pieces the flanks of the long unwieldy Roman column, with their assailing wings.

Precisely similar to this catastrophe, was that of the British column at Fontenoy, where the French and English forces reversed their usual mode of fighting—the latter attacking in column, the former resisting in line. Precisely similar was the check and overthrow of Lannes' terrible column at Aspern. And, with but one exception, precisely similar even to the smallest details, were the whole tactics of the last decisive charge at Waterloo. The exception is this, that whereas the Punic line of battle at Cannae became concave, from convex, by the retrogression of the centre; the British line at Waterloo underwent the same change by the advance of its flanks.

In both actions the attacking column plunged into a concave line, carrying all before it; until its head was checked by the steadiness of the resisting centre, its flanks ravaged by the onslaught of the wings, and, to complete the parallel, in both cases, its rear torn to pieces by a charge of cavalry, its own cavalry having been long before expended—for at the close of the bloody day of Cannae, Hasdrubal, returned from the slaughter of the Latin horse, broke in upon the rear of the still struggling legionaries, and closed the conflict by such a butchery as history but seldom has recorded.

Strange results followed this catastrophe. All the Southern allies deserted from Rome's authority, except the Latin name; and, even of these, twelve colonies refused their contingents. Still Rome disdained to treat; and Hannibal, unable, for want of artillery or of sufficient disciplined and steady infantry, to attack her walls, was compelled to maintain the war in the Southern provinces. From that day forth the Romans fought no more pitched battles; and, having regular supplies, while Hannibal was compelled to forage for his subsistence, they could rarely be forced into action. Whenever he did so, indeed, his superiority of resource and ability inevitably told; but the war was henceforth changed into a war of sieges; and in these Hannibal fought at disadvantage, for his cavalry could not be brought to bear, and his infantry were, as I have before observed, inferior to the lemons.

Still, never were the talents of the great Carthaginian so conspicuous as in these later campaigns, when the Romans selected none but soldiers of proof, and those soldiers had learned strategy even through being beaten by Hannibal. His manoeuvres about Tarentum; his marches to and fro, dealing tremendous blows on all hands; his presence seeming almost ubiquitous, cannot fail to remind the reader of Napoleon's finest campaign, in my opinion, which terminated with the abdication of Fontainbleau.

His reappearance before the walls of Capua, when confident that he was leagues distant before Tarentum, the Romans, by a vast combined movement, had surrounded that city, and already exulted in the sure prospect of its fall, only to vanish like morning shadows before the mere splendour of his presence, seen on the distant summit of Tifata, surrounded by his veteran invincibles, is so complete an antecedent to Napoleon's similar reappearance at Dresden, and the scattering of the allies, that if the names and geography were changed one narrative might do for either.

When on his removal to the south, the Romans gathered again about the fated walls of Capua, and fortified themselves in their leaguer with lines of circumvallation and countervallation which mocked his army's strength, what decision could he sounder, what conception grander, what execution more masterly than that of his forced march upon Rome itself in the hope of drawing them from their half-won prey? What more romantic than his actually hurling his javelin over the Colline gates of Rome, and wasting the immediate territory of the city with the sword and fire before the very eyes of her senators? It is true the Romans did not raise the siege, and that to his great regret they did take Capua; but that in no wise detracts from the correctness of his military principles, or the magnificence of his military achievements.

This was in the sixth year of the war; for five years more he struggled on with varying success, but unvarying courage and conduct; in the eleventh year Hasdrubal, his brother, followed in his footsteps from New Carthage to the Alps, passed them, and entered Italy with powerful reinforcements, which might well have changed the fortunes, would certainly have protracted the duration, of the war. But he was intercepted by vastly superior forces, concentrated against him by means of Claudius Nero's splendid forced march from one to the other end of the Peninsula, utterly defeated and killed.

This was the great, the *one* great Roman achievement of the war; and it was disgraced by a deed of the foulest atrocity, Hannibal's first information of his brother's defeat, was that brother's pale and bloody head cast over the entrenchments of his camp. Yet he had sought for Flaminius' body to give it honourable burial; and when Marcellus was slain, he buried his remains with all honour, and sent his inurned ashes to his son.

The defeat of Hasdrubal was the real downfall of all Hannibal's prospects of success; for it had long been evident that his single army could not effect the destruction of the Roman Republic; and Carthage with Spain now wrested from her grasp, could offer him no aid. Indeed, she was, ere long, to be so hard pressed at home, as to require his all-powerful arm, alas! no longer powerful to preserve her. All he could now do, was to act on the defensive; and he did that as brilliantly and effectively, as he had before assumed the offensive. Before he was recalled to fight at home for the very existence of Carthage, he had maintained himself for seventeen years in the heart of an enemy's country, without reinforcements, supplies, or moneys except what he took from the enemy; he had traversed and retraversed every portion of the peninsula, from the Po to the Gulf of Tarentum, wasting it with fire and sword at his own will; he had won three pitched battles, which are to this day the admiration of all strategists; he had beaten every force that ever met him in the field; he had never suffered a defeat; and when he withdrew from the shores of Italy, he did so, not that the Romans drove him thence, but that Carthage needed him elsewhere.

At Zama he was overpowered, not vanquished; for the Romans were superior, in both numbers and quality, of both horse and foot. And the Numidians, to whose irresistible onset and impetuous horsemanship Hannibal had, in great part, owed his previous successes over the Romans—for with their thundering charge he terminated the crisis of almost every battle, crushing their indomitable infantry under foot, after having broken and exterminated their weak cavalry—were now arrayed under the savage and revengeful veteran Massinissos on the side of Scipio.

There was little manoeuvring in this action, but much hard fighting; and it was won in the end by the stubborn hardihood of the Roman reserve of *Triarii* brought fresh into action with their long spears, after all the forces of the Carthaginians had been successively wearied out and cut to pieces.

Scipio gained no laurels by that victory beyond the barren honour of being styled the conqueror of Hannibal, whom all men of all countries knew to be his better.

And Rome earned eternal disgrace by her persecution, even unto the death, of the aged, friendless, helpless exile, during whose life-time she could not but tremble.

Take him for all in all, not looking for virtues incompatible with the times, the country, and the state of society in which he flourished; weighing what he did against the means with which he did it; judging his acts by his motives, and his character by his conduct; I think we shall not err in pronouncing him, one of the purest patriots, and *the greatest captain*, without exception, whom this world has yet seen, or perhaps will see for ever.

ALSO FROM LEONAUR
AVAILABLE IN SOFTCOVER OR HARDCOVER WITH DUST JACKET

THE FALL OF THE MOGHUL EMPIRE OF HINDUSTAN *by H. G. Keene*—By the beginning of the nineteenth century, as British and Indian armies under Lake and Wellesley dominated the scene, a little over half a century of conflict brought the Moghul Empire to its knees.

LADY SALE'S AFGHANISTAN *by Florentia Sale*—An Indomitable Victorian Lady's Account of the Retreat from Kabul During the First Afghan War.

THE CAMPAIGN OF MAGENTA AND SOLFERINO 1859 *by Harold Carmichael Wylly*—The Decisive Conflict for the Unification of Italy.

FRENCH'S CAVALRY CAMPAIGN *by J. G. Maydon*—A Special Correspondent's View of British Army Mounted Troops During the Boer War.

CAVALRY AT WATERLOO *by Sir Evelyn Wood*—British Mounted Troops During the Campaign of 1815.

THE SUBALTERN *by George Robert Gleig*—The Experiences of an Officer of the 85th Light Infantry During the Peninsular War.

NAPOLEON AT BAY, 1814 *by F. Loraine Petre*—The Campaigns to the Fall of the First Empire.

NAPOLEON AND THE CAMPAIGN OF 1806 *by Colonel Vachée*—The Napoleonic Method of Organisation and Command to the Battles of Jena & Auerstädt.

THE COMPLETE ADVENTURES IN THE CONNAUGHT RANGERS *by William Grattan*—The 88th Regiment during the Napoleonic Wars by a Serving Officer.

BUGLER AND OFFICER OF THE RIFLES *by William Green & Harry Smith*—With the 95th (Rifles) during the Peninsular & Waterloo Campaigns of the Napoleonic Wars.

NAPOLEONIC WAR STORIES *by Sir Arthur Quiller-Couch*—Tales of soldiers, spies, battles & sieges from the Peninsular & Waterloo campaingns.

CAPTAIN OF THE 95TH (RIFLES) *by Jonathan Leach*—An officer of Wellington's sharpshooters during the Peninsular, South of France and Waterloo campaigns of the Napoleonic wars.

RIFLEMAN COSTELLO *by Edward Costello*—The adventures of a soldier of the 95th (Rifles) in the Peninsular & Waterloo Campaigns of the Napoleonic wars.

AVAILABLE ONLINE AT **www.leonaur.com**
AND FROM ALL GOOD BOOK STORES

ALSO FROM LEONAUR

AVAILABLE IN SOFTCOVER OR HARDCOVER WITH DUST JACKET

AFGHANISTAN: THE BELEAGUERED BRIGADE by G. R. Gleig—An Account of Sale's Brigade During the First Afghan War.

IN THE RANKS OF THE C. I. V by Erskine Childers—With the City Imperial Volunteer Battery (Honourable Artillery Company) in the Second Boer War.

THE BENGAL NATIVE ARMY by F. G. Cardew—An Invaluable Reference Resource.

THE 7TH (QUEEN'S OWN) HUSSARS: Volume 4—1688-1914 by C. R. B. Barrett—Uniforms, Equipment, Weapons, Traditions, the Services of Notable Officers and Men & the Appendices to All Volumes—Volume 4: 1688-1914.

THE SWORD OF THE CROWN by Eric W. Sheppard—A History of the British Army to 1914.

THE 7TH (QUEEN'S OWN) HUSSARS: Volume 3—**1818-1914** by C. R. B. Barrett—On Campaign During the Canadian Rebellion, the Indian Mutiny, the Sudan, Matabeleland, Mashonaland and the Boer War Volume 3: 1818-1914.

THE KHARTOUM CAMPAIGN by Bennet Burleigh—A Special Correspondent's View of the Reconquest of the Sudan by British and Egyptian Forces under Kitchener—1898.

EL PUCHERO by Richard McSherry—The Letters of a Surgeon of Volunteers During Scott's Campaign of the American-Mexican War 1847-1848.

RIFLEMAN SAHIB by E. Maude—The Recollections of an Officer of the Bombay Rifles During the Southern Mahratta Campaign, Second Sikh War, Persian Campaign and Indian Mutiny.

THE KING'S HUSSAR by Edwin Mole—The Recollections of a 14th (King's) Hussar During the Victorian Era.

JOHN COMPANY'S CAVALRYMAN by William Johnson—The Experiences of a British Soldier in the Crimea, the Persian Campaign and the Indian Mutiny.

COLENSO & DURNFORD'S ZULU WAR by Frances E. Colenso & Edward Durnford—The first and possibly the most important history of the Zulu War.

U. S. DRAGOON by Samuel E. Chamberlain—Experiences in the Mexican War 1846-48 and on the South Western Frontier.

AVAILABLE ONLINE AT **www.leonaur.com**
AND FROM ALL GOOD BOOK STORES

ALSO FROM LEONAUR
AVAILABLE IN SOFTCOVER OR HARDCOVER WITH DUST JACKET

THE 9TH—THE KING'S (LIVERPOOL REGIMENT) IN THE GREAT WAR 1914 - 1918 *by Enos H. G. Roberts*—Mersey to mud—war and Liverpool men.

THE GAMBARDIER *by Mark Severn*—The experiences of a battery of Heavy artillery on the Western Front during the First World War.

FROM MESSINES TO THIRD YPRES *by Thomas Floyd*—A personal account of the First World War on the Western front by a 2/5th Lancashire Fusilier.

THE IRISH GUARDS IN THE GREAT WAR - VOLUME 1 *by Rudyard Kipling*—Edited and Compiled from Their Diaries and Papers—The First Battalion.

THE IRISH GUARDS IN THE GREAT WAR - VOLUME 1 *by Rudyard Kipling*—Edited and Compiled from Their Diaries and Papers—The Second Battalion.

ARMOURED CARS IN EDEN *by K. Roosevelt*—An American President's son serving in Rolls Royce armoured cars with the British in Mesopatamia & with the American Artillery in France during the First World War.

CHASSEUR OF 1914 *by Marcel Dupont*—Experiences of the twilight of the French Light Cavalry by a young officer during the early battles of the great war in Europe.

TROOP HORSE & TRENCH *by R.A. Lloyd*—The experiences of a British Lifeguardsman of the household cavalry fighting on the western front during the First World War 1914-18.

THE EAST AFRICAN MOUNTED RIFLES *by C.J. Wilson*—Experiences of the campaign in the East African bush during the First World War.

THE LONG PATROL *by George Berrie*—A Novel of Light Horsemen from Gallipoli to the Palestine campaign of the First World War.

THE FIGHTING CAMELIERS *by Frank Reid*—The exploits of the Imperial Camel Corps in the desert and Palestine campaigns of the First World War.

STEEL CHARIOTS IN THE DESERT *by S. C. Rolls*—The first world war experiences of a Rolls Royce armoured car driver with the Duke of Westminster in Libya and in Arabia with T.E. Lawrence.

WITH THE IMPERIAL CAMEL CORPS IN THE GREAT WAR *by Geoffrey Inchbald*—The story of a serving officer with the British 2nd battalion against the Senussi and during the Palestine campaign.

AVAILABLE ONLINE AT **www.leonaur.com**
AND FROM ALL GOOD BOOK STORES

www.ingramcontent.com/pod-product-compliance
Lightning Source LLC
Chambersburg PA
CBHW031621160426
43196CB00006B/222